*Journey
in Faith
Series*

D1360451

Church

Our Faith Story

*Catholic High School
Teacher's Edition*

**by
Beth Lowry Speck**

General Editors
John S. Nelson, Ph.D.
Catherine Zates Nelson

Special Consultants
Rev. James T. Mahoney, Ph.D.
Rev. Peter Mann
Sr. Ruth McDonell, I.H.M.
Sr. Marie Paul, O.P.
Sr. Dominga M. Zapata, S.H.

Contributors
Elinor R. Ford, Ed.D.
Eileen E. Anderson
Eleanor Ann Brownell
Joyce A. Crider
Mary Ellen McCarthy
William M. McDonald
Joan McGinnis-Knorr
William J. Reedy
Joseph F. Sweeney

The content of this program
reflects the goals of *Sharing the
Light of Faith* (NCD).

Sadlier
A Division of
William H. Sadlier, Inc.
New York
Chicago
Los Angeles

Nihil Obstat
Rev. Donald J. Tracey
Censor Librorum

Imprimatur
✠ Raymond J. Gallagher
Bishop of Lafayette-in-Indiana

February 16, 1981

The nihil obstat and imprimatur are
official declarations that a book or
pamphlet is free of doctrinal or
moral error. No implication is
contained therein that those who have
granted the nihil obstat and imprimatur
agree with the contents, opinions, or
statements expressed.

Assistant Project Director:
  Sr. Ruth McDonell, I.H.M.
Project Editor: Sr. Jane Keegan, R.D.C.
Managing Editor: Gerald A. Johannsen
Design Director: Willi Kunz
Designer: Grace Kao
Photo Editor: Lenore Weber
Photo Researcher: Mary Brandimarte
Photo Coordinator: Martha Hill Newell

Home Office:
11 Park Place
New York, N.Y. 10007

ISBN: 0-8215-2920-X
123456789/9876543210

Contents

3

Additional Chapter Features:

- **Student Involvement:** recurring opportunities for sharing concerns, raising questions, internalizing experiences.
- **Challenges:** questions and activities which reinforce and extend the learning experiences of the chapter.
- **Prayer Reflection:** opportunities for personal prayer and communal sharing based on the theme of the chapter.

Authors

John S. Nelson, Ph.D.
Moral Growth
Lifestyles
General Editor:
Journey in Faith Series

Director, Division of
Adolescent Religious Development
Fordham University

Catherine Zates Nelson
General Editor:
Journey in Faith Series

Co-Author of Sadlier
Lord of Life Series
Grades 7 & 8

Paul E. Bumbar
Faith

Supervisor of Child Care
St. Agatha's Home of the
New York Foundling Hospital
Nanuet, N.Y.

Anthony J. Cernera
Social Issues

Assistant Director, Bread for
the World Educational Fund

Sr. Regina Coll, C.S.J.
Death and Dying

Campus Minister
Queen's College, N.Y.

Judith Craemer
Old Testament:
Hebrew Scriptures

Teacher, Los Angeles Unified
School District
Los Angeles, CA

Patricia Curley
Social Issues

Chairperson, Religion Department
St. Helena's Commercial High
School, Bronx, N.Y.
Chairperson Bread for the World
Bronx Chapter

Sr. Mary Dennison, r.c.
Church

Assistant Director of the
Graduate School of Religious
Education
St. Thomas University
Houston, TX

Gloria Durka, Ph.D.
Faith

Associate Professor of Religious
Education and Theology, Graduate
School of Religion and Religious
Education, Fordham University.
Director of Division of Family
Ministry

Peter F. Ellis, S.S.L.
New Testament:
Christian Scriptures

Professor of Biblical Theology
Graduate School of Religion
and Religious Education
Fordham University

Judith Monahan Ellis
New Testament:
Christian Scriptures

Religious Education Coordinator
St. Denis — St. Columba Parish
Hopewell Junction, N.Y.

Thomas V. Forget
Social Issues

Chairperson, Manhattan
Chapter, Bread for the World

Rev. Robert J. Hater, Ph.D.
Ministry in Catholic
High Schools

Theologian for Studies in Spirituality
and An Active Spirituality for a
Global Community Program
Cincinnati, Ohio

Brennan R. Hill, Ph.D.
Jesus

Director of Parish Programs
Office of Religious Education
Diocese of Albany, N.Y.

Gloria Hutchinson
Prayer and Worship

Free lance writer
Former high school teacher
and religious education
coordinator
Brunswick, ME

Rev. James T. Mahoney, Ph.D.
Church

Assistant Superintendent of
Schools for Religious Education
Diocese of Paterson, N.J.

George McCauley, S.J., D. és Sc. Rel.
Prayer and Worship

Associate Professor of
Theology, Graduate School
of Religion and Religious
Education, Fordham University

Nadine McGuinness, C.S.J.
Old Testament:
Hebrew Scriptures

Director of Master's Program
in Religious Studies
Loyola-Marymount University
Los Angeles, CA

Rev. Frank J. McNulty, S.T.D.
Lifestyles
Professor of Moral Theology
Immaculate Conception Seminary
Darlington, N.J.
Vicar for Priests
Archdiocese of Newark
Mahwah, N.J.

Joanmarie Smith, C.S.J., Ph.D.
Death and Dying

Associate Professor of
Philosophy, St. Joseph's
College, Brooklyn, N.Y.

Joanne Roach Stickles
Lifestyles

Religious Education Coordinator
Most Holy Name Parish
Garfield, N.J.

Consultants

Dr. Elinor R. Ford
Vice President and Publisher
William H. Sadlier, Inc.

Joyce A. Crider
Assistant Editor in Chief
William H. Sadlier, Inc.

William M. McDonald
Project Director
Journey in Faith Series
William H. Sadlier, Inc.

Eleanor Ann Brownell
National Consultant
William H. Sadlier, Inc.

Sr. M. Jeannine Curley, R.S.M.
Secondary Religion Chairman
Religion Department Chairman
Immaculate Conception
Diocese of Memphis, TN

Rev. Peter Mann
Theologian and Producer
Diocesan Television Center
Uniondale, NY

June O'Connor, Ph.D.
Assistant Professor of Religious
Studies
University of California
Riverside, CA

Sr. Dominga M. Zapata, S.H.
Consultant: Spanish Division
Archdiocesan Center of CCD
Chicago, IL

Eileen E. Anderson
Vice President and
Assistant Publisher
William H. Sadlier, Inc.

William J. Reedy
Vice President and
Director of Catechetics
William H. Sadlier, Inc.

Ruth McDonell, I.H.M.
Assistant Project Director
Journey in Faith Series
William H. Sadlier, Inc.

Mary Ellen McCarthy
Regional Sales Manager
William H. Sadlier, Inc.

Rev. John E. Forliti, D.Min.
Director of Religious Education
Archdiocese of St. Paul and
Minnesota, MN

Sr. Rosemary Muckerman, S.S.N.D.
Supervisor, Secondary Schools
Archdiocese of Los Angeles, CA

Sr. Marie Paul, O.P.
Associate Director of Youth
Ministry/Catechesis
Archdiocese of Newark, NJ

Joseph F. Sweeney
Vice President and
Editor in Chief
William H. Sadlier, Inc.

Gerard F. Baumbach
Assistant Director of
Catechetics
William H. Sadlier, Inc.

Joan McGinnis-Knorr
Director of Market Research
Manager of Consultant Services
William H. Sadlier, Inc.

Rev. Michael J. Carroll
Assistant Superintendent of
Schools
Archdiocese of Philadelphia, PA

Rev. James F. Hawker
Director of Religious Education
— Schools
Archdiocese of Boston, MA

Dr. Samuel M. Natale, S.J.
Associate Professor
Psychology and Management
Col. of Business Admin.
St. John's University, NY

Lawrence J. Payne
Director, Office of Black
Ministries
Diocese of Galveston-Houston,
TX

Introduction

The *Journey in Faith Series* is offered to contemporary Catholic youth and to those who minister with them to assist in the study of the Catholic Faith. It provides the catechetical component of youth ministry in Catholic high schools and parish schools of religion. The series addresses the needs of youth at a critical stage of their faith development. Each of the texts provides opportunities for the sharing of faith experience and the building of Christian community.

The *Journey in Faith Series* is designed to meet wider youth ministry goals such as:

● That both young people and adults realize that they are a ministering community, that is, people who help each other in their journey of faith.

● That each one become more knowledgeable about the community's doctrines, heritage, rites, symbols, values, and great persons. As a community we share rich traditions.

● That in this shared journey each one find his or her own way of praying, serving, and becoming his or her own best self. We are a community who cherishes the uniqueness of each of its members.

The *Journey in Faith Series* was prepared by a catechetical team whose members have journeyed in faith with young people in schools and parishes.

Many of the team members are biblical scholars, theologians, psychologists, and educators. They offer from their disciplines the best of today's thinking for responding to faith questions and for sharing faith experiences.

The Series directly reflects the goals of *Sharing the Light of Faith: National Catechetical Directory for Catholics of the United States*. The Series applies in a practical way the wisdom of *Sharing the Light of Faith*. From this document, may we cite one passage in particular to express what is central to *Journey in Faith*:

"The source of catechesis, which is also its content, is one: God's word, fully revealed in Jesus Christ and at work in the lives of people exercising their faith under the guidance of the magisterium, which alone teaches authentically. God's word deposited in scripture and tradition is manifested and celebrated in many ways: in the liturgy and 'in the life of the Church, especially in the just and in the saints'; moreover, 'in some way it is known too from those genuine moral values which, by divine providence, are found in human society.' Indeed, potentially at least, every instance of God's presence in the world is a source of catechesis." (#41)

The *Journey in Faith Series* is true to *Sharing the Light of Faith* in another way. In matters of doctrinal substance, it is clearly and explicitly Catholic. It makes use of a wide variety of learning processes.

The Series recognizes and respects the enormous range of backgrounds and experiences of those who may be using these books. It does not shy away from its task of evangelizing and catechizing explicitly the Good News that is Jesus Christ.

The Series strikes a balance between *input* from the catechist or youth minister and *discovery* by the young person through individual and group activity.

Again, to cite *Sharing the Light of Faith*:

"It is significant that many adolescents apparently stop thinking about religion long before they consciously reject it. Various reasons are suggested. . . . To the extent that these explanations are valid, the answer seems to lie in adapting catechesis to the mental age of young people, and allowing them to question, discuss, and explore religious beliefs. . . . If such steps as these are taken; if young people are provided with models of faith which they perceive as credible and relevant; if they are challenged to confront the fullness of religious truth — then there is reason to hope that, as they grow older, adolescents will progress in faith and religious practice and suffer no delay in the process of religious maturation." (#200)

To assist catechists, this series includes a handbook which relates the *Journey in Faith Series* to the catechetical component of youth ministry programs in schools and parishes.

Student Materials

The texts pictured in the top row were designed primarily for ninth and tenth grades; those below for grades eleven and twelve. However, they are not limited to these levels and could be used in the curriculum wherever appropriate.

Moral Growth: A Christian Perspective, John S. Nelson, Ph.D.
This text focuses on the dynamic relationship between personal and moral growth. The processes of decision-making and the stages of personal development are examined as ways by which this growth takes place.

Old Testament: Hebrew Scriptures, Nadine McGuinness, C.S.J., Judith Craemer
This text presents important themes of the Hebrew Scriptures which speak to some life questions of Christians today: human relationships and law, personal and social morality, the dignity of persons, the recurring Passover experience in our lives.

Prayer and Worship: Praise the Lord with Gladness, George McCauley, S.J., D. és Sc. Rel., Gloria Hutchinson
This text encourages students to examine concepts and practices of prayer — both individual prayer and the liturgical prayer of the Church. The emphasis is on the sacraments and prayer which express the relationship of a life lived in God's presence.

Death and Dying: A Night Between Two Days, Joanmarie Smith, C.S.J., Ph.D., Regina Coll, C.S.J.
This text explores death as experienced by all humans, as reacted to in various religious traditions, and as understood in the light of Christian faith. In Catholic Christian tradition this text explains that the resurrection of Jesus is the promise of new life.

Lifestyles: Shaping One's Future, Rev. Frank J. McNulty, S.T.D., John S. Nelson, Ph.D., Joanne Roach Stickles
This text is designed to assist students in coming to a deeper appreciation of their sexual and vocational identity. The student is challenged to consider the various vocations which reflect a mature Christian lifestyle.

Social Issues: A Just World, Anthony J. Cernera, Thomas V. Forget, Patricia Curley
Examining the Scriptures as the foundation for our involvement in and concern for the value of human life, this text helps the student to examine ways to solve some of the complex social issues of our time.

Support Materials

New Testament: Christian Scriptures, Peter F. Ellis, S.S.L., Judith Monahan Ellis
This text helps the student to understand the value of the Christian Scriptures as a source of knowledge to establish a relationship with Jesus. The New Testament writings exemplify what it means to be a member of the Christian community.

Church: Our Faith Story, Sr. Mary E. Dennison, r.c., Rev. James T. Mahoney, Ph.D.
Through a study of Christian Scriptures and Church life, this text develops the "story" of the Church as the community of Christ. The students are encouraged to see how their own personal stories form part of the Christian community's story.

Spirit Masters
The *Journey in Faith Spirit Master Paks* are available through William H. Sadlier, Inc. These worksheets are designed to encourage dialogue about the themes of the chapter. The teacher will find them a resource for facilitating the student's journey of faith. The Pak also includes an attitudinal and informational survey to be used by the students at the beginning of the course.

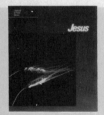

Jesus: God's Son with Us, Brennan R. Hill, Ph.D.
This text helps the students to answer the two questions put by Jesus to his first disciples: "Who do people say that I am?" "Who do you say that I am?" In so doing, they are helped in developing their own faith in who Jesus is and what meaning he has in their lives.

Faith: Becoming True and Free, Gloria Durka, Ph.D., Paul E. Bumbar
This text presents faith as an ongoing, developing process. Students are helped to see the gift of faith as the dynamic force which shapes our personalities and relationships.

Ministry in Catholic High Schools, Rev. Robert J. Hater, Ph.D.
This book helps teachers reflect on their role as ministers in the Catholic High School. Models for ministry are offered and analyzed. Concrete suggestions are presented to improve and expand that ministry.

About This Guide...

Each chapter of this Guide builds upon the following components:

Objectives: what we intend the students to know, to feel, to do as a result of this learning experience. We recognize that, in sharing faith and moral values, individual freedom plays an important role. Hence some of our objectives may be beyond empirical measurement or verification.

Orientation: a sense of the chapter — its relationship to what precedes and what follows, its internal flow, logic, and structure. The orientation's purpose is to maintain a good progression from chapter to chapter and within the chapter itself.

Life Experience Focus: a statement of how the content and process of the chapter arises from or is related to the wider life of the adolescents. According to its subject matter, a chapter may stay totally within the life experience of the students or it may begin with their life experience, move on to items from the Christian community's tradition, then return in reflection and application to their everyday lives.

Background on Content: a statement for the teacher, in more technical terms, of the theology, biblical scholarship, or human sciences which underlie the substance of the chapter. The authors of this series have tried to present the best of recent scholarship in nontechnical language for the students.

Teaching Notes: practical indications on how to present the chapter section by section. For ease in reference, Teaching Notes for each chapter are divided into three parts and they follow the section headings found in the student text. One feature of the Teaching Notes is the reference to the *Journey in Faith Spirit Master Pak* which contains 24 worksheets for use throughout the course. They are reproduced in miniature at the back of this Guide, and they may be obtained from William H. Sadlier, Inc.

Prayer and Worship Experiences: possibilities for personal prayer or communal celebration at different moments of the learning experience. This section may refer not only to the "Prayer Reflection" at the close of each chapter in the student text, but also to other items in the chapter where prayer is appropriate.

Service Projects: ways in which students can live out the knowledge and attitudes which have become more their own through the learning experience. Granted there are difficulties of programming service activities for adolescents, such a dimension, however, is very important to their growth in faith, and to the carrying of that faith into civic and secular life.

Independent Study Projects: items which lend themselves to library research, further reading, oral or written presentations. The student texts are designed more for group learning than for individualized instruction, yet they are open to personalized assignments.

Resources: selected audiovisual and print material for use by the teacher and, at times, by the students. These materials represent some of the sources researched by the authors of both the student's text and the teacher's guide.

Outline
of the Text

Using the method of a personal story, this text brings the student to an awareness of the journey of faith that is taken by those who participate actively in the life of the Church. Through a solid understanding of the scriptural foundations of the Church, the student will appreciate our continuing participation in the story of Jesus' Good News in the Catholic Christian tradition.

By use of a journal technique the students link together the story of the Church with their own. Drawing upon the experiences of the student's life, the course will gradually lead the student forward in a journey towards an acceptance of responsibility to be a full participant in the Church.

The priority of worship, the role of the parish, and the different approaches to Church constitute major themes of the course.

Through an understanding of the history of the Church, students can better determine their own attitudes about the Church and how those attitudes might change or grow in the future.

The major objective of this course is to join the story of the Church, the community of believers in Jesus Christ, with the student's story so that the student will realize that the Church's story becomes our story.

The following overview is given to provide the teacher with the scope of the entire text:

Chapter One — **Writing Your Story** deals with the student's own story of his or her life and the importance of one's personal lifestory to the growth of the Christian community.

Chapter Two — **Jesus: The Father's Story** considers the ways in which Jesus invited people to experience the love of God through his ministry of word, community, service, and celebration, and how they are continued in the Church today.

Chapter Three — **The Father's Story in the Church** gives us a picture of the early Christian community and some of the problem situations which challenged the followers of Jesus.

Chapter Four — **Understanding Our Story** presents various models of the Church to help the student reflect on the reality of the Church today. The marks of the Church challenge the student to make the Church visible in life.

Chapter Five — **Living the Story Together** leads the student to a consideration of the roots of the Church in the Hebrew Scriptures, and shows how in Jesus a new covenant began in which his followers became the new people of God.

Chapter Six — **Sharing Our Story** traces briefly the story of the Christian community from the time of St. Paul to the present day. In each era persons of vision and hope are presented to show how God continues to be with his followers.

Chapter Seven — **Proclaiming Our Story** describes the task of the Christian community in bringing the good news of the kingdom to the rest of the world. Evangelization and catechesis. are shown as central to faith development.

Chapter Eight — **Celebrating Our Story** calls the student to develop an ''attitude'' of celebration. Each of the sacraments is considered as a celebration of the Christian community.

Chapter Nine — **Acting on Our Story** presents the Church community as an agent of Jesus Christ in trying to meet the needs of the poor, the hungry, the oppressed, and those who are alone in the world. Action on behalf of justice is presented as a mark of a follower of Christ.

Chapter Ten — **Our Story Takes Shape** looks at the Church as it is experienced in the parish community and describes the various ways each person's talents can be utilized. The Rite of Christian Initiation is described, and future concerns of the parish are explored.

1

Writing Your Story

Text Pages
4–21

Objectives

Knowledge: To help the students realize the significance of their own individual lifestories as a frame of reference for understanding the story and meaning of the Church.

Attitude: To lead the students to appreciate how their own lifestories intersect with and mirror the larger story of the Christian community's journey so that they will understand and value their participation in it.

Practice: To have the students write their own lifestories by identifying significant persons, events, and experiences in their past and present lives.

Orientation

The opening chapter of the text introduces the theme of story which underlies the entire book. The concept of lifestory or personal journey is presented as both a universal experience and a significant influence upon our attitudes toward life.

It is important that the theme of story reach the students on a personal level. For this reason a major activity in the chapter is to have the students write about their own personal journeys from birth to now. In the text the Church and the human community are presented as integral to one another. Students will need direction to be able to see their own lifestories as microcosms of the Church's story—a story of human effort and struggle, of success and failure, of being saved by a loving God over and over again. The teacher should help the students understand that the Church's story shapes them, and that they in turn have a responsibility for shaping it. Ultimately they should be led to the realization that the larger picture of Church community is more complete and enhanced by sharing in it.

"What's In a Story" (text pages 4–6) introduces the concept of story very simply by mentioning the universal appeal of stories as well as the variety of types which exist. An immediate connection is made between one's personal lifestory and the Church's story.

Bill Robinson's negative experience on a basketball team (text pages 5–6) concretizes the significance of giving attention to lifestories. Most students can identify with and remember negative experiences, but may not yet have begun to realize the importance of *how* we remember them. The pain and hurt are all too easily remembered, but a tremendous growth potential exists if, in remembering those feelings, decisions are made to alter future circumstances. This is important to emphasize now so that it can be used as a point of reference in later chapters.

"Family Stories" (text page 7) expands on the idea of how much we are shaped by our families and in turn shape them. Knowledge about family can bring us into more intimate relationships with one another. Still, adolescence is often an age when a natural strain occurs between parents and children. Family ties are fragile and tenuous today because of the frequency of broken and separated families. Some students may wish to avoid or even negate their thoughts about family history. Nonetheless, their history is a part of them. Here again an atmosphere of trust is necessary so that the level of rapport between teacher and students can be reached.

"Special People" (text page 8) develops the notion of belonging to peer groups outside of the family circle. Students will readily identify with this since peer acceptance is such a crucial need for young people. Use this interest as a step toward introducing the Church as Christian community with Jesus as its source and life.

In the "Christian Community's Story" (text pages 8–10) the parallel is drawn for the students between themselves and their story, between themselves and the Christian community's lifestory. Its focus is on Jesus' own story and on stories he told, as well as the stories about the followers of Jesus.

"Our Story Is Ongoing" (text pages 10–11) expands the idea of Church and sketches a profile of its members and their purpose, attitudes, and way of life. This section brings out the reason why it is so important to know the Church's story by elaborating on a previous point. Knowing *how* our story shapes us can help students understand themselves better and gain a sense of direction. Such personal growth can affect the way they shape the future of the Church.

In "My Own Sense of Direction" (text pages 12–16) the students are encouraged to write their own lifestories by stepping back and looking at their lives up to now. The first step is the construction of a lifeline from remembered persons, events, and experiences. The process expands in *Model for The Book of Life*. The purpose is to help them internalize their journey and thereby discover more about their remembered past.

The final step of the process occurs in "Reflecting on Our Story" (text pages 17–19). Here the students are led to a deeper appreciation of their own experiences, both good and bad, through the practice of reflection, a vital component for growth during the journey of life.

Life Experience Focus

Because of the physical and emotional upheaval taking place in young people, introspection is often a common occurrence for them during this period of their lives. As a result, adolescents tend to magnify their minor blemishes and faults as well as their negative experiences. Through the painful transition from the child into the adult, and from their ideal world into the real world, young people tend to look at others with a very critical eye, especially those outside their peer group. Estrangement may occur between young people and authority figures. This period usually lasts until the young person is more able to understand and accept the fragile reality of humanness.

The personal nature of this chapter requires the teacher to be keenly aware of the heightened sensitivity of the students. If a loving and understanding climate is created in the classroom, many opportunities for personal growth can be realized by the students.

Background on Content

"Storytelling Theology" has flourished rapidly in recent years. What is new about it is its incorporation into contemporary spirituality. Spiritual directors today are focusing people's attention on the sacredness of each unique lifestory. Through prayerful examination of their past experiences, people are more able to see how God has been acting in their lives. This can help people to discern the movements of God in the present.

In a world where media bombardment is constantly capturing the young person's attention, "journal keeping" can provide a means for becoming more attuned to what is happening *within* the events of life. The Journal Workshop Process includes periods of quiet time to allow the feelings which surround remembered events to emerge. It is recommended that the teacher provide such an atmosphere while the students are working on *The Book of Life*. Quiet time may be foreign to the students initially, but it is all the more needed by them. More journal activities will be provided throughout this Guide. It is suggested that the teacher refer to Ira Progoff's writings for further explanation (see *Resources* for this Guide chapter).

The sharing of lifestories, especially of one's faith experiences, in both spoken and written word, is a vital element in the ministry of evangelization today. In so doing, a person gives testimony to the power of the Spirit in this world. Witness talks such as these are known to motivate the listeners to greater faith in God. It has been found that they are especially effective for high school students at retreat programs. Students should have the opportunity for this type of sharing after *The Book of Life* activity.

Storytelling theology is not really new, but rather as ancient as the human race. It is inherent in our Judaeo-Christian tradition. Jesus used stories to teach profound truths. He was influenced by the use of story in the cultural traditions of his Jewish ancestors. The gospels are not histories, but stories about Jesus which were first shared orally as testimonies of faith. Our eucharistic liturgy celebrates anew the story of God's love expressed through his Son Jesus.

The lifestories of Jesus' followers who have lived out their faith-inspired values have motivated others down through the centuries. The students are invited to be part of this process. This chapter should cultivate their sense of awe at the preciousness of life and heritage that is theirs. It is not too soon to challenge them to explore the deeper level within life's events!

Teaching Notes 1

Text Pages
4–7

What's In a Story

1. To introduce the theme of story, ask the students a few questions about their interest in stories, such as the following:
- What kinds of stories do you like best?
- What types of characters do you enjoy or relate to most in books?
- What stories do you remember from your childhood as "favorite"? For example, fairy tales. (This could be done orally or by having the students complete *Worksheet #1.*)

Whichever means you use, encourage the students to share their interests with the group. Use this as an "ice breaker" to get them talking to one another about a non-threatening topic.

2. Use a word association technique such as, "The word 'Church' makes you think of . . ." to initiate the topic of Church. Direct the students to express the first word that comes to mind when they hear the word "Church."
    a. Accept each response that is given in a non-judgmental way and list on the chalkboard or on a transparency to keep it before them. Be aware that some students may refrain from contributing because of their negative views about Church.
    b. After a number of responses have

been given, ask them where they think these impressions may have come from. Next to each word on the list, write the suggested source.
    c. Then have students analyze what was said by asking them if the words on the list are positive ones or negative. Allow time for any discussion or any airing of feelings which might arise from this activity. The manner in which this initial discussion about Church is handled could either encourage or limit the degree of honesty and openness that students will bring to successive discussions.
    d. Have each student write a descriptive paragraph about the Church according to their own individual understanding of it now. Tell them that these will be referred to later in the course. Have them conclude their descriptions by answering the question, "Where do you see yourself in your picture of the Church now?"

Collect the papers and plan to use them as a measuring point at the end of the course to see what growth, change, and development of their understanding has occurred during the learning process.

3. After the reading of Bill Robinson's story (text pages 5–6), lead a discussion on the students' reactions to it along these lines:
- How did Bill Robinson feel as a benchwarmer?
- Should the coach have acted in this way with his players?
- What would you have done if you were the coach of this team?
- What do you think might have improved the situation for the team?
- Why is teamwork important? How does a team develop it?
- How did this experience affect Bill's decisions in his adult life?
- Have you ever had an experience like Bill Robinson's? How did you handle it?
- Do you think you could make your experience work for you the way Bill made his work for him? Please explain.

15

Offer encouragement and opportunity for the students to share their experiences from the exercise that follows about an important event in their lives (text page 6). Ask them to explain why it is so meaningful. For some students it may be difficult to single out one event as being so influential. For others, the pain involved in their experience—loss of a parent through death or divorce, a sickness, handicap, or a failure in themselves—may prevent them from being able to share it. The teacher should be keenly aware of how students are responding. What might *seem* to be non-participation may in fact be quiet suffering and intent listening.

A key point to focus on is the *kind* of learning that a person might gain from the events in their lives. Invite the students to share their thoughts about how and what others may learn from their experiences. Since students at this age are so influenced by their peers, this sharing activity should provide much food for thought. The film *A Day in the Life of Bonnie Consolo* might have much to say to students in conjunction with this section. Bonnie was born without arms but lives a normal life as a wife and mother. (See *Resources* for this Guide chapter.)

Family Stories
1. Move into the next section on "Family Stories" (text page 7) by asking the students to recall any funny stories connected with a past celebration of the holidays in their family. Give one or two examples from your own childhood to get them started. Undoubtedly every family has had some funny experiences at holiday times. Telling these should provide some amusement, and at the same time pave the way for a more serious approach to family.

Next ask students these questions:
● Which member of the family do they know best? least? Why?
● Who do they think they are most like?
● What kind(s) of experiences did each of their parents have in high school?

(If they are unable to answer this question, tell them to find out at home.)

2. The exercise which follows calls for a prayerful setting. To prepare students for it, have them close their eyes and then lead them in a short breathing exercise. When they are in a more relaxed, quiet state, have them recall an unhappy time when they felt farthest away from their family. Try to get them to identify the feelings they had, and what caused them. Then have the students write about it in a conversational form to God. Ask that they conclude it with a petition of some nature, for example:
● asking God to heal the hurt they feel;
● asking God to help them forgive someone else who caused this painful situation;
● asking God to help their families grow closer to one another;
● asking God to help them understand their families better or be more patient toward them.

It is good to end this reflection on a positive note. Repeat the breathing and picturing process again, but this time have the students visualize a time when they felt *closest* to their family, and were very happy. Once again, have them write a descriptive conversation-prayer to God about this experience. Invite any students who wish to share their family memories to do so.

3. Either of two appropriate films would be an excellent supplement for this section, *Grandpa Doc* or *Peege.* Each film depicts a young person remembering the vibrant life that a grandpa shared with them. Through the use of flashbacks, it is apparent to the viewer how in each of these films the young person has been shaped and influenced by the loving grandparent.

Conclude this section by pointing out that both happy and unhappy feelings occur, and that both are an inevitable part of life.

Teaching Notes 2

Text Pages
8–11

Special People

Use *Worksheet #2* to expand the concept of belonging beyond the family unit. While the students are filling out this worksheet help them by pointing out certain characteristics that one might admire, be drawn to, desire to emulate so as to make them a part of themselves.

When this is completed, have the students work in groups of four to compare their special persons and groups and to draw up a list of any characteristics that are common.

List the common characteristics on the chalkboard or the transparency. Help them to realize that in a community many times we share common experiences even when the events have been individual and separate ones. This is an important point to be emphasized so that the students can move from the self to the community mindset with as much continuity as possible.

The Christian Community's Story

1. Common experience should be a natural point for introducing the concept of Christian community by comparing the students' worksheets with the reason such a community was initially begun—"their experience of the presence of Jesus Christ in their lives" (text page 8). As the community grows so does the understanding of Jesus among the community of believers.

The community's common experience of Jesus came through the medium of stories in two different ways. Jesus' use of the parable, a story form, was his primary method of teaching people profound truths about God his Father and about themselves. (For more information on the use of parable, see Brennan Hill's text *Jesus: God's Son with Us* in Sadlier's *Journey in Faith* Series.) The other type of story is *about* Jesus—the gospel account, a collection of remembered words, events, and experiences that were told and retold from different points of view and that kept his presence alive to his followers. (See *New Testament: Christian Scriptures* by Peter Ellis in Sadlier's *Journey in Faith* Series.)

2. One way of introducing (or recalling) the concept of parable for the students is through a short film. *The Stray;* or *Right Here, Right Now;* or *Willie* would provide an excellent visual example of a parable Jesus told in a modern-day setting. Depending on the level of maturity in the group you might wish to show *The Parable,* a contemporary Jesus-story. (See *Resources* for this Guide chapter.)

3. In order to convey a sense of the power of the parables of Jesus and of their effect on the Christian community throughout the past 2000 years, assign each group of three students a certain parable to read and then rewrite in a different historical time setting. You can either assign the time period or have them pick out of a box a slip of paper on which the time setting is briefly described. The ability level of your students will determine how much help they will need for this assignment. They can use their history books to provide themselves with background. The list of parables is as follows:
- The Pharisee and the Tax Collector—Luke 18:9–14
- The Laborers in the Vineyard—Matthew 20:1–16

- The Rich Man and Lazarus—Luke 16:19–31
- The Good Samaritan—Luke 10:25–37
- Parable of the Seed—Matthew 13:3–23

It may be necessary to clarify the meaning of the parable first before the students begin the task of rewriting it in a different historical period. Have them read their creative stories to the class and have the class be prepared to explain each parable's point as seen in this new setting. Very often the parables reveal different things to different people. This should be pointed out as a part of the beauty of the parables— their mystery and significance.

Our Story Is Ongoing

This activity is intended to show the enduring quality of the words of Jesus as well as the span of time during which the people of the Christian community have witnessed to the words of Jesus. It is important that the students focus not only on the past—but on the present and the future as well. Jesus Christ is Lord of history but it is a story that encompasses yesterday, today, and tomorrow.

Have the students write down what each parable says to them personally. Show the connections between the parables of Jesus with history and ultimately with our own lives by elaborating on the quote (text page 10). A point to emphasize here is the value of having a sense of direction. Knowing where we have come from, where we are now, and where we are going can be a great challenge fo adolescents who tend to live only in the present.

The short film *The Shopping Bag Lady* can be used to bring out this point. (See *Resources* for this Guide chapter.)

Teaching Notes 3

Text Pages
10–21

My Own Sense of Direction

1. The effectiveness of the next activity (text page 12) will depend on preparation, that is, how well the students understand what they are doing and why. Assure them that this activity will be very helpful for their inner growth, which only they and God can see and measure.

2. Illustrate the lifeline for them on the chalkboard and take time to explain the directions for coding the significant items. Your own willingness to reveal a few items that might be on your lifeline might give them more confidence to enter into this activity.

3. Establish a reflective atmosphere by playing quiet instrumental background music, such as ''Be'' or ''Dear Father'' from the *Jonathan Livingston Seagull* album. (See *Resources* for this Guide chapter.)

4. Before they move into the stage of descriptively writing their ''Book of Life,'' repeat the breathing technique which was taught earlier in the course. This will help them to relax and allow their deeper thoughts to surface. Move among them while the students are working on this project, answering questions and making suggestions. The section on faith experiences will be difficult for them to describe on their own. Here again, the sharing done by the teacher can help the students to learn a great deal.

5. When the students are ready for the section on ''Who Are You?'' have them share their responses with one another. Be affirming toward each response and make it a positive experience. The ability of the students to be open about themselves and their feelings will be important to discussions in the future.

Reflecting on Our Story

1. Have the students write in their journals a reflection on their feelings about this chapter, answering the following questions:
- How did I feel while writing my life story?
- Am I able to see how my story fits in with others' stores?
- Do I want to know more about this community called Church to which I belong?
- Do I want to know more about myself and my commitment to Jesus?

2. Use one of the prayer experiences (See *Prayer and Worship Experiences* for this Guide chapter) to help the students internalize what they have learned about self and about story.

3. For a closing exercise have the students put all their life stories together in a pile. Then each student arbitrarily chooses someone else's. Give the students time to read the other person's story and to write a letter to the author about some significant points that struck them while reading, as well as any feelings they have concerning the life story. The reader should be sensitive to the fact that the author has written very personally and is sharing a very important part of themselves with another.

The purpose of such an exercise is to build up
a sense of trust and of community sharing,
experiences that will be used again
throughout the book.

4. Return the life stories to their authors and
have the students read the comments.
Write on the board "My Story" and have
the students brainstorm their feelings about
the comments from the other students.
Bring the students to a consensus of opinion
in the brainstorming session about the
meaning of community and how sharing
our experiences enables us to come together
and see one another as a part of
ourselves.

Prayer and Worship Experiences

1. Have the students bring to class a poem or the lyrics to a song that says something to them about their life story. In a reflective setting with instrumental music in the background, have the students share their verses allowing time for shared reflection.

2. Play the Neil Diamond song "I Am, I Said." Distribute paper with the words "I Am, I Said" on the top of the page and ask the students to write a prayerful response. Collect the responses and read them reflectively to the students. Then replay the song and allow time for a spontaneous prayer response.

3. Do a prayer service on life stories:
- Opening: Invite a student to read the prayer from text page 21.
- Scripture Reading: Psalm 139.
- Silent Reflection: Have the students compose their own prayers in which they offer their book of life back to God. In addition, direct them to choose one particular thing from their books that they feel should be prayed about. Have them spend this quiet time talking to God about it, either in writing or simply in their own hearts. If any students wish to share their prayers aloud, invite them to do so.
- Closing Song: Use a record or have students sing an appropriate song about life, such as "Yahweh" or "Take, Lord, Receive," both by John Foley, S.J.

Service Projects

1. Have the students make a list of their own individual gifts and talents. Identify those students with similar gifts, putting them into groups of three and giving them the option of offering some kind of service in their home, school, or family. Each group must formulate a plan and decide which gifts or talents will be used. Each group should choose a different place for providing their service. Direct them to choose projects which will help them to affirm who and what they are.

2. Provide time for the groups to meet together and discuss their experiences so that they can report to the class. Each group should be prepared to explain its project to the others and also to explain how it made them know themselves better.

Independent Study Projects

1. Have the students conduct research into their family trees, using many different sources, such as the geneological library, relatives' recollections, antiques, memorabilia, etc. Have them piece together a family story traced from the beginnings of their families to the present.

2. To get in touch with someone else's story and see how life experiences influence other's values, have the students interview a non-family member about his or her life story and write a report that will illustrate what they have learned in this chapter.

3. Have the students read a biography or an autobiography of a person in history who interests them. Have them analyze that individual's life story and prepare a written profile of the person's feelings about self, the major influences upon his or her life, and a summary of what this study says to them in contrast to their own life stories.

Resources

Audiovisual

Grandpa Doc, 30 minutes, color.

Peege, 28 minutes, color. Phoenix Films.

A Day in the Life of Bonnie Consolo, 17 minutes, color. Barr Films, Pasadena, CA 91107.

The Stray, 15 minutes, color. TeleKETICS Film. Franciscan Communications Center, Los Angeles, CA 90015.

Right Here, Right Now, 17 minutes, color. TeleKETICS Films.

Willie, 1S minutes, color. TeleKETICS Films.

The Shopping Bag Lady, 21 minutes, color. Learning Corporation of America, NY: 10019.

Parable, 15 minutes, color. Broadcasting and Film Commission of National Council of Churches, 457 Riverside Drive, New York, NY 10027.

"I Am, I Said." Song by Neil Diamond from the album *Neil Diamond/His 12 Greatest Hits.* MGA Records, 100 Universal Plaza, Universal City, CA.

"Be" and "Dear Father." Songs by Neil Diamond from the album *Jonathan Livingston Seagull,* Columbia Records, CBS, New York.

Print

P. Ellis, J. Ellis. *New Testament: Christian Scriptures.* Journey in Faith series. New York: W. H. Sadlier, 1981.

J. Fowler, S. Keen. *Life Maps: Conversations on the Journey of Faith.* Minneapolis, MN: Winston Press.

B. Hill. *Jesus: God's Son with Us.* Journey in Faith series. New York: W. H. Sadlier, 1981.

I. Progoff. *At a Journal Workshop.* New York: Dialogue House Library, 1980.

I. Progoff. *The Practice of Process Meditation.* New York: Dialogue House Library, 1980.

R. McBrien. *Catholicism.* 2 vols. Minneapolis, MN: Winston Press, 1980.

J. E. Westin. *Finding Your Roots.* New York: St. Martin's Press, 1977.

"Storytelling and Theology." *New Catholic World* Ramsey, NJ: Paulist Press, March/April, 1979.

Good News Bible. American Bible Society. New York: W. H. Sadlier, 1976.

Sharing the Light of Faith: National Catechetical Directory for Catholics of the United States. Washington, D.C.: United States Catholic Conference, 1979.

23

2

Jesus: The Father's Story

**Text Pages
22–39**

Objectives
Knowledge: To lead the students to a greater understanding of Jesus and his ministry as the foundation of the Church.
Attitude: To develop in the students a positive awareness of what it means to be a Christian in the world today.
Practice: To enable the students to see and follow Jesus as the model for a Christian way of life.

Orientation
The underlying premise of this chapter is that the more students know Jesus, the more they will know and understand God. That experiential knowledge of Jesus should motivate students to enter into more loving relationships with God and with others in the human and Christian community. Continuing the theme of story begun in Chapter 1, the text expands upon the basic point that each person's life is influenced by other people who have made a significant impression.

In "Our Rediscovery" (text page 22), the students' attention is focused immediately on Jesus, the most significant person in

the story of the Church. Rather than simply reviewing what students already know about Jesus, the text involves them personally and actively in the study of Jesus. They are asked to recall and to write the life of Jesus as they understand it from their own experience. This approach provides another step in the journal writing process begun in Chapter 1. Students are then given a reflection activity to help them (and you) assess the scope of their knowledge and their feelings about Jesus and to see what ideas may have evolved out of the writing exercise. The time and care devoted to the handling of this section will be invaluable. The section concludes by drawing a parallel between the students' writing exercise and the process through which the gospels were formed.

The next section, "Mission of Jesus" (text page 26), identifies the threefold mission of Jesus. The text then speaks of goals that students can hope to accomplish in future chapters related to each area of Jesus' mission. The section entitled "Ministry of Jesus" (text page 28) explains the word *ministry* and illustrates the transforming love of Jesus' ministry by the story of the Samaritan woman. The exercise which follows (text page 28) challenges the students to reflect further on the life and purpose of Jesus in relation to their own purpose and mission in life. Students should be assisted in recognizing and discovering the opportunities for realistic service that are all around them and which they might overlook.

"Different Ways to Minister" (text page 29) briefly explains the different ministries of prayer, proclamation, and service as exemplified in Jesus' life. This section serves as an introduction and a link to the next four parts of the chapter. The remainder of the student text in this chapter is an unfolding of a quote from *Sharing the Light of Faith:* "the Church continues the mission of Jesus. . . . This one mission has three aspects: proclaiming and teaching God's Word, celebrating the sacred mysteries, and serving the people of the world. Corresponding to the three aspects of the Church's mission and existing to serve it are three ministries: the ministry of the Word, the ministry of worship, and the ministry of service." (#8)

In "Ministry of Word" (text page 29) the text highlights the power of Jesus' spoken word to transform people. Students are challenged to think about his power by doing an exercise on the meaning of several parables. Jesus' ministry of service is first examined in "Ministry of Community Building" (text page 30) and then in "Ministry of Serving and Healing" (text page 34). The students consider the meaning of each ministry by examining key passages in the Scriptures and by applying the meaning of these texts to their lives.

The section "Ministry of Celebration" (text page 34) makes a connection between the celebrations that are part of our everyday lives and the celebration that is integral to prayer and worship. Each type of celebration should overflow into and nourish the other. The accompanying exercise (text page 35) allows the students time to apply this concept of celebration to their experience of the Mass.

Life Experience Focus

Adolescents need inspiring models to help them develop and strengthen appropriate value systems for themselves. In order for a strong Christian value system to be developed, students will need help in seeing the genuine human qualities of Jesus. Jesus' relationship in prayer with the Father in turn guided his human growth as well as the sense of his mission and purpose in life. For the emerging adult, this point is significant. As the students' own relationship with God develops, so too will their sense of identity and their awareness of their own special purpose in life.

An affective approach is used for this study of Jesus and his ministry. This is important for the fostering of students' relationships *with* Jesus, as well as for attaining intellectual knowledge *about* him.

This approach is well supported by *Sharing the Light of Faith* which speaks about the variety of methods that are needed for an appropriate catechesis.

"The experiential approach is not easy, but it can be of considerable value to catechesis. Catechists should encourage people to reflect on their significant experiences and respond to God's presence there. Sometimes they will provide appropriate experiences. They should seek to reach the whole person, using both cognitive (intellectual) and affective (emotional) techniques." (176)

Background on Content

Contemporary theology offers much speculative input about the consciousness of Jesus. It is commonly agreed that Jesus' understanding about who and what he is grew out of his study of the Hebrew Scriptures, out of his prayerful relationship with his Father, and out of his own openness to the events and circumstances of his life.

Gerald O'Collins, in his book *What Are They Saying About Jesus?,* offers a concise summary of recent theories about this topic; Monika Hellwig does also in *What Are the Theologians Saying?* (See *Resources* in this chapter.) Although these are only speculative, such ideas about the consciousness of Jesus can encourage young people in their search for identity. Students can relate more closely to Jesus as they realize that he experienced a similar struggle in attempting to understand his own identity.

Lawrence Kohlberg, the developmental psychologist from Harvard University, testifies to the importance of behavioral models, especially for young people. In Kohlberg's studies of human moral development, described as a sequential movement through six successive stages, Kohlberg found that people are drawn towards the higher stage above them by hearing and observing others. For this reason Kohlberg strongly advocates that teachers encourage students to articulate their choices in given moral situations and to express aloud the reasons behind their choices. Kohlberg's insight points up the importance of a careful examination of the words and actions of Jesus, especially in his interactions with others. The time spent on this type of study in an atmosphere that is conducive to patient searching will be invaluable for students.

Teaching Notes 1

**Text Pages
22–26**

Our Rediscovery

1. Begin this chapter by asking the students if they know about any famous people whose lives made a significant impression on many others. List all their suggestions on the chalkboard and ask them to explain why the person was such an influence in each case. Be sure that students notice the particular quality which influenced the others; for example: loyalty, dedication to a cause, determination, courage, etc. If you can add examples from your own experience, it will increase the effectiveness of the lesson. Examples:

- Eric Heiden, winner of five gold medals for speed skating in the 1980 Winter Olympics; an example of determination and perseverance.
- Tai Babilonia, the world-champion ice dancer from California, who lost her chance to compete in the 1980 Winter Olympics at the last minute due to an injury to her skating partner, Randy Gardner; an example of acceptance of a great disappointment.
- Brian Piccolo, the professional football player who continued playing despite the pain of cancer until it abruptly ended his young life; an example of courage to his teammates, especially to Gale Sayers. (See *Resources* in this Guide chapter.)

- Betty Ford, wife of former President Gerald Ford, who admitted her battle with alcoholism and drugs, giving courage and hope to many people.

2. Ask the students to reexamine their journal-writing activity from Chapter 1 (text page 4), especially the section they wrote about the significant people in their lives. Impress upon the students the fact that many people influence our lives in a number of different ways. Some of the people will remain constant, while others may come and go or be part of our lives for only a brief period. As the main character said in the movie *I Never Sang for My Father*, "Death may end a life, but it does not end a relationship." No matter how long the time period, the people who make a difference in our lives are the ones who have left a lasting impression.

Point out to the students that Jesus is a person who had a profound effect on individuals, even though he may have had only a brief encounter with a person, as shown in the story of Jesus and the Samaritan woman (John 4:1–42). Moreover, keeping alive Jesus' story continued to inspire people down through the centuries. Jesus' presence—preserved in the gospels, celebrated in the Liturgy, and kept alive in faith—continues to influence people today. Ask the students to write in their journals a short paragraph entitled "Who and What Jesus Is to Me." If time permits, invite them to share their descriptions aloud, but do not exert any pressure on them to speak. Be aware that students may be reluctant to speak on such a personal topic. As a preparatory exercise to this activity use *Worksheet #3* which asks the students to reflect on and respond to Mark 8:27.

3. Step 1 in the activity about memories of Jesus (text page 24) calls for ten statements about Jesus; fewer than ten would be acceptable if students find ten difficult. Much of this will depend on the background and makeup of the group. Having the students exchange their selected statements in smaller groups (step 2, text page 24) will help those students with limited knowledge. In addition, all the students will be better prepared for the activity of writing Jesus' story (step 3, text page 25).

4. Point out that the activity in step 3 (text page 24) is similar to the writing of the "Book of Life," a student activity done in Chapter 1. If the students are an advanced group, teach them to write Jesus' life story according to the method of Ira Progoff as he describes it in "Towards Inner Relationship," Chapter 12 of his book *At a Journal Workshop.* (See *Resources* in this Guide chapter.) Progoff's process begins with a brief description of the relationship between you and the person chosen. The next task is to write a list of the "stepping stones," as he calls them, of the other person's life. In order to gain an inner perspective of the person, one steps inside that person's shoes, so to speak, and records the events of the other person's life. These are listed in the first person, beginning with, "I was born," and so on.

Quiet time should be established for the experience of a shared presence with the other person, which is likely to occur, and for the opportunity to reflect on the experience. An inner dialogue may also naturally arise. If time permits and your group seems to be capable of it, this method has been found very effective for individuals as well as for groups.

5. Here are some optional ways of accomplishing the task of reexamining the students' knowledge about Jesus:
- Have the students plan a modern film version of Jesus' life.
- Organize a presentation of a TV show—"This Is Your Life, Jesus."
- Plan a TV talk show in which three or four key people who knew Jesus well are interviewed.
- Create a series of ten telespots to focus peoples' attention on the ten most important experiences in Jesus' life.

Whatever will best help your students to become more in touch with the personhood of Jesus is the desirable goal and the heart of this chapter.

6. At the completion of this activity, show the parallel between the students' task and the writing of the gospels. The process is basically the same:
- recalling experiences and events;
- selecting those of major importance;
- reflecting on the meaning of the events;
- committing the events to writing;
- further reflection upon it all.

Teaching Notes 2

Text Pages
26–28

The Mission of Jesus

1. Ask the students what the word *mission* means to them. Relate the word to Jesus' life and purpose as described in the text (pages 26–27). Have the students look through the gospels for examples of each of the three major areas of Jesus' mission.

2. Next, have the students role play the scene in the Gospel of Luke where Jesus reads aloud the scroll from Isaiah in the synagogue and identifies it with himself (text page 27). Set the tone for the dramatization by giving whatever background information might be necessary; for example: the meaning of the passage, the role of the synagogue in Jewish life and tradition. Select a mature student to read the text as he or she feels Jesus would have read it. Have the rest of the group imagine themselves hearing it as the assembled body in the synagogue and responding to it as they think those persons may have responded.

Let them describe their feelings afterwards. Direct the students to draw conclusions about Jesus' understanding of his mission from the Father, and about the reactions of the people of his time to Jesus' proclamation. Emphasize how faithful Jesus was to the carrying out of his mission, despite the opposition of public opinion.

3. Have the students complete *Worksheet #4* on the mission of Jesus.

The Ministry of Jesus

1. Prepare the students to read the story of the Samaritan woman (John 4:5–42), by giving them this background information. Explain the hostility of the Jews towards the Samaritans since the time of the Northern Kingdom's collapse in the eighth century B.C. After the Assyrian takeover of Israel, the people of Samaria intermarried with the pagan Assyrians and allowed idol worship at pagan shrines. Faithful Jews regarded this as an unforgivable infidelity and ostracized the Samaritans. In addition to this, the Jews treated women as inferior beings. For Jesus to stop and converse with this woman was a shocking event therefore on two counts.

2. Have the students do a personality sketch of Jesus and of the woman based on their observations of this scene. Begin this task by having them list characteristics of each one on the chalkboard. Ask the students why they think Jesus made such a profound impression on the woman. Make sure that students notice Jesus' attitude of forgiveness and acceptance as well as the woman's feelings of shame about herself. Jesus is reflecting the compassionate love of God for every person, regardless of what one may have done or not done. This point demands strong emphasis.

3. Direct students to the reflection questions at the end of this section (text page 28) and read slowly through the questions with them to insure understanding of them. Then establish a quiet reflective atmosphere, perhaps by using the breathing techniques taught in Chapter 1 and guide the students to hear each question as if spoken to them personally by Jesus. One way to do this is to have them add their own name at the end of each question, for example, "What parts of my story seem to be like your own, (name)?" Suggest to the students that they write their answers and all these reflections in their journals.

Teaching Notes 3

**Text Pages
29–39**

Different Ways to Minister

Put the four ways to minister on the chalkboard and have the students list persons, groups, or works which typify each ministry. Here are a few examples:
The Ministry of the Word
- priests
- deacons
- lectors
- catechists

The Ministry of Community Building
- parish councils
- prayer groups
- committee to welcome new parishioners
- youth groups

Ministry of Serving and Healing
- volunteer work in hospitals
- reading for the blind
- meals on wheels for elderly people
- working in a nursing home

Ministry of Celebration
- hosting a picnic for workers in a telethon
- liturgy committee
- committee for planning parish socials

The more examples students hear the more opportunity they will have for discovering their own unique role in the Church.

Ministry of the Word

1. Have the students read a parable of their choice and decide what it was that drew the people to listen to Jesus. Tell them to notice who listened to Jesus, what it was that he said, how and why they listened, and what it meant to them. You want the students to become more aware of how powerful the Word of Jesus is.

Worksheet #5 provides a helpful format for this activity.

2. After students have worked on the exercise individually, have them share their observations in small groups and also explain what the parable means to them.

3. Direct students to the parables in the text (page 30). Have them read the parables or have students role play them. Allow time for a discussion about the meaning of each one. Ask the students to apply the meaning of each parable to a situation in today's world. The point here is to show how the ministry of the Word is as powerful now as it was in Jesus' time.

4. Have the students complete *Worksheet #4* to supplement these activities on the ministry of the Word.

The Ministry of Community Building

1. Tell the students to imagine themselves living in Jesus' time. If they can capture a sense of what community was for the apostles, it will help them to examine what community is for them today.

Explain the setting for the events in chapter 2 of the Acts of the Apostles and then have the students read it slowly and carefully, being particularly attentive to the feelings and reactions of the people who were present there. Put the names of the apostles on the board and assign each student to write a diary account of what it felt like to be an apostle of Jesus, especially after Jesus' death. Let them reread any parts of the gospels if they wish to get a clearer picture about any of the apostles. Tell them to write as if they were "in the shoes of that apostle" and to include the feelings of the apostle as they might have been on the day described in Acts 2.

Have the students volunteer to share these diary accounts with the rest of the group. This should be an enjoyable exercise in which the students can become more familiar with the apostles.

2. The following activity is designed to facilitate the ability to listen and accept.

a. Have the students work in pairs. In each group of two, tell one person to be the listener and the other to be the speaker. The speaker will have a two-minute period to talk about himself or herself to the listener. They then will reverse the roles and repeat the task. When the second two-minute period is ended, each partner will tell the other what he or she heard and the other will affirm or deny it.

b. After the process is completed, have each pair introduce one another to the rest of the group and comment on anything in the other person's story that impressed them.

c. Once the entire group has spoken about their experience, lead a discussion on questions such as these:
- How did you feel when you were the speaker?
- How did you feel as the listener?
- What did you gain from doing this exercise?
- What do you think this might have to do with building community?

Ministry of Service and Healing
1. Using the example of a contemporary person, introduce this ministry to the students. Two well-known examples are Mother Teresa of Calcutta and Fr. Bruce Ritter who ministers to runaway children in New York City.

There will be many resources available to introduce Mother Teresa to the students. One of the best is the film *Something Beautiful for God,* a moving portrayal of her work with the poor. Many magazines and books have done feature stories about Mother Teresa (see *Faith: Becoming True and Free*

by Gloria Durka and Paul Bumbar) and Fr. Ritter (see *Moral Growth: A Christian Perspective by* John Nelson). These might be made available for students. (See additional *Resources* for this Guide chapter.)

2. Once the students have examined the work of service, brainstorm with them the various elements involved in the ministry of healing and serving. List these on the board for future reference.

3. Follow this exercise with the one on Jesus' ministry of healing and serving (text page 34).

a. Having the students read the passages and answer the questions individually or in groups.

b. Refer to the brainstorming list on the board and ask the students to make comparisons between Fr. Ritter's or Mother Teresa's work and that of Jesus.

c. Next to the comparisons of the contemporary person and Jesus have the students write down ways in which they can give service in their home, school, parish, and local communities.

d. Try to make the student be as specific as possible and invite them to experience the ministry of healing and service by actually carrying out a work of service they have chosen.

The students may be overwhelmed and begin to feel inadequate to compare anything they could do to serve that could equal what they have been exposed to. Suggest to them that gifts and talents are different and they only need to be willing and open to find how they can best heal and serve others.

Ministry of Celebration
Moving On

1. Begin the section (text page 34) by having students investigate how Jesus celebrated during his lifetime. Tell them they must choose a gospel and find where and how and with whom Jesus celebrated. This can be done individually or in groups.

Once the students have compiled a list, have them share their findings and conclusions about Jesus' ability to celebrate all aspects of life.

2. Ask the students to read the account of the Last Supper (Matthew 26:17–30, Mark 14:12–26, Luke 22:7–23), giving their impressions of this celebration and its importance and significance for Jesus and his apostles as well as for us today.

From this experience direct the students to plan their own celebration of liturgy, one that is intimate and conducive to community building, with emphasis on the ministry of the Word.

3. Students are asked to examine once again their feelings about Jesus and answer the questions that follow (text page 37).

4. Once they have completed the questions have them refer to their papers with the question "Who or what Jesus is to me." As a conclusion to this study of Jesus and his ministry, have them reread their descriptions to see if any changes have occurred in their thinking and feelings, and to help them understand why.

The point to be emphasized is how we constantly grow and change as we grow closer to Jesus and experience him in our lives.

Prayer and Worship Experiences

1. The reflective thoughts the students wrote in their journals about Jesus can be used as readings in a prayer service. Arrange the room so that students feel comfortable. Have the students share their reflections, with time for prayer response. Quiet music in the background could also add to the atmosphere.

2. Have a student who is accomplished in dance put movements to the song "By My Side." Plan a prayer service that has the dance as the introduction, followed by a reading of the Last Supper (Matthew 26:20–30, Mark 14:12–26, Luke 22:7–34), with an explanation of the Word by a student who has prepared it. Give time for reflective response. Invite the students to express any petitions aloud, if they wish, and conclude by reciting the Our Father.

Service Projects

1. Have the students choose a ministry for which they would like to volunteer. For instance, a student could chooe to teach in a catechetical program of the ministry of the Word of their choice. If the choice is the ministry of community building, they might approach the parish council with the suggestion that a parish function which fosters community be initiated and offer to work on the committee.

If they choose ministry of service and healing, the best place to find out the needs would be the social service center, where volunteers are always needed and appreciated.

Finally, if they choose the ministry of celebration the liturgy committee would be a good place for students to volunteer to be involved in planning parish liturgical celebrations.

2. Have the students write about their experiences and responsibilities. Plan to have them share these at a later point.

Independent Study Projects

1. Have the students choose a gospel and with a study guide (as in the *Good News Bible*) read the gospel and the notes that accompany it. Have them write a report on it, including any new insights into the Jesus story and how this project helped them to understand Jesus more fully.

2. Have the students interview people who are involved in the ministries studied to find out what motivated them to continue in their work. Sharing these experiences with the class might be helpful to the students in deciding what ministry they are most suited for.

3. Go to the diocesan offices and interview the chancellor or the bishop concerning his vision of the ministries of Jesus and how he sees them in his diocese—his vision of the future in his particular diocese as well as in the Church as a whole.

Resources

Audiovisual

Parable. A film. Council of Churches. 475 Riverside Drive, New York, NY 10027.

Godspell. Record album.

Jesus Christ. Set of four filmstrips. TeleKETICS. Franciscan Communication Center, 1229 South Santee Street, Los Angeles, CA 90015.

Print

Good News Bible, Catholic Study Edition, New York: W. H. Sadlier, 1979.

R.E. Brown. *Jesus, God and Man.* Milwaukee: Bruce, 1967.

P. Bumbar, G. Durka. *Faith: Becoming True and Free.* New York: W.H. Sadlier, 1981.

E.J. Ciuba. *Who Do You Say That I Am?* New York: Alba House, 1974.

J.D. Crossan. *In Parables: The Challenge of the Historical Jesus.* New York: Harper and Row. 1973.

M. Hellwig. *What Are the Theologians Saying?* Dayton: Pflaum Press, 1971.

R.P. McBrien. *Catholicism.* Minneapolis: Winston Press, 1980.

J. Nelson. *Moral Growth: A Christian Perspective.* New York: W.H. Sadlier, 1981.

G. O'Collins. *What Are They Saying About Jesus?* New York: Paulist Press, 1977.

J.B. Phillips. *Your God Is Too Small.* New York: Macmillan, 1961.

I. Progoff. *At a Journal Workshop.* New York: Dialogue House Library, 1975.

D. Senior. *Jesus: A Gospel Portrait.* Cincinnati: Pflaum-Standard, 1975.

B. Vawter. *This Man Jesus: An Essay Toward a New Testament Christology.* New York: Doubleday, 1973.

Sharing the Light of Faith: National Catechetical Directory for Catholics of the United States. Washington D.C.: United States Catholic Conference, 1979.

3

The Father's Story in the Church

Text Pages
40–59

Objectives

Knowledge: To give the students an understanding of the workings of the early Church and its similarity with today's Church.

Attitude: To help the students to be able to appreciate the problems of the early Church as an inevitable part of true community and to parallel this realization with their own experience.

Practice: To help the students to analyze a problem-solving process used in the early Church and be able to apply it in their own parish situations.

Orientation

The chapter "The Father's Story in the Church" aims to give the students a clear understanding of what occurred with the apostles at the death and resurrection of Jesus, and how the early Church grew and prospered. It presents some of the problems and decisions faced by this newly-found community. By examining these the students may grow toward a better understanding of the Church.

The life experiences of the teenager's attempt to save the child and the outcome of her own rescue being left untold gives the students something to grasp that is more a part of their own life experience. The text draws the student from this life situation to the one that the apostles had after the death of Jesus.

Using such a powerful experience helps the students realize—in a limited way—the emotions that the apostles might have had at that crucial time in their lives. Basically, what the authors are trying to do is have the students get in touch with the experience of the despair the apostles must have felt with the death of Jesus so that they can in some way get a taste of the incredibility of the resurrection that followed. The first scriptural reference in Luke (text page 42) further clarifies the experience for the students. The resurrection is now a reality.

Once that has been established for the students, the next step is the Pentecost experience that molds the apostles into the persons who are to establish and guide the newly-found Church with the help of the Spirit. The juxtaposition of scriptural texts and human examples from everyday life further clarifies the message of Pentecost.

In the section "The Challenge to Continue the Story" (text page 44), the students are asked to make choices on how the Spirit might be realized in their own decisions. All the choices are realistic ones that can help the students find out how they best respond to the call of the Spirit in their lives. These options are later identified as similar to the ones the apostles had. The aim is to give the students a sense of continuity with the past.

In the section entitled "Continuing What Jesus Had Begun" (text page 46), the students take another step in discovering the workings of the early Church by learning what the apostles did at the very beginning.

The first priority for the apostles was building community. The students are taken through the process by moving from the Scriptures to their own experience. The *Rite of Christian Initiation for Adults* is introduced and identified as the normative model in the Church today. Because it so clearly shows how the Church responds to building community, it provides an excellent explanation of the importance of community building in the early Church.

The NCD document *Sharing the Light of Faith* further clarifies this point: "The Church is a community of people assembled by God, whose members share the light of Christ. Within this assembly all enjoy a basic equality. All are called to holiness. All are united by close spiritual bonds. All share 'one Lord, one Faith, one Baptism' (Ephesians 4,5). This is the basis of community building for the Church of the apostles' time just as it is the basis for all adults who call themselves members of the Church today." (94)

In this same section the students are asked to consider the impact of the early Church on that time frame and culture. The Acts of the Apostles (2:47) tells us that the Christians enjoyed "the good will of the people. And every day the Lord added to their group." The phenomenon of Jesus' death and resurrection witnessed in the lives of his followers profoundly affected their world.

The next important aspect that is brought to light is the celebrative or commemorative ritualization of the Eucharist and how this internalized the message that Jesus had left his followers. This strengthening of community helped them to share with one another, to reach out to those in need, and to take responsibility for others.

It is here that the humanness of the early Christians is introduced. It should be emphasized and made real to the students. The examination of problems that occurred in the Church can give them a way of dealing with problems that occur in the Church today.

Draw the attention of the students to the frequent references in the Scriptures to the role of the Spirit in this early Church. To see that the apostolic community never assumed to seek solutions on their own but rather would reflect and pray for guidance in all matters concerning their community is important.

Lastly, the students are asked to draw conclusions from their understanding of how the early Church solved human problems to corresponding experiences they may have. The aim of this effort is to help them to internalize the message, so that the connections with the coming chapters may be facilitated.

Life Experience Focus

The content of this chapter is probably one which most students are least aware of: the second part of the story of Jesus. Although they know the facts about the death and resurrection of Jesus, they may never have considered what an impact this must truly have had in the world at that time. Nor will they have really thought too seriously about the role the apostles played in setting up the basic structure of the Church.

Since this is most likely the case, it is essential that the teacher be able to parallel the experiences of the early Church with experiences of the students. The recognition that the early Church was made up of people like ourselves—weak, sinful, hopeful, saved, Spirit-filled—bridges the gap of 2000 years. Not only will the students grow in understanding of the early Church but they will also be able to grow in appreciation of how their Church continues to grow in the present.

It is important to explore with the students the concept and the reality of the Spirit. This is an abstract concept that they, at this developmental stage, cannot fully comprehend. They can, however, begin to understand that it is precisely through the action of the Spirit that the community of those who follow Jesus are united (Ephesians 2:18–19), sent to the world (Acts 5:3; 9; 10:19), and saved (Titus 3:5; 7).

Background on Content

The reality of the death and resurrection of Jesus and the commitment of the apostles to continue the work of Jesus is the background of this chapter.

Scholars point out that the Church's origin was founded in Jesus the Lord, and with the guidance of the Holy Spirit the apostles began to live that manifestation daily. Many of those who came in contact with Jesus' followers were so impressed with the love and concern these people had for one another that they wished to be like them, to be *with* them. The community grew rapidly and—as is so true of most human situations—as the numbers grew, so did the problems. The Acts of the Apostles makes this very clear!

The world has changed considerably since the apostolic era, but it is the same Spirit which guides and impels the followers of Jesus today. It is this link we must rely upon in order to see the authenticity of our Church—the Church of our fathers in faith.

Sharing the Light of Faith concludes:"Arising from an outpouring of the Spirit, the Church is a divine mystery; but as people of God and pilgrim, it is also a human reality. These themes come together in the image of the Body of Christ, especially when the Church celebrates its identity in word and sacrament, an identity that is rich in its heritage and continually growing in understanding itself as sacrament." (80)

Teaching Notes 1

**Text Pages
40—44**

To Be Continued . . .
1. Ask the students to describe how they think they would feel and what they could do if they were friends or relatives of the teenager in the story (text page 40). Some questions that might be asked are:
- Would they stay at the scene even though they knew they could do nothing there?
- Would they want to be alone or would they rather be with others who felt the same way?
- Considering the circumstances, would they be able to hope or would they instead prepare themselves for the worst?

2. To make it even more dramatic, before reading the story hand out character cards that assign the students to be specific characters. Then read the story and have them react in character. For instance, the emotions of the young child's parents are going to be different from those of the teenager's parents. Let them get really involved before you tell them there is no ending to this story yet.

3. After the students are fully aware that you truly do not know the ending, parallel the emotions of the students with those the disciples must have had over the death of Jesus before the resurrection.

Have the names of Mary the mother of Jesus, Mary Magdalene, and the apostles on the back of your character cards and then ask the students to go through the same process in the character of one of these followers of Jesus.

4. Have the students try to recall the feelings these people had about Jesus up to the time of his arrest and their commitment to him. Then have them go through the emotions of the arrest, the trial, and the crucifixion. Help them to come to a realization of the complete and total despair and unbelief the apostles must have experienced.

The Father's Story Continues Too
1. Allow sufficient time for the students to internalize the experience of the death of Jesus before moving into the following activity.
   a. Have the students read the Easter accounts in the gospels. Concentrate on the passage from Luke (text page 42) that recounts what was said to the women at the tomb. Say: We are so familiar with the Easter message that we can easily fail to understand how stunning and overwhelming a reality it was. Try to put yourself in the position of these women:
- How would you have reacted?
- Could you have easily accepted the explanation?
- What would have been your reaction: disbelief? total shock? joy?

   b. When the students have decided whether they could accept the women's experience, divide them into two groups, one that could believe and one that could not. In these groups ask the students to discuss the situation, their reactions, their reasons.

   c. After providing sufficient time for discussion, ask the students to debate their position. If at any time anyone wants to change their mind concerning their feelings they have the freedom to do so.

The point of this exercise is to get the students in touch with the mixed reactions and confused feelings the apostles must have had during the first few hours of realizing that Jesus had indeed risen.

2. Once the debate has run its course give the students an opportunity to make a final decision about their feelings. Then read chapter 24 from the Gospel of Luke, having the students jot down their reactions while still acting in the character of an apostle.

3. Once Jesus has appeared and gone again have the students try and recreate not only their feelings of seeing him again but also how they have been changed because of his coming. Remember that in Luke the gospel ends with Jesus ascending to heaven and that Acts opens before the apostles receive the Holy Spirit, so once again the followers of Jesus are left to their own human emotions.

4. Read chapter 2 of Acts, with the students still reacting in character, and relate the feelings and emotions.

This should be the point where the students stop being the apostles and assume their own identity.

5. Write on the board the word CHALLENGE. Then read the scriptural reference from Acts to the class (text page 43). Discuss: Accepting a challenge does not always mean that we understand everything that we are being asked to do. At the very heart of a challenge is insecurity.

6. The following prayer was written by Thomas Merton. Have the students read it quietly, prayerfully, then ask: Do you feel that these words reflect the challenge of Pentecost for the followers of Jesus—including yourself?

"My Lord God, I have no idea where I am going. I do not see the road ahead of me. I cannot know for certain where it will end.

Nor do I really know myself, and the fact that I think I am following your will does not mean that I am actually doing so.

But I believe that the desire to please you does in fact please you. And I hope I have that desire in all that I am doing. I hope that I will never do anything apart from that desire.

And I know that if I do this, you will lead me by the right road though I may know nothing about it.

Therefore will I trust you always though I may seem to be lost and in the shadow of death. I will not fear, for you are ever with me, and you will never leave me to face my perils alone."

Teaching Notes 2

Text Pages
44–48

The Challenge to Continue the Story

This section (text page 44) takes the students further into the experience of Pentecost, and the challenge that confronts them: How the apostles will act on this new spirit that has entered their lives.

a. The exercise on text pages 45–46 asks the students to examine options and decide upon courses of action in light of the words of Jesus in Matthew 28:19-20 (See text page 44). The aim is to help the students further empathize with the dilemma of "what to do now?" which the apostles must have had.

b. Direct the students to the choices (text page 45) and ask them to decide which action seems best for them. Once they have chosen, ask the students to join the group that is made up of those who made the same choice.

c. Have large pieces of newsprint for each group and instruct the students to put down all the reasons why they made that choice and why they think it is the best course of action.

d. Once all students have filled in their newsprint ask the group to present the case for their choice to the larger group.

e. After all the groups have had a chance to present and explain their choice, open the floor to a vote. During the decision-making time, anyone who wants to suggest further reasons may do so.

f. Now it is time for the group to come to a consensus of opinion, which means they must make a choice which everyone can feel comfortable and work with.

Point out that this is the process the apostles must have used in deciding how they would best manifest the Spirit in their lives and carry out the mission of Jesus. Through this type of process, along with prayer and reflection, the apostles began to build a Church—a community of believers.

Continuing What Jesus Had Begun
Jesus' Ministry: Building Community

1. Have the students read the excerpts from the Scriptures in the text (page 46). Ask:
- Why do you think that the building of community became a priority?
- What are the elements that appear in the formation of this community?
- What is your opinion of these elements? Are they important? Would you have chosen others? If so, what would these be?

2. List on the board the elements found in the early Church community (for example, sharing of meals, prayers, possessions; care for the needy; love for each other; spreading the name of Jesus). Brainstorm for elements we find in our present Church community. List these on the board. Note and discuss similarities, differences, and reasons for these.

3. Introduce *Worksheet #6* as a way of analyzing some decisions made by the early Christian community.

4. Have the students analyze one other type of community with which they are familiar and the social, emotional, physical, or spiritual relationships of the members of this community. Have them select the hallmark of that community—the most recognizable sign of its members. Read again Acts 4:32.

5. This can be an appropriate place to point out that people can belong to communities for different reasons and that they can respond in different ways: they can be *dependent, independent,* or *interdependent.* Discuss these terms with the students and examine the effects each type of behavior can have on an individual and on a community.

Draw a comparison between what we know of the early Church community and that of a contemporary community which was self-destructive—that of the Rev. Jim Jones. Taking time to clarify this phenomenon for the students can be extremely important. Questions of peer pressure, blind allegiance to a powerful personality, and relinquishment of personal responsibility are all issues that affect students at this age level. The comparisons should help strengthen their appreciation and care for the Church while placing in perspective such extremes as the Guyana commune.

6. Have some volunteer students prepare a TV commentary for the "33 A.D. Television News" in which they describe this new group called "Christians." Suggest that they interview a member of this community or describe what they feel will be the effects of such a group on the larger public.

7. Write on the board: Rite of Christian Initiation for Adults. Ask the students what they think this expression means. After a brief explanation of the Rite, show students a filmstrip about it, if possible, such as "Baptism: Invitation Into the Christian Community." (See *Resources* for this Guide chapter.)

If the filmstrip is not available have a guest speaker who is involved with the new Rite in your diocese come and talk to the students about this significant step in our Church.

Following the filmstrip or lecture, discuss with the students the differences between their own baptism and the new Rite.

Remember to be sensitive to the fact that infant baptism includes a manifestation of the *parents'* faith. Students at this age are often in the process of rejecting traditional parental values as they strive for independence and some will no doubt raise the issue: "Baptism was my parents' choice, not mine. Why do I have to live with it?" It is essential for the teacher to make the point that the *parents* have the *option in faith* to baptize an infant and raise it in their faith. It is at Confirmation that we are given the right and responsibility to choose to strengthen our commitment to Christ.

The main point of the discussion should be the aspect of *community* in this Rite. It is much like the community the early Church was striving for. The new Rite is an attempt to revitalize that experience in the Church.

Jesus' Ministry: The Word
1. To help the students grasp the power and enthusiasm present in the early Church, acquaint them through map study, filmstrips, etc. of the Holy Land and the world in the first century A.D. Discuss with them the difficulties and perils of travel, the poverty and insignificance of the small Christian community. How can we account for its growth?

2. After reading text page 48, have the students turn to Timothy 3. List on the board the qualities of a good leader. Ask: Do these still apply today? Are there any other qualities you would add to this list?

Jesus' Ministry: Celebration
This is an appropriate place to explain the difference between the synagogue experience of the Jews and the celebration of the Eucharist.
  a. Have the students break into two groups: one group represents the community of Jews who worship in the synagogue, the other the new Christian community that breaks bread together to commemorate the presence of Jesus.
  b. Have each group research their prospective rituals and present their findings in a dramatization to the class.

c. Once both have demonstrated their respective rituals, hold a discussion on the possible reasons for the split between these two communities. Remind the students that both communities were Jewish.

This experience and discussion should help clarify for the students why the followers of Jesus substituted for the Sabbath Day rituals the new ritual given them by Jesus himself: the breaking of bread and the drinking of the cup in his name.

Teaching Notes 3

Text Pages 49–59

Jesus' Ministry: Service and Healing

1. Ask a student to read aloud the text from John 13:34–35 on the new commandment. Remind students that Jesus had just washed each apostle's feet before he said this, setting an example of loving service.

2. Ask the group to imagine what kind of people the community cared for and what type of care was given. Relate this to the present day by means of the exercise about the spirit of Christian service (text page 49).

Problems! Problems! or One Headache After Another

1. Ask the students to try and decide what kind of problems these early Christian communities might have encountered. List these on the board. As the list develops, the students might see that the problems fall into observable categories such as: human weakness, political pressure, geographical problems, internal authority, individual interpretation of Jesus' mission, etc.

   a. Ask them how they would try and solve these problems, what tactics they would use, and what support they would need.

   b. Discuss some of the ways in which the early communities solved their problems (text pages 50–53). The students' discussion of the problem and its solution will give the teacher an indication of what needs to be clarified before they get into the following exercises. Make certain that the students are able to identify the problem, explain why it occurred, state the solution, and then be able to evaluate the solution proposed as well as the final outcome. The effectiveness of the following exercise hinges on their understanding of the sample given.

c. Direct the students to read over the three problems that are stated, choose the one they would like to work with, and then move into groups of three. Worksheet #6 can facilitate the students' decision-making process. It follows the above process and can be used with all three problem situations.

d. Once there seems to be an understanding of the problems and the proposed solutions, bring the students to an understanding of the human elements involved by means of role playing. Assign students to re-enact the trial of the apostles before the Sanhedrin and the High Priest in Acts 5; the scene between Peter and Cornelius in Acts 10:1–17; and the debate between the Jerusalem community of apostles and elders and Paul and Barnabus in Acts 15:6–29.

e. Once the roleplaying exercise has been completed, ask the groups to share their reactions and open up a general discussion so that points concerning the workings of the early Church can be clarified.

2. Now it is time to parallel what the students are learning about the early Church with experiences in today's Church.

a. Read the section about the youth group of St. Henry's parish (text page 55) so the students can get an understanding of the parallel.

b. After reading the account analyze the situation at St. Henry's by using the same process applied to the problem of the early Church.

c. Have the students move into groups according to their own parishes, if possible, and ask each group to speak about one problem facing them in parish life today.

d. Once the problem is identified ask the students to use the process the early

Church used to find a solution. Have the groups share their findings with the others.

3. Have each student group organize a plan of offering their solutions to an appropriate parish group or committee. Be sure that they are committed to the problem and to seeing the solution through.

4. The next step is to help the students internalize the material they have dealt with in this chapter. Have them reflectively read the poem "The Church in Our Day" (text page 56) and spend some time alone reacting to the thoughts expressed. Have them write their reactions in their journals.

Suggest that they reflect for a moment on the ideas developed in this chapter. Let them associate freely and put the ideas on the board as they are expressed. Give them freedom enough to explore their feelings concerning the early Church and how we today are trying to learn from that experience. Have them add these reflections to their journals.

A Look Ahead

1. Have the students read to themselves the section on page 57 "A Look Ahead" and to add to their journals their feelings concerning what lies ahead of them in this course. Ask them to be honest about what they have learned as well as their feelings about what is yet to come.

2. When the students have had an opportunity individually to get in touch with how they feel about this chapter, write on the board "The Father's Story in the Church" and go over with them the questions found at the end of the chapter (text page 58). As the discussion progresses, be sure to add your own views and thoughts.

3. Discuss with the group possible explanations of why Jesus left his followers without a completely organized plan. What difficulties did this make for his Church? What advantages do you think it gave the early community?

4. Ask the students to make a connection with their own lives. What if there were a fool-proof plan assigned them for their lives: follow the plan and success is assured.

- What would that do to them as persons?
- How would it affect the whole community?
- What is the essential wisdom behind Jesus' leaving the Church in the hands of those who followed him?
- What responsibilities does that place on Christians?

5. Ask the students to reflect on how they themselves can make Jesus present in their lives, where they are comfortable with him, and areas where they might need help in doing this.

6. Have the students choose one area in which they would like to concentrate on making Jesus present, and in their journals have them explain their choices and keep an account of their efforts—both their successes and their failures.

7. Have the students complete *Worksheet #7* on the continuing mission of Jesus.

Prayer and Worship Experiences

1. Have the students recreate an early Eucharist experience in which they reflect on Jesus' story, break bread, and drink from the cup to remember his presence. Since this event occurred within the context of a meal it would be appropriate to have a meal as part of the experience.

2. Use the prayer found at the end of the chapter (text page 59) as the beginning of a prayer experience. After reading the section "To Make Jesus Present . . ." have a large piece of newsprint available to the students. Ask them to write on it ways in which they feel that Jesus shows his love for them. Allow time for reflection on these responses, then read the gospel passage of the vine and the branches (John 15:1–17). You may want to have someone offer a reflection on the reading or have the students reflect privately or both. Close the prayer with a song the students know such as "Be Not Afraid," and then have them read silently the prayer that ends the chapter.

3. In a quiet, reflective atmosphere show the film *The Dancing Prophet* (see *Resources* for this Guide chapter). Such a prayer experience can help the students to recognize their need both for individual growth and for commitment to a community. Draw the attention of the students to what Doug Krenshaw says at the end: "I don't want to be greater than, I want to be part of . . ." Use that as a beginning for a prayer reflection in which the students individually reflect on how they can best be "a part of." Writing their thoughts in their journals can help them to internalize their feelings.

45

Service Projects

Just as the early Church saw community building as an important priority, so should it be for any community which identifies itself as Christian. Suggest that interested students sponsor a "Faith Night" to which they will invite other students, faculty members, and parents. The object of the evening is to share faith within a community setting. Begin the evening with an "ice-breaker." Divide into small groups and ask people to respond to the question: Who is God in my life right now?

Following these small group sharings, bring the entire group together for discussion. It is helpful to have some significant background information to present—input concerning the faith relationship of both a personal and communal nature.

In closing, offer night prayer, a time when all share in the thanksgiving for the evening and for each other. This can be structured according to the needs of the group, but again it should be simple and not too long.

This project could be continued on a monthly basis, with different people from the group encouraged to sponsor an evening. Special celebrations at Thanksgiving and Christmas and during Lent are also good opportunities to further community.

Independent Study Projects

1. Have the students read a biography about Peter or Paul, or do some research about the first century of Christianity. Have them prepare written reports about the life and times of one of these followers of Jesus who were also leaders in the Church community.

2. Have the students go to the parish and investigate ways in which it builds community. Have them find out as many as they can and choose one that looks interesting. Have them interview the people involved in that particular one, asking specific questions concerning the feelings on community and how that group builds community in the parish. The students can report their findings to the group.

3. Have the students initiate ways in which they can build community in their homes. One way to begin such an endeavor is to have a festive family meal. At the meal they can discuss ways in which their families can build community in the home and have someone write down the ideas. They can then choose the one most liked by the whole group and plan to do it in the week ahead.

Resources

Audiovisual

"Baptism: Invitation Into the Christian Community." One of an eight-part filmstrip series. Paulist Press, 545 Island Rd., Ramsey, NJ 17446.

The Dancing Prophet. A 15 min. color film. TeleKETICS. Franciscan Communications Center, 1229 South Santee Street, Los Angeles, CA 90015.

Service Christian Ministry Series. Set of 4 filmstrips: "Extraordinary Ministry of the Eucharist," "Music Ministry," "Ministry of Lector," and "Ministry of the Baptized." Paulist Press, 545 Island Rd., Ramsey, NJ 17446.

The Widow's Mite. 21 min. color film. TeleKETICS.

Ruby Duncan—A Moving Spirit. 15 min. color film. TeleKETICS.

Mission to Love. 17 min. color film. TeleKETICS.

Paradox. 10 min. color film. TeleKETICS.

"Be Not Afraid" by Bob Dufford, S.J. on the *Glory and Praise, Vol. I* album. North American Liturgy Resources, 10802 North 23rd Avenue, Phoenix, AZ 85029.

Print

Good News Bible. American Bible Society. Catholic Study Edition. New Yori: H. Sadlier, 1979.

N. Barclay. *The Promise of the Spirit.* Philadelphia: Westminister Press, 1979.

R. Brown. *Community of the Beloved Disciple.* Ramsey, NJ: Paulist Press, 1975.

New Testament Essays. Milwaukee, WI: Bruce Publishing Company, 1965.

R. Brown, K. Donfried, J. Reumann, eds. *Peter in the New Testament.* Ramsey, NJ: Paulist Press, 1974.

F. Bruce. *New Testament History.* New York: Doubleday, 1972.

J. Dupont. *Salvation of the Gentiles: Studies in the Acts of the Apostles.* Ramsey, NJ: Paulist Press, 1979.

R. Karris. *What Are They Saying About Luke and Acts?* Ramsey, NJ: Paulist Press, 1978.

L. Keck. *The New Testament Experience of Faith.* St. Louis, MO: Bethany Press, 1976.

R. McBrien. *Catholicism.* 2 vols. Minneapolis, MN: Winston Press, 1980.

G. Montague. *Holy Spirit: Growth of a Biblical Tradition.* Ramsey, NJ: Paulist Press, 1976.

G. O'Collins. *What Are They Saying About the Resurrection?* Ramsey, NJ: Paulist Press.

D. Stanley. *Apostolic Church in the New Testament.* Ramsey, NJ: Paulist Press, 1974.

E. Tetlow. *Women and Ministry in the New Testament.* Ramsey, NJ: Paulist Press, 1979.

M. Warren. *Resources for Youth Ministry.* Ramsey, NJ: Paulist Press, 1978.

The Rite of Christian Initiation: Historical and Pastoral Reflections. New York: W. H. Sadlier, 1979.

Journey in Faith: An Experience of the Catechumenate. New York: W. H. Sadlier, Inc., 1979.

Sharing the Light of Faith: National Catechetical Directory for Catholics of the United States. Washington, D.C.: United States Catholic Conference, 1979.

4

Understanding Our Story

Objectives
Knowledge: To help the students understand the concept of Church by the presentation of models.
Attitude: To enable the students to see the many aspects of the Church and to accept its universality.
Practice: To make it possible for the students to find the model most beneficial to their own understanding of Church and to live it more fully.

Orientation
This chapter will bring the student to today's Church by first using a life experience of what Church probably meant to them as children and how this meaning grew and took on a different shape with their own maturity. An experience of growth is one that is evident throughout the chapters. As we speak of different models and points of importance to our faith, we are coming to understand how our Church took on new meaning as it grew and flourished.

The chapter opens with "The Experience of Church" (text page 60) by having the students identify their own experiences of being part of the Church community. The first task of the teacher is to find out what association students make with the word

"Church," an association that initiates the learning process. This experience is followed by an exercise (text page 60) which will help to identify the positive and negative feelings associated with Church by the students. These many individual reactions need to be exposed, scrutinized, and understood.

The next step is to introduce the concept of the Church as mystery. Here again the students' limited understanding of abstract thought must be considered. Quotes from various sources are used for explanation as well as for clarification. This is probably the most feasible way for helping the students to grasp the concept fully. From the understanding of Church as mystery the students are asked to look at models that help explain this mystery in its most important aspect.

In the section "More Than One View "(text page 62) the five models of the Church are introduced and the key to understanding the models is presented: how one understands and interprets the reality of a thing is the "model" one uses for explaining it. For the students of St. Mark's the way in which each one envisions the school clearly indicates a unique model, a special frame of reference.

"Model 1—Church as Institution" (text page 64) puts emphasis on the organization of the Church and its mode of expressing its beliefs. "Model 2—Church as Community" (text page 65) focuses on the membership of the Church—the people who unite in fellowship and unity of faith. "Model 3—Church as Sacrament" (text page 66) speaks of the Church as the sign of God's presence and love in the world. The fourth model, "Church as Herald" (text page 66) points to the message and to the Church as the speaker and teacher of the good news of Christ. The final model sees the "Church as Servant" (text page 67) and emphasizes the role of service to the world.

In "Your View of the Church" (text page 68) the students are called to reflect on the various models as ways to grow in understanding of the Church, recognizing that no one model tells all. The students are then asked to develop their own model of the Church incorporating those elements which they feel are essential, significant. This activity leads naturally into "Identifying Our Church"(text page 68) which focuses on the distinguishing marks of the Church: "To Be One" (text page 70), "To Be Holy" (text page 72), "To Be Catholic" (text page 73), and "To Be Apostolic" (text page 74).

This chapter moves between the two poles of the visible and the invisible, the mysterious and the concrete, the speculative and the factual. The aim is both to broaden the students' perceptions of the Church and deepen their understanding of it.

Life Experience Focus

Up to this point in their religious development young people have most probably never thought very seriously about the Church and their place in it. Their most frequent associations with Church are with the concepts of rules and ritual. At this stage of growth when adolescents begin to question and challenge any external authority, it is appropriate that they be confronted with the multiple aspects of the Church and the diversity of its mission in the world—rooted in service and love.

The models of the Church are introduced in the context of a life situation which is recognizable and authentic. The aim is to move the students from an experience with which they can identify to the more abstract speculations of Dulles' *Models of the Church.* It is thus hoped that new and broader understandings of the Church can be grasped so that their appreciation of and commitment to the Church can grow.

By having them use the information provided in their own lived experience of Church the teacher can encourage them to make it their own so that the word "Church" becomes a living reality and a challenging possibility both now and in the future.

Background on Content

The background for most of this chapter can be found in *Sharing the Light of Faith* in Chapter IV, "The Church and Catechesis; Part A: Meaning of Church." This section clarifies the essential elements of our faith.

Each model of the Church presented in this chapter is identified and explained in this section of *Sharing the Light of Faith.* This same NCD chapter also presents the catechesis for the marks of the Church which are developed according to what the Directory calls our guidelines for the future.

For purposes of simplicity and clarity, this text has selected one of the many sources used in developing this catechesis of Church: Avery Dulles' *Models of the Church.* In the chapter, his ideas are presented in outline form in order to facilitate recognition, identification, and understanding in the young person. Dulles' concepts of the Church and the effect these perceptions have had on the Christian community past, have now in the present, and will have in the future are both clear and profound.

Several of the models may be quite familiar to the students already; others may be new to them and challenge them to respond in new ways. In order to know what Church is in its fullness we must take forms and articulations—no single one of which provides the complete expression, but all of which taken together can make the reality of Church much more real and present to the world in which we live.

This chapter gives the students basic sound knowledge of what Church does and is. The students who can grow in this informed appreciation can find in these models a basis for decision-making concerning their place in and commitment to the Church.

Teaching Notes 1

Text Pages
60–64

The Experience of Church

1. Begin this section by asking students to recall their earliest memories of "Church."

a. You might create an open atmosphere by sharing one or two experiences from your past. Allow time for students to share their stories and memories, which can be a mixture of both amusing and distressing stories. Draw this to a close by pointing out the fact that as a person gets older, the Church comes to mean different things. Once again, illustrate this in your own life.

b. Help students concretize and articulate their feelings about Church now, first by having a large piece of newsprint with the word *CHURCH* in large letters in the middle. Invite the students to write down anything they associate with the Church. This should follow after the completion of their own personal "graffitti board" (text page 60).

c. Have students answer the questions in the exercise emphasizing the need for reflection. It is important that they give both their positive and negative experiences so that a complete and honest picture can be seen. This should also be true for the graffitti board.

d. Once the students have reflected and written down their answers to the question call on various individuals to share their thoughts with the class. Be prepared for students to express many different ways of thinking about the Church. It should be emphasized that this is understandable and normal. Do not become defensive in response to the shared views of the students. Such behavior might close their minds to any further learning.

51

2. Question the students about the meaning of Pope Paul VI's definition of the Church as mystery (text page 60). Elaborate on the idea of ourselves as mystery (text page 62). Do we ever fully know ourselves, or any other human person? Again, if you are able to share a discovery—recent or past—about yourself, the lesson will be effectively demonstrated. Be sensitive to the fact that this topic may generate a great deal of interest within the students. Allow time for adequate discussion and questioning about mystery.

More Than One View

1. Suggest to the students that looking at models might help them understand the Church better. Parallel the way an architect uses models (text page 62) to introduce the students into this mindset. Once the comparison has been made the introduction of Dulles' material should be that much easier. A simple introduction will suffice because in-depth discussion will follow the life experience that illustrates the models.

2. Have the students complete *Worksheet #8* as a help in keeping the life experience and models of the Church in order.

a. First have the students read the entire story about St. Mark's students. Ask the students to summarize each point of view about what should happen at St. Mark's. When a consensus of opinion has been reached, instruct the students to write down each viewpoint under the appropriate person's name.

b. The worksheet should look like this:
Harry
organization:
purpose:
structure:

June
message:
spirit:

Mickey
symbols:
celebration:

Joe
need:
service:

Sara
welcoming:
hospitality:

Such a focal point will help the students keep track of the various models that they will cover. To be able to bring it back to a name and a point of view will help students be able to make the transition from the familiar to the new concepts and help them in stablizing and internalizing these concepts.

c. Now introduce the models that each person identifies with by listing them on the line of the worksheet so that the students identify the familiar.

d. To end this section, have the students look at the worksheet and note the explanations of the viewpoints that go with the models. Have the students identify the differences. Then ask them how these students are able to remain together as a group since they see things so differently. Lead students to the realization that "difference" is healthy and normal and growth-producing. Emphasize this for the students so they can see that more important things than differences keep us together and that those differences help us respond to many more people.

This worksheet is continued in Teaching Notes 2, page 54.

Teaching Notes 2

Taking a Closer Look

This section (text page 64) takes the student from fictional life experiences to the notional models of the Church given by Avery Dulles, S.J. Each time you speak of a model it might be helpful to identify the student who is associated with the model. Since this is abstract and therefore difficult material the more association that is made for the students the easier the learning will be.

Model 1—Church as Institution

The best way for the students to learn about each of these models is to pick out the features themselves. There are seven features to look for in this chapter for each model. The students must supply them from reading the text.

a. Make this activity into a competitive search—who can find the most features for each of the models of the Church given. Some features the students might select for the model "Institution" are:
- the visible building
- the organization
- the structures
- the creeds
- the form of worship
- the appointed offices the roles and duties of each

b. As the features are identified, have the students explain what they mean by each feature, such as, the visible building being the need for a Church structure. Each feature should be noted on the worksheet.

c. Another teaching aid in doing the models is to outline the features on an overhead transparency so that the students get a sense of how the features fit together with the model.

d. Now have the students look at the questions (text page 64) and answer them on the worksheet, highlighting the three most important ones. This will help clarify their understanding of this model as well as to see that it will continue to change in the years to come.

Model 2—Church as Community

Present this section in the same way.

a. The seven features would include:
- fellowship of members
- people of God
- various ages
- different lifestyles
- different nationalities
- common ways of expressing beliefs
- oneness in spirit

Again, each time the students point out a feature, have them explain it in their words and understanding.

b. After the students have picked out the features direct them to the questions in the exercise (text page 65) and have them try to imagine what this would be like. Ask them to identify the 500 in the parish by groups and then explain how each group lives out the reality: "We are the community of the Church."

For example: some of the 500 are family groups. How could family members live out this belief? As they try to describe the responses of the various groups, students will grow in understanding of the task at hand as well as the challenge posed by such a question. Ask them to record three of the most important responses that would truly express community, as they see it.

Model 3—Church as Sacrament

The features needed to be found are:
- symbol
- inner reality love

● reminds us of presence of Jesus in our midst
● who we are
● what we are called to be

b. When these features have been identified and discussed have the students read the quote from Matthew 5:14–16 (text page 66) which further explains this model. Then ask them to listen to the song "Light of the World" from *Godspell*.

c. Reinforce these identifications by finding similar features in the scriptural reference as well as in the lyrics of the song.

d. Direct the students to write in their journals the answer to the questions posed in the text (page 66). Provide time for reflection before writing and encourage the students to be both precise and personal in their responses. The new knowledge they have received from this chapter should help them take a step toward learning more about the sacraments.

e. When they have finished their journal entries, ask the students to choose the three most important needs the sacraments can fulfill for followers of Jesus.

Model 4—Church as Herald

1. The features that can be brought out are:
● message entrusted to us by Jesus
● sharing gospel with others
● people conscious of God's love
● preaching
● teaching
● official message to be passed on
● people formed by the Good News

In the discussion of these features which follows it might be a good idea to concentrate on the preaching and teaching because these are two elements with which the students have had experience. The way to approach this would probably be from the vantage point of how would Jesus want us to preach and teach, to herald to Good News. The students can probably come up with many viewpoints that will help them internalize the model.

2. Once the students have explained how they would preach and teach, direct them to the question (text page 66). Brainstorm with them the messages of Jesus. Where these have been listed on the board have the students work in small groups to single out what they feel is the primary message of Jesus—the one that is absolutely essential to an understanding of his mission. By doing this activity, the students take their experience a step further: they must decide not only *how* they would preach and teach but also exactly *what* they would want to communicate.

Now that they have provided some substance to these features, ask them to fill in the needs that this model will be able to fulfill for the Church in the future.

Model 5—Church as Servant

1. This model has the following seven features:
● helping people
● serving people
● working for justice
● aiding the poor
● ministering to the sick and elderly
● counselling those in trouble
● global struggle of injustice

a. Have the students find a scriptural basis for each of the above elements. They will need assistance in doing this activity but it is an excellent opportunity for them to learn how to use the Concordance to the Bible.

b. Discuss each feature in the group, sharing the Scriptures they have found.

2. Direct the students to the illustration of the Last Supper and the scriptural reference (text page 67) that explains what Jesus wants us to do. Then ask the students what they see as possible for them in their own lives in order to make this model meaningful. From this discussion the students should be able to write down three needs that this model makes them aware of for their future.

3. Direct the students to complete *Worksheet #8* which began this chapter. Ask whether they see the need for all of these models in the Church. Have them compare the contents of the worksheet with their graffitti board as the text directs.

a. If there are any words that do not seem to fit, encourage the students to write them on the back of the worksheet. When they have completed the exercise deal with the ones that do not fit.

b. As the students finish the front of the worksheet, direct them to the back and ask them to put the positive and negative images in two columns. Explain that Dulles never intended to say these five were the only ones; other models could be added.

c. Allow students to express their negative feelings but now move them to focus on the more positive aspects as well. Remind them during the discussion that the Church is human and just as they are not completely perfect, neither is the Church. This is a reality the students need to admit and get into their way of viewing the Church.

4. To internalize their experiences of models have the students break into five groups, choosing the model that best explains their understanding of Church.

5. In any way the group wishes, have the students make a symbol that characterizes their model and what that model signifies. These symbols can be used in a prayer service at the end of the lesson.

Teaching Notes 3

Identifying Our Church

1. To introduce this section, have the students identify themselves by taking out any form of personal identification which they might have—library card, student ID card, social security card. Since they may not have too many different kinds of identification, ask students what other forms they think they might have in the future. Discuss the meaning and value of signs of identification. Ask: What other things serve as signs of identification? Brainstorm these and list the responses on the board.

2. Point out that the Church also has marks that identify what the Church is. Write on the board the four marks of the Church in large letters as heads. Then brainstorm again with the group to identify how these marks are gifts to us and how they are tasks to us, challenging us to be truly Christian.

To Be One

1. A good way to illustrate the concept of the oneness of the Church would be to use the film *Hello In There* (see *Resources* for this Guide chapter). This film tells the story of a woman who has the need to be one with others although she is continually alienated and cast off from others. This film can serve as a catalyst to spark instant discussion about unity among ourselves.

2. Following the discussion, ask the students to consider other ways in which unity can be manifested. Ask them to read the scriptural reference from the Last Supper (text page 70). The Eucharist is a powerful metaphor expressing Jesus' desire for union with us.

3. Elaborate on the point that unity does not mean *uniformity.* Illustrate this by discussing the various ways different ethnic groups celebrate the Eucharist (text page 71).

4. Have volunteer students select one part of the liturgy such as the "Lord, Have Mercy" or the "Our Father" and present slides and/or recordings of ethnic interpretations to show the variety of liturgical expressions that can exist and yet which are still considered "in unity."

5. Direct the students to the exercise on unity and uniformity (text page 72). Ask students to look up the exact meaning of the words. Discuss the question on different ministries, being open and attuned to deeper questions which students may have about this. As a conclusion to the discussion, read 1 Corinthians 12:4–7 on Gifts from the Spirit.

To Be Holy

Have the students take time to read the excerpt about St. Bernard (text page 72). Assign each student to investigate the life story of *one saint* to find out why this person was thought to be "holy." Have them report their findings to the group and discuss each report. After they have investigated what others did to be holy, ask the students to take out their journals and write down two or three specific ways in which *they* could be "holy" in their everyday lives.

To Be Catholic

1. Ask the students to research the meaning of the word "catholic." If some say "universal," have them explain what that means. Brainstorm for things (ideas, customs, trends, etc.) which they feel can be called "universal" or "catholic." Ask them in what sense can we say our Church is catholic or universal.

2. Direct the students' attention to the quote from St. Paul (text page 74). Have them clarify exactly what the quote means before directing them to the exercise (text page 74). Have students answer the questions individually and then share them with the class.

Make sure that students understand that, although when we are speaking about the Church, the People of God, we are referring to those persons who have encountered Jesus Christ in the Catholic Church, yet we do not exclude from the meaning of the term Church others whose lives are directed by the message of Christ.

To Be Apostolic
1. The students will be able to recognize the meaning of the word "apostolic" as far as it having roots in the word "apostles" but a second step should be introduced: the connection between being apostolic and the preaching of the gospel.

Have the students look at the exercise (text page 75) and spend some time reflecting on these questions. The points they wrote previously about holiness will probably help the students in their responses to these questions.

2. Return to the four headings on the board and ask the students to try to identify the meaning of each mark with an example of how each can be manifested in the world today.

3. Break the class into three groups; assign each group one "challenge" question (text page 76). Give the groups ample time to discuss their question and come up with an adequate solution. Have the groups present their responses to the class.

4. Have the students complete *Worksheet #9* as a conclusion to this chapter.

5. If possible, show the film *An Arrow of Light.* (See *Resources* for this Guide chapter.) This film presents varied dimensions and facets of the experience of *Church*—institution, worshiping community, servant healer, hopeful people, etc. The involvement of Christ with his people is portrayed by a young man in modern dress.

Prayer and Worship Experiences
1. The symbols made by the students can be used as the center of a prayer service. Begin the service with the song "Earthen Vessels." Then have a student who has been chosen to write a reflection on the symbol read that reflection. After each reading allow time for individual responses.

2. Plan a prayer service on the theme of light. Place a single large lit candle in the center of the group and provide a smaller candle for each person. Begin with a reading from Matthew 5:14—16. Allow time for quiet reflection as the song "Light of the World" (from *Godspell*) is played. Invite the students to share how they feel about being called to bring light to the world. As they finish have them light their candle from the large candle. End with the Lord's Prayer or the prayer at the end of the chapter (text page 77).

3. Conduct a prayer reflection around the concept of mystery. Read again Pope Paul VI's quote about Church as mystery (text page 60). Play the record "Listen" from the Weston Priory album of the same title. Allow time for silence and for spontaneous prayer. Close with appropriate music.

Service Projects

1. The students have been dealing with the model of servant. Have them make a list of all the situations that need to be healed and served in their school. Pick the five that mean the most to the students and create a plan to put these into action that will actually take place, a plan that is concrete and realistic.

2. A group of students who are interested in the sacrament model of the Church could begin a liturgy group to help plan the liturgies or volunteer their services to the existing group to do some liturgical art for each celebration. There are many books available that can provide the students with ideas for liturgical art.

Independent Study Projects

1. The institution model of the Church could be interesting to research. Have the students find out how the diocese is organized into the parishes and the deaneries. Make a diagram of the structure with the connection of the Catholic bishops and Rome.

2. For a project on the herald model of the Church the students could attend various services with different people preaching and compare and contrast the messages delivered (and heard!). Have them prepare and present a report to the group on what they have observed.

3. For the servant model of the Church suggest that some students volunteer to tutor students in areas they might need help with after school.

This should be cleared through the principal but it could be a tremendous service both for the younger students and the school.

4. The sacrament model project could center around a celebration coming up soon at school. A group of students could volunteer to be responsible for the celebration and coordinate the liturgy to give it special meaning and significance.

5. For the community model of the Church suggest that the students volunteer to sponsor the Faith Night that is described in Chapter 3—possibly in conjunction with one of the larger celebrations of the year such as Thanksgiving and Advent.

Resources

Audiovisual

Hello In There. 21 min. color film. TeleKETICS. Franciscan Communications Center, 1229 South Santee Street, Los Angeles, CA 90015.

Hope—Lutherans and Roman Catholics in Dialogue. Set of 4 filmstrips. TeleKETICS.

"Earthen Vessels." Song by John Foley, S.J. on the albums *Earthen Vessels* or *Glory and Praise Vol. 1.* North American Liturgy Resources, 2110 West Peoria Avenue, Phoenix, AZ 85029.

An Arrow of Light. 15 min. color film. Boston Catholic TV Center, Boston, MA.

"Listen." Song by Gregory Norbert, OSB on the album *Listen Together in*

Images of the Church. 14 min. color Insight film. Paulist Productions, P.O. Box 1057, Pacific Palisades, CA 90272

"Light of the World." Song from *Godspell* album. New York: Bell Records.

The Church: A Believing Community. 16 min., filmstrip. Paulist Press, Ramsey, NJ.

Print

Good News Bible. Catholic Study Edition. New York: Wm. H. Sadlier, 1979.

A. Dulles. *Models of the Church.* New York: Doubleday, 1974.

J. Dunning. *Values in Conflict.* Cincinnati, OH: Pflaum Press, 1976.

J. Hardon. *The Catholic Catechism.* New York: Herder & Herder, 1977.

M. Hellwig. *Tradition: the Catholic Story Today.* Dayton, OH: Pflaum Press, 1974.

R. McBrien. *Basic Questions for Religious Educators.* Paramus, NJ: Newman Press, 1980.

R. McBrien. *Catholicism.* Minneapolis, MN: Winston Press, 1980.

J. McKenzie. *The Roman Catholic Church.* New York: Holt, Reinhart and Winston, 1969.

G. Sloyan. *How Do I Know I'm Doing Right?* Revised Edition. Dayton, OH: Pflaum-Standard, 1976.

Sharing the Light of Faith: National Catechetical Directory for Catholics in the United States. Washington, D.C.: United States Catholic Conference, 1979.

5

Living the Story Together

Text Pages
78–97

Objectives

Knowledge: To help the students gain a sense of the history of God revealing himself and of a people responding; to see this story as the roots of the Christian community.

Attitude: To enable the students to appreciate the faith struggles of their ancestors, and to realize their responsibility in continuing to shape this story of the Church.

Practice: To have the students construct a time line identifying the significant people, everts, ard experiences in the Church's story in the Bible.

Orientation

The life situation that opens the chapter in "A Surprise Ending" is typical of an adolescent—the students should identify with the chapter immediately. Looking into our ancestry continues to be a very popular pastime. For 13 years, Alex Haley traveled around the world, conducted interviews, searched through old records, and then wrote his compelling story in the book, *Roots.* When *Roots* was shown in a 12-hour TV special, millions of viewers shared in Haley's search for his past. This reference to Alex Haley will help students recall how searching for one's roots became so popular; it will also help them grasp the idea that looking into our past can help us grow in our commitment to the present and future.

The section entitled "The Story of Our Religious Roots" (text page 81) parallels the Bible's use of "In the beginning" with the typical fairy story beginning "Once upon a time." The comparison of the opening phrase of Genesis to the opening phrase of fairy tales gives the students a familiar reference point between themselves and ancient Hebrews. In hearing either phrase, one knows for certain that a favorite and well-known story is about to follow.

To speak about these symbolic stories as ones which contain and express life's deeper questions is an importart point to establish before introducing the historical characters who heard the voice of God revealing himself. What follows in the student text is an historical overview of call and response in the experiences of God's people.

The way history is written facilitates the students' involvement with characters and important events. Each time there is an important point to be covered, or a new character to be introduced, the students get a sense of the importance through the style of writing. The use of the Scriptures also gives the students a sense of rootedness.

Before beginning a sketch of the New Testament history, the students are given time to absorb the material as well as internalize the meaning in the section "Time Out to Think" (text page 87). The purpose of this section is to relate the previous material highlighted in the Old Testament with the students' life experiences. After considering the stories of Cathy and Tony and their respective responses to God's call, the students are asked to reflect so that they might ask these questions of themselves and examine their own responses to God's call.

In "The Story of Our Roots Continues" (text page 91) the students resume the study of the Church's story as it is told in the New Testament. Before introducing Jesus, the Messiah, the text describes the milieu into which he came.

As Richard McBrien states in his book *Catholicism,* "The more one knows about and understands the social, economic, political, and religious situation at a time of Jesus, the more intelligently one will be able to interpret the New Testament's faith in him as well as the import and impact of Jesus' words and deeds upon his contemporaries." This is exactly what we are asking the students to do in a way that is commensurate with their level of thinking. The historical treatment concludes with a glimpse at the people of the early Church community. The students are asked to see these people in relation to themselves and identify with the challenges they faced. It is hoped that this study will foster a sense of continuity in the students—the recognition that *they* are the Church community *now*.

In the final section, "The End Is But the Beginning" (text page 94), a number of real-life situations are cited as examples of the unlimited possibilities open to young people of today's Church. It is the author's hope that the impact of the past will be more than just a story—that it will be an impetus to motivate our students into prayerful actions on their own journeys of faith!

Life Experience Focus

Justification for this chapter is well-founded in *Sharing the Light of Faith.* The Directory states: "Between 12 and 18 many young people either begin to abandon the faith of their childhood or become more deeply committed to it.

There is a tendency for young people around age 13 to regard much previous teaching about religion as childish, in the erroneous belief that there is no coherent and mature explanation for what they have learned earlier. Resolution of the conflict between faith and reason, formerly thought to take place by age 20, now appears to be occurring earlier. These developments must be taken into account in preparing catechetical programs and materials for young people facing or about to face a crisis of faith." (#200b)

It is evident that there has been a decline in faith values and religious practice among many of our young people. Rejection of the Bible is part of this attitude and unfortunately many young people never go beyond a limited introduction to this integral part of the Christian message. The treatment of the Scriptures in this chapter follows the observations and recommendations of the NCD. Our students are often confused and bored by the language and thought of the Bible. It is important, therefore, that the catechesis be adapted to their age, and their stage of religious development, and that it be presented through dialogue as opposed to "indoctrination."

Therefore, in treating the material in the chapter, the teacher must be well prepared to give sound and correct explanations; be honest enough to admit he or she may not have all the answers to students' questions about the Bible; be sincere in encouraging and also joining students' efforts to search for truth; and be careful to insure that this study of Scripture is not only intellectual and academic but also affective and experiential (see Guide for Chapter 1).

It is essential that the students look at the Scriptures in such a way as to say, "What is here for me? What are these events and people in the past saying for my life?" More often than not, they tend to look at the Bible as "too old and too remote a part of the past" to be able to have any relevance to their lives today. The teacher can perform a real service for them by helping the students to see the Bible as the living Word of God speaking to them not only today, but also tomorrow. Helping students to see that the Bible *is* their story, in fact is every person's story, is the task at hand. Spending time establishing this concept will reap results as the study progresses.

This subject matter of the Old Testament, however, will require very delicate handling with respect to the psychological stage of the adolescent. Many of the stories in Genesis and Exodus, especially, are very familiar to them. The stories have most likely been learned in a very concrete manner; perhaps they have been seen on TV or in a movie version. For adolescents to make the transition to seeing biblical truths in an allegorical way is a giant step! Teaching them that the stories in the first 11 chapters of Genesis are symbolic, rather than factual, events often causes traumatic results. It raises questions about the credibility of previous teachers or even the credibility of the whole Bible. In general, adolescents tend to resist an intelligent, adult understanding of the Bible because of their own insecurity. They have heard these stories repeated since childhood, as "gospel truth." As students cling fiercely to the old and familiar, the teacher must help them to see that the truth has *not* changed; the students are the ones who have changed, and they must be willing to stretch and expand their thinking process. Much patience, sensitivity, and repeated explanation is required of the teacher.

Background on Content

The importance of the Scriptures in the life of the Church is well-attested by the *National Catechetical Directory* as it states: "Catechesis studies scripture as a source inseparable from the Christian message. It seeks ways to make biblical signs better understood, so that people may more fully live the message of the Bible. (Cf 2 Tm 3, 14–17) . . . .

The term 'biblical signs' refers to the varied and wonderful ways, recorded in Scripture, by which God reveals himself. Among the chief signs to be emphasized in all catechesis are: the creation account, which culminates in the establishment of God's kingdom; the covenant made by God with Abraham and his descendants and God's new Covenant in Jesus Christ which is extended to all people; the parallel, but far more profound, passage from death to life accomplished by Christ's paschal mystery. Underlying all as an authentic biblical sign is the community of believers—the People of Israel, the Church—from among whom, under the inspiration of the Holy Spirit, certain individuals composed and assembled these holy writings and transmitted them to future generations as testimony to their beliefs and their experience of grace." (43)

Chapter 5 treats each of these key themes in such a way as to help students gain a sense of history shaping them and giving them an identity with God. The text highlights many of the major events, key personalities, and pivotal experiences in both the Old and New Testaments. Bold headlines and flowing phrases are set in a type of free verse to point up an essential characteristic of each major topic. Such a format gives the teacher the option of providing either an in-depth treatment or a brief coverage of any given topic.

Students should be taught the basic tools needed for intelligent reading of the Bible on their own. These include the following:

● how to read and write a "citation" correctly, for example, 1 Samuel 9:18-23 as "the first book of Samuel, Chapter 9, verses 18 through 23";

● how to locate and read "notes" providing background or explanatory matter, located at the bottom of a page of text in the Bible;

● how to read the "parallels," also located at the bottom of the page of text, and be able to use them;

● how to use a "biblical concordance" for ease and facility in locating passages about selected topics.

Reference materials will be found in *Resources* for this Guide chapter.

Teaching Notes 1

**Text Pages
78–97**

A Surprise Ending

1. The life situation opening the chapter is one which students can easily relate to because Jerry's emotions are ones that are honestly felt by students their age.

a. Ask the students to initiate the same kind of conversation with their parent(s) as Jerry did. *Worksheet #10* could help students organize their interviews, and *Worksheet #11* could help them reflect on the experience of discussing their birth story with their parents.

b. If these are not available to you, direct students' questions along these lines:

● Factual Information: date and place of birth; time and day of the week; weight, height, color of hair and eyes; those present at birth; any significant circumstances before, during, or after the birth.

● Feelings Involved: how your mother and father each felt about this birth; grandparents' reactions; reactions of brothers and/or sisters (if any); other.

Encourage students to enter into conversation with their parent(s) about any of these points if they feel so inclined or to discover a particular point of interest or poignancy. Because of the personal nature of this assignment, students should not be made to share the results. However, offer the opportunity for sharing in an atmosphere of acceptance and respect. The results of sharing these aloud could be very inspiring, and could also strengthen the students' bonds of community among themselves. Here again, the teacher can give examples by sharing from his or her own experience and so encourage the students to do likewise.

c. To help the students benefit most from this interview direct their post-interview thinking. Have them reflect on questions such as:

● What did I learn from the interview—either about myself or my family?

● What impressed me most about this experience?

● How did I feel about myself after the interview?

● How did I feel about my parent(s) after the interview?

This reflection activity should be written in students' journals. This entry could be incorporated into one of the concluding Prayer Experiences or become the occasion for an immediate prayerful experience.

2. Ask the students what they know about *Roots*, either from seeing it on TV or from reading the book. Bring out the significance of the story of the African, Kunta Kinte, that was passed down to each generation in Haley's family, and the often repeated story of Kunta Kinte lifting his child up to the stars as he named him and made him a member of the tribe. Point out that story-telling is integral to every culture and people. This is an important foundation for understanding the contents of the Book of Genesis.

The Story of Our Religious Roots

1. Ask the students if doing the interview with their parents raised any other questions aside from physical birth in their minds, such as:

● Where does life come from?

● How does life truly begin and where does it go?

● How does life end or continue?

Suggest some of these questions, if students do not think of them at the moment. You want to call their attention to this deeper pondering about life's mysteries.

2. Have them open their journals to the Lifeline done in conjunction with Chapter 1 and write these questions at either end of their lifeline. Tell them to add any other questions that are mystery to them in the appropriate places anywhere along their lifelines.

3. Direct the students' attention to the text's explanation of the first eleven chapters of Genesis as being a "prologue" to the human experience of God. Clarify the meaning of the word prologue and the meaning of symbolism. Make a comparison between the questions that students wrote previously on their lifelines and the similar questions that ancient Hebrews were pondering. Explain that the ancient people expressed these questions in story fashion, according to the custom of that period in history.

4. Ask students to recall one or two stories from Genesis that are familiar to them, for example, the story of Adam and Eve, the tower of Babylon, the story of the temptation in Eden, etc. Have the stories read aloud from the Bible text. Ask them what question or truth might be contained in each story, and what might have been the Hebrew's attitude towards that mystery. Carefully work your way through this section. If students reject the concept as incorrect, keep assuring them that truth is still contained in this part of the Bible, whether we interpret it literally or contextually. The truth does not change; our way of understanding truth does change.

5. Explain the symbolism found in these stories. Have students read the notes on the text as found in their Bibles. It is essential that they see the difference between symbolic story and factual history as recorded in the story of Abraham, Genesis 12. An excellent filmstrip entitled *Understanding Genesis* could provide a fine summary of these concepts (see *Resources* for this Guide chapter).

Teaching Notes 2

**Text Pages
82–87**

Abraham, Founding Father

1. This section begins salvation history. Have the students construct a time line which they will keep adding to as the study progresses. After leaving an introductory space on it marked by a broken line, have them begin the chronology with the date 2000 B.C. and mark it "Abraham."

2. In the first section about Abraham, have the students relate to what Abraham must have been feeling as he perceived this strange message to leave home, and after he actually did it. A few examples from life may be effective, such as, leaving friends and familiar surroundings to go off to high school, having to move from one's home to an entirely different location. Make the point that we are often more open to God's call when we are in new or different surroundings. Abraham received the promise from God only after he was in his new location. More can be said about this openness to God when you are dealing with the desert experiences of the Israelites in Exodus (text page 83).

3. Abraham marks the beginning of recorded history in the Bible, even though the history is "folk history," or oral tradition. He is the first known person who said "yes" to God. Have the students keep a list in their notebooks of all such persons named in the text who responded affirmatively to God. Next to the person's name have them characterize the call and the response. This can be used for reflection in the section "Time Out to Think" (text page 87). *Worksheet #12* could also serve this purpose.

4. Direct the students to outline the genealogy from Abraham to the twelve sons of Israel, using selected passages in Genesis. Point out the brief summary of many years of history in Exodus 1:1–14. It explains what caused the enslavement of the Hebrews in Egypt, and describes the situation in which the heroic figure of Moses appears. Students should record his name and significance on the time line in the approximate year 1250 B.C.

From Slavery to Freedom

1. Here again, focus on the call and response of Moses and what Moses' feelings might have been realistically. Since many students may have seen the Hollywood film version of Moses, it may be hard for them to see Moses' humanness and the Exodus events as less than magical phenomena. A point to stress here is the power of God, and the wonders each of us may be involved in if we allow that power to work in us. Ancient peoples believed in God's power and expressed their belief in extraordinary descriptions of it, as "the Red Sea parting," etc. Explain the plagues, the manna, the quail, and the water from the rock in the desert as natural occurrences, as indeed they were and are even today. The lesson to emphasize is the "faith view" of the Israelite people. In the phenomena of nature, the people looked beyond the events themselves and saw the power and presence of a saving God.

2. Assign the students to work in groups of three or four on the exercise about the covenant (text page 83). Let each group select two terms of the covenant and show how each of them can be applied today. Have each group report this to the entire group.

David—King After God's Own Heart

1. The next step is to get in touch with how the Israelites handle being the chosen people (text page 84). To be clear and concise have the students read the quote about the peoples' cry for a king and then ask them why a king would be wanted.

2. David is the next personality. Once again fact and fiction may be mixed up and some sorting out needed. Have them read all the material on David before discussion and characterize David's call and response. Give them time for any clarification needed. Point out David's strengths and weaknesses as realistically as possible for students. Have them write a personality sketch of David, concluding it with the thing they admired most about David. It is important to spend time on David's popularity with his people; he is admired not only for his strength and governance, but also for his support of the covenant and encouragement of worship in the life of his people. Students need to understand this for a clearer concept of the Messiah.

God Called Forth Prophets

1. The next section (text page 84) deals with the divided Kingdom and the era of the prophets. To change the pace a bit have the students choose either the Northern or Southern Kingdom and plot the fate of either side according to their choice.

2. The time line should show the split as well as the progression of both kingdoms.

3. Have the students read the excerpts from the prophets Amos and Hosea and explain each passage. These two individuals should be included on the students' list of key figures as well as a description of each one's call and response. Amos was called to challenge social injustice, and his response was to keep the covenant with Israel. Hosea's call was to unconditional love, and his response was to redeem a remnant of Israel.

4. Have the students work in groups of three or four to complete the exercise (page 85).

Prophets in Exile

1. In this section, the students might role play scenes from each prophet's life. Let them work in two groups to research the lives of Jeremiah and Ezekiel in the Bible. Each group will depict one or more situations from each prophet's life, with scenes that involve the prophet's words and the people's response. This will give students an experiential insight into these two individuals and what it cost them to follow God's call.

2. Be sure to include Jeremiah and Ezekiel on the students' list of persons called, and also to add them to the time line.

3. The exercise on the psalms (text page 86) is important for two reasons. It should enable students to get a sense of the emotions of the people in exile—their feelings about God, life, suffering, longing, homeland. The exercise can also offer a fine opportunity for teaching students to pray with the psalms. Establish a quiet atmosphere. Direct the students to be quiet and center themselves by using the breathing exercise taught in Chapter 1. Then have them read one line of the psalm at a time very slowly and reverently. Pause quietly before going on, and allow the Word of God to penetrate. Tell the students to be aware of any thoughts or feelings that may arise, and to enter into conversation with God about those thoughts or feelings. This prayer activity might be more effective if the students have already completed the exercise. Conclude the prayer by playing a record of one of the psalms. (See *Resources.*)

4. To point up the anticipation of the Messiah, have the students read the Messianic prophecies in the Old Testament:

- Zephaniah 9:9–13
- Isaiah 7:14–16
- 2 Samuel 7:16
- Micah 5:1–4 and 7:6
- Isaiah 53

Let them work in groups and report what they have discovered to the entire group.

Teaching Notes 3

Time Out to Think

1. Ask the students to look over their list of people in the Old Testament who responded to God's call. Aside from the uniqueness that is evident in each one's response, focus the students' attention on an important point made in the text (page 88) that each of these individuals put aside their natural uncertainties and trusted God. Only in so doing did they become extraordinary people.

2. Relate the experience of call and response to the students' lives by discussing the two life situations, Cathy Woods and Tony Peratta, and completing the exercise (text page 88).

The Story of Our Roots Continues

1. One way of having students appreciate the cultural milieu in which Jesus lived is by comparing the opposing groups of the times to political groups holding different opinions today. Pharisees, Sadducees, and Zealots of Jesus' day can be likened to the Liberal, Conservative, and Extremist thinkers today. Have the students work in three groups and prepare reports.

2. There was yet another group who lived apart and practiced a stricter fidelity to the law, remained celibate, and worshiped in their own way among themselves, apart from the Temple or the synagogue. These were the Essenes. Some might compare them to religious groups or cults of today. List these on the board for students to write in their notebooks. They should also record them on their time lines.

Mary, the Mother of Jesus

1. Elaborate on the description of Mary's role and qualities (text page 91). Mary can be a powerful model for students—as a young person who was fully human, fully Christian, and fully woman, and who opened herself fully to the power of God. Here again, point up the tremendous trust Mary had at every stage of her journey of faith. The filmstrips "Woman of Faith" and "Magnificat" are excellent audiovisuals for providing a "new look" at the Mother of Jesus (see *Resources* for this Guide chapter).

2. Have students write an article for a magazine introducing Mary to people of today. They may include references from the gospels for the article.

Church—A Community

Ask students to read the passage from Acts 5:40–42 to get a sense of the apostolic spirit after Pentecost. In treating the story of the early Church community the examples of Paul, Stephen, and Barnabas will be effective with students. The story of Stephen's trial and subsequent stoning in Acts 7 could be role played by the entire group. Such courage should be highlighted. Have students read 1 Corinthians 12:12, 25–27 and Ephesians 4:16 in addition to the passage in the exercise (text page 93) to grasp the full import of Paul's vision of Christian community. Ask: How does it compare with your own?

The End Is But the Beginning

The last section of the chapter relates the text to students' lives. It brings back the point that this *is* their story. *They* are the Church *now*. Discuss the examples of youth group activities given in the text (page 95) and ask students for other examples.

Prayer and Worship Experiences

1. Have the students choose a psalm from the ones read in the chapter. Begin the service with the song "Isaiah 49" (see *Resources* for this Guide chapter). Read the psalm reflectively; then ask for a prayerful response from the students concerning the chapter. Include some opportunity for prayers of petition concerning calls and response to the Lord that the students see as important, for example, praying for the continued commitment of Mother Teresa who was called by God to minister to the dying and destitute of India. An appropriate song to conclude would be, "I will Play Before the Lord" (see *Resources* for this Guide chapter).

2. Use the lifeline as the focal point of a worship service having students recall their feelings and understanding of the personalities that are part of salvation history. Each student could compose a prayerful reflection to be read. A good song to be part of this service would be "Great Things Happen When God Mixes Us" (see *Resources* for this Guide chapter). Then use the closing prayer of the chapter.

Service Projects

1. Suggest that some students offer to teach CCD or religious instruction in their local parishes. If high school students are not permitted to be actual catechists, have them offer their services as aides or as tutors for one or two hours a week. Ask them to record in their journals their thoughts and feelings about this experience.

2. Choose an individual whose call and response to the Lord is one that you admire. Volunteer to spend some time helping the person in his or her work and see if you can get in touch with how he or she sees the call and how he or she responds to that call. Interview the person to make sure that your perceptions are valid.

Independent Study Projects

1. Do an in-depth study of Mother Teresa of Calcutta. Find out about her childhood and her call to go to India, as well as her life in India and her dedication to the dying and destitute of her adopted country. A report to the group would be beneficial for all.

2. To nurture interest in the early Church have a student choose a personality studied in the chapter and do a report on that person, first reading excerpts from the Bible, then going to other sources for their interpretations.

3. Do some further research about one of the prophets not mentioned in the text. Prepare a report on the prophet's life and how it influenced his message to the people of God.

4. Look up information about some of the famous women in the Old Testament, such as Ruth, Deborah, Esther, or Judith and prepare a report about their responses to God's call.

Resources

Audiovisual

"Isaiah 49." Song by Rev. Carey Landry, on the album *I Will Not Forget You.* North American Liturgy Resources, 2110 West Peoria Avenue, Phoenix, AZ 85029.

"Be Not Afraid" on the album *Earthen Vessels* by the St. Louis Jesuits. North American Liturgy Resources.

"I Will Play Before the Lord." Song by Bob Dufford, S.S. on the album *Glory and Praise Vol. 1.* North American Liturgy Resources.

"You Are Near" on the album *Neither Silver Nor Gold* by the St. Louis Jesuits, and also on the album *Glory and Praise, Vol. 1.*

"Great Things Happen When God Mixes Us." Song by Carey Landry on the album *Glory and Praise, Vol. 1.*

Roots. Series of 12 filmstrips, 48 min., color. Boston University Krasker Memorial Film Library, 765 Commonwealth Ave., Boston, MA 02215.

Understanding Genesis. A two-part color filmstrip. Thomas S. Klise Co., P.O. Box 3418, Peoria, IL 61614.

"Woman of Faith" and "Magnificat," two of a four-part set of filmstrips, each 17 minutes, on *Mary.* TeleKETICS. Franciscan Productions, 1229 South Santee Street, Los Angeles, CA 90015.

Print

F.F. Bruce. *New Testament History.* New York: Doubleday, 1972.

R. Brown. *Biblical Reflections on Crises Facing the Church.* New York: Paulist Press, 1975.

P. Ellis. *Men and Message of the Old Testament.* Collegeville, MN: Liturgical Press, 1976.

H. Daniel-Rops. *Daily Life in the Times of Jesus.* New York: Hawthorn Books, 1962.

N. Flanagan. *Salvation History.* New York: Sheed and Ward, 1964.

W. Keller. *The Bible as History: A Confirmation of the Book of Books.* New York: William Morrow, 1956.

R. Karris. *What Are They Saying About Luke and Acts?* New York: Paulist Press, 1980.

J. McHugh. *The Mother of Jesus in the New Testament.* New York: Doubleday, 1975.

J. McKenzie. *Dictionary of the Bible.* Milwaukee, WI: Bruce Publishing Co., 1965.

——————. *Light on the Gospels.* Chicago, IL: Thomas More Association, 1976.

Good News Bible. Catholic Study Edition. New York: Wm. H. Sadlier, Inc., 1979.

Sharing the Light of Faith: National Catechetical Directory for Catholics in the United States. Washington, D.C.: United States Catholic Conference, 1979.

The Jerome Biblical Commentary. Englewood Cliffs, NJ: Prentice-Hall, 1968.

J. Dunn. "Who Do You Say That I Am?" *U.S. Catholic.* April 1974.

G. McCauley. "The Values of Jesus." *New Catholic World.* May/June 1974.

E. Carroll. "Theology on the Virgin Mary: 1966-1975." *Theological Studies.* 1976.

G. Friedman. "Tommorow's Church Today: Cleveland's Kaleidoscope Experience." *St. Anthony Messenger.* June 1979.

P. Stuhlmiller. "Biblical Education." *PACE 10* (*Professional Approaches for Christian Educators*) Winona, MN: St. Mary's Press, 1979.

R. Wild. "The Spirit in the New Testament." *St. Anthony Messenger.* 1975.

6

Sharing Our Story

Text Pages
98–117

Objectives
Knowledge: To acquaint the students with the history of the Church in order to identify significant people and experiences that have shaped the Church today.
Attitude: To enable the students to come to a realistic understanding of both the human element and the Divine Presence in the Church since its beginning.
Practice: To help the students to identify the cycle of history observable in each era of the Church's history.

Orientation
This chapter will take the student through a brief panoramic view of Church history, a view that will give a sense of what kind of journey the Church has been on through the ages, as well as a glimpse at various personalities who have been instrumental in shaping the Church's story.

The introductory situation in this chapter makes a connection with the previous chapter by recalling another school experience in the life of the student named Jerry. After completing a course on Church history, Jerry's feelings are very typical and realistic: he was surprised at learning more than he expected!

Reading about Jerry's experience subtly conveys to the students objectives which they too can achieve by studying the chapter. In the section "A New Impression" (text page 98) the cyclic pattern of history is recalled from Chapter 5. Learning about this pattern will provide an important tool for developing an analytical sense in students. A skill such as this is invaluable for their future use.

"Peter and Paul: Success and Failure" (text page 101) presents two important models for adolescents. Time spent here will reap rewards later. Seeing the human elements in Peter and Paul will help students identify with the first leaders of the Church. For students to realize Peter and Paul's humanness will also set the tone for the rest of the chapter—an honest look at the story of the Church and its people.

In "Persecution: Love Is Stronger Than Death" (text page 101) students will not only deal with the persecutions of the early Christians but also examine the Christian oppression going on in various parts of the world today. In this section the burden is placed on the students to explain and justify their own faith, which is a good experience for them.

The next section, "Freedom and Recognition" (text page 103) offers a glimpse at the truth that out of evil often comes unexpected good. The formulation of the Creed, the Church's response to the early heresies, illustrates this truth. Studying this section should shed a new light on the Creed for students.

In "Making a Difference," (text page 104) the treatment of Augustine lends itself to many important concepts for students, whether in the lessons learned from Augustine's conversion or from his philosophy and teachings.

The section on "Monasticism: A Counter-Culture Movement" (text page 104) provides a look at the Church's contribution to the preservation of civilization as well as exposure to an important movement in spirituality. Adequate time and attention should be given here to the students' own spirituality and prayer life.

"Saints and Scholars: A New Mood" (text page 106) offers a good opportunity for students to apply the skill of historical analysis to this period. Vocational instruction and discussion would be very helpful here also.

In studying the 20th century, you will want to emphasize the people behind the experiences. The more students learn about the lives of the individuals mentioned in the last section "From Peak Times to Bleak Times" (text page 111), from Luther to John Paul II, the more effective their learning will be. Above all, emphasize a sense of compassion and forgiveness towards human faults and play down a judgmental attitude in the students. In the final analysis our just and merciful God alone is the Judge of us all.

Life Experience Focus

Because the content of this chapter is similar in scope to the last one, the students are asked to absorb a great deal of content. The setup of this chapter, however, provides the student with information followed by an exercise to help them reinforce and internalize the material.

Since there is so much history to be covered the text is designed to involve the students as fully as possible. The concept here is that the more the students feel a part of the action, the more they will absorb and make their own.

Another factor that will demand attention is the *honest* picture of the Church being shown, with its virtues and glories as well as its foibles. The good will most probably be accepted but the human weaknesses and mistakes may need more careful handling in order that the students accept the whole picture. This age group tends to see things as "black and white;" they need to be helped to realize that most of life consists of the shades of grey in between. The "black and white" of situations is rare and infrequent, although some people live as if such clear-cut extremes are common. Adolescents fall into this category and can remain in that stage of perception unless we help them to see life realistically. To give them an honest picture now will be doing them a service. You will be developing in them attitudes of compassion, forgiveness, and hope in dealing with the experience of failure, whether it be their own or someone else's failure.

History is a key to our lives that should help us understand who we are and what we can become. If we call ourselves Christian, then experiencing the history of the Church will help us get in touch with our own unique call, how we respond to it, and what that call can mean to the world around us. Ultimately this is the final result we seek with the students as they become more involved with the history of the Church.

Background on Content

This chapter continues the story of the Church by identifying key events and personalities that shaped our Church thoughgut the ages. *Sharing the Light of Faith* says: "The Church, founded by Christ, had its origin in His death and resurrection. It is the new people of God, prepared for in the Old Testament and given life, growth, and direction by Christ in the Holy Spirit. It is the work of God's saving love in Christ." (93)

As we look closely at the journey of the Church community down through the centuries, this quote takes on even more importance.

From the time of Peter and Paul to the present, the Church has been led by very human individuals who many times failed because of their own personal weaknesses. In spite of this, the Spirit worked in and through each of the people and the Church has survived.

The point that is essential for the students to be able to grasp from this chapter is "the impact that history had on the Church, and the Church upon history" as Richard McBrien states in his work entitled *Catholicism.*

All the events are a part of history; all the personalities are a part of a historical framework. The Church is a unique gift from God that has molded and shaped both throughout the centuries. For the students to get in touch with how and why this all occurred is to begin to make the history of the Church their own.

The events and personalities that are presented for the students have been chosen so that they can come to an understanding of the Church and recognize its successes as well as its failures. Throughout each experience, even disasters, the members have grown closer to the source because their fidelity has prevailed.

Sharing the Light of Faith sums up this point by saying; "The Holy Spirit preserves the Church as Christ's body and bride so that, despite the sinfulness of its members, it will never fail in faithfulness to Him and will meet Him in holiness at the end of the world." (93) We are constantly challenged by the Spirit to be faithful and even when we fail there is always a way back to the Father; all we have to do is choose to continue our journey of faith as part of his Church.

Teaching Notes 1

**Text Pages
98–102**

A New Impression

1. Since Jerry's realization is a common experience, ask the students for examples of situations involving similar feelings; for instance: after a party, a date, a class or a course that they dreaded. Do they remember feeling afterwards that it turned out to be better than they had expected? Then ask them how they feel now about studying Church history and about saints in general. Do they have any favorite saints? Are there any they pray to? What makes a person a saint? Have them list characteristics which they think a person would need in order to be considered a saint.

2. List the cycle (text page 100) on the board and have the students copy it into their notebooks. The list can be used as a reference point while they are studying different eras in the history of the Church. Review the pattern to insure their understanding of it.

3. Give emphasis to the point made in the text about the presence of the Spirit being more certain because of the humanness observable in the Church's members (text page 98). Ask students if they agree or disagree with Jerry's conclusion. Raise this question again after the study of this chapter has been completed.

4. Direct the students to the exercise (text page 100) and conduct an open discussion about stereotyping and the causes for it. Conclude this section by having students write a brief description on "The Church As I See It."

Peter and Paul: Success and Failure

1. Ask the students to read the following passages in the gospels which reveal Peter's mistakes and failures:
Matthew 16:21–25; Jesus calls Peter Satan.
Matthew 26:31–35; Jesus predicts Peter's denial; Peter denies it.
Luke 22:54–62; Peter denies Jesus and then realizes what he has done.
Matthew 14:22–32; Peter walks on the water and then sinks.
Matthew 26:36–46; Peter falls asleep in the garden when Jesus needs him.
John 13:2–10; Jesus washes the apostles' feet; Peter protests.

Spend time working through these scenes with the students, having them notice the words and attitude of Jesus as well and those of Peter. For additional emphasis, have them read:
John 21:15–19; Jesus' triple questioning of Peter's love.
Matthew 16:13–19; Jesus praises Peter and calls him the "rock."

Be sure the students notice how Jesus never gave up on Peter but kept forgiving him and challenging him to new growth. Stress the fact that Peter, on his part, was open to learning and to trying again.

2. Ask the students to write a biographical sketch of Paul showing the change in Paul's lifestyle and attitudes. Let them use excerpts about Paul from Acts or from Paul's own words about himself taken from his letters. A few examples are:
Acts 22:3–4; Paul speaks about persecuting the followers of Jesus.
Acts 26; Paul on trial speaks before King Agrippa.

2 Corinthians 11:16—12:10; Paul speaks about his sufferings.
Philippians 3:12—14; Paul's philosophy.

3. Use the concluding exercise, about standing up for one's beliefs (text page 101), to relate this lesson to concrete experiences in the students' lives. They need to be made aware that the qualities exemplified in Peter and Paul still exist and can be cultivated in themselves.

4. Have the students complete *Worksheet #13* as a way of increasing understanding of the personalities of Sts. Peter and Paul.

5. Have the students choose a contemporary problem in the Church, the United States, the world, or their school. Approach it like this: "If Peter (or Paul) were here today, how would he handle this problem? What advice would he give?" Compose a letter or a speech as you think Peter (or Paul) might have addressed the situation selected.

6. Plan to include some lessons on motivation related to the experiences of success and failure illustrated in Peter's and Paul's lives. Time spent on this topic will be invaluable for adolescents. Marilyn Vanderbur, the former Miss America, distributes an excellent mini-course of films and discussion guides on the topic of motivation. Her program was shown at the NCEA in the 1970s and has been used effectively in schools throughout the country. (See *Resources* for this Guide chapter.)

Persecution: Love Is Stronger Than Death
1. After students read the text, ask them to explain why the Romans would feel as they did towards the Christians. Try to elicit the point that ignorance often breeds suspicion.

2. Have the students role play a scene between Romans and Christians, either as a debate, a trial, or an interview on a talk show. Whatever the scenario, let the task be for each side to explain the ritual of the Eucharist as each of them perceives it. This activity should generate a great deal of thinking for the entire group. If it is a debate or trial, let the rest of the group pass judgment on each side. As a follow-up, students could be asked to write a critique on the explanation of the Eucharist that was given.

3. To show that the pen is mightier than the sword, assign the students to write "Letters to the Editor" (of the *Roman Times*) in support of the Christians' beliefs and in praise of their courage and heroism. Write letters of protest to the newspaper or to the Emperor. Write letters of encouragement and consolation to an imprisoned Christian. Lastly, have them each write a letter defending themselves as Christians. In the letter, they should explain the specific things they do and the practices they believe in which verify that they are Christian.

4. Conduct a group discussion on the meaning of the quote: "The blood of the martyrs is the seed of the Church" (text page 102). Assign students in groups of three or four to prepare a visual display to accompany their essay about the meaning of the quote. Let them use slides, posters, a film, a collage of words and/or pictures or original sketches and drawings. This could be done in conjunction with the research assignment on "Persecution in the Church Today." Be sure to provide time for students to share the results of their research since the information will be very revealing for most of them. The visual assignment could provide a setting for a short prayer service to conclude the study about persecutions. Encourage the students to pray for both persecuted and persecutors in the countries where oppression exists.

Teaching Notes 2

**Text Pages
103–113**

Freedom and Recognition: New Life, New Errors

1. Explain to the students the major erroneous teachings about Jesus and about salvation that arose in the early centuries. Have them take notes on these:

Gnosticism: a belief that the spiritual world alone is good and the material world is wholly evil. Only those who are given direct knowledge (*gnosis*) by God are saved.

Arianism: Jesus is a lesser god, created by God and dependent on him. Jesus is not divine, but is rather the adopted son of God, and he was not born of Mary.

Nestorianism: a belief that made a complete distinction between the human nature of Jesus and the Second Person of the Trinity, who dwelled in the human nature of Jesus.

Donatism: a belief which placed an emphasis on the holiness of the individual person. One could not belong to God's Church if one was unholy.

Pelagianism: A belief that man has an exaggerated magical power by nature to do good; he has no need for divine grace and can be saved by his own power.

Manichaeism: a later development of Gnosticism. Manichaens believed in two kingdoms—based on two principles or natures—of light and darkness, good and evil, God and matter, each in conflict with the other. Man was considered a prisoner of Satan and could only be freed by a strict self-discipline.

Emphasize the point that these errors or heresies brought about a good result. It made the Church clarify its beliefs and set them down in writing for its people.

2. Explain what a Church council is by referring to the account of the first council of Jerusalem in 49 A.D., described in Acts 15:1–21. After analyzing this event, elaborate on what a Church council does. Ask if students think a council might be necessary in the Church today and why.

3. Since the Creed contains the basic teachings of the Church, distribute copies of the Nicene Creed to the students. Ask them to examine it closely. Question them on the meaning of each phrase and clarify any that might be confusing or unclear. Direct them to the question at the end of the exercise (text page 103) about what part appeals to them most.

4. Another option might be to have the students compose a creed in their own words as an expression of their personal beliefs.

Making a Difference

1. Read through this section with the students, answering any questions and elaborating on Augustine's early life and subsequent philosophy. Recall the heresy of Manichaeism studied in the last section and point out that Augustine had been a follower of Mani, its founder, during his early years. Students can relate to Augustine more easily when hearing about his failings and recklessness in his youth. Ask students to explain how a person like him could be so looked up to by the Church community. Stress that Augustine, like Peter, did not give up on himself.

2. In conjunction with the exercise (text page 103), provide time for students to share their interviews. Perhaps a talk show or a role-playing situation might be arranged as a means for effective and enjoyable sharing of their work.

Monasticism: A Counter-Culture Movement

1. Ask if anyone knows the meaning of the term "counter-culture movement." If no one knows, give examples of counter-culture groups such as the hippies, the Yippies, the Weathermen in the 60s, and the cult groups of the 70s. Recall the Essenes studied in Chapter 5 as another example. Point out that the followers of Jesus were considered a counter-culture movement, as evident during the persecutions. Help the students to see that a radical following of the gospel message is and will always be in opposition to the prevailing values of the society. The eternal struggle between good and evil is at the heart of this reality.

2. Show the filmstrip or slides about the Benedictines at Weston Priory in Vermont, *The Gift of Community.* (See *Resources* for this Guide chapter.) This will give students a good picture of contemporary monasticism. Since the tone of the filmstrip is meditative as well as instructive, provide the opportunity for an appropriate response after its viewing.

Anticipate many questions about the brothers and their works, about the location of the monastery in Vermont, and about this kind of vocation. Help the students to be aware of what they may be feeling—peaceful, happy, a sense of God's presence. Ask why they think a person would choose to live this way of life. Use the discussion questions in the exercise (text page 106) in conjunction with the filmstrip.

3. Play some of the records by the brothers of Weston Priory. (See *Resources* for this Guide chapter.) Have the words of the songs available and discuss the words and the music in relation to people of today's world and their renewed interest in prayer and spiritually. Ask students if they have ever made a retreat or gone to a prayer meeting. Would they like to do this? Perhaps a day of prayer and reflection could be planned along the lines of a monastic day.

4. Have the students complete *Worksheet #14* on the monastic life.

Saints and Scholars: A New Mood

1. Take time to look again at the cycle of events explained at the start of this chapter (text page 106). Help students to notice the sequence of events in this time period in reference to the human cycle. For example, out of the decline of civilization after the barbarian invasions a new life was being born and nurtured in the monasteries. Education was beginning; it would flourish and prosper in the Medieval Period. In other words, try to help students step back and look at historical events analytically while you are rounding out the picture for them.

2. Explain the difference between monks and mendicants (text page 107) and between active and contemplative religious life. Seeing the new type of religious orders emerge in the 12th century, such as the Franciscans and the Dominicans, should help students to understand this basic difference in religious response. Show the students how the response is determined by the needs of the times. With the new development of towns, the religious response is outward, to a ministry *among* the townspeople, rather than calling the townspeople to go *apart* from the town. Relate this point about appropriate religious response to the needs of the times to situations in the world today. Ask students to give examples of what religious orders are doing today. If students are only aware of teaching as a ministry, give examples of the variety of religious responses being made today; for example: prison work, parish ministers, political offices, social action groups, spiritual direction, drug and alcohol abuse centers, to name a few. Be open to the students' questions and mixed reactions about the appropriateness of religious to be engaged in these ministries. Help students to see that as times changed in history, new ways of ministering to people evolved. One thing remains constant throughout all times: living a life of prayer and deepening one's relationship to Jesus Christ are always an essential factor in religious life.

3. Tell the students to compose a letter to a friend explaining why they have chosen to enter a religious community. Let them choose a particular group, either an active or a contemplative order. Have information and materials available about the different orders, such as Dominicans, Franciscans, Carmelites, Augustinians, Cistercians, Benedictines, etc. Assuming that the friend does not understand anything about religious life, the letter should include the following:
  ● What is the daily routine of their life?
  ● What kind of ministry do they engage in?
  ● What do their vows mean?
  ● What are their requirements? What are their benefits?
  ● What is the reason for chosing this life?

4. Have the students break into groups of three or four. After examining the duties of a Christian in the Church precepts (text page 110), have them explain the value behind each precept. Let each group choose two precepts and prepare an explanation of them for someone who does not understand Church laws. Allow time for these to be expressed aloud for the entire group. This will give you a chance to be aware of their limited understanding and to clarify any confusing ideas about the precepts.

Doing the last question in the exercise puts the responsibility on the student to again "step into the shoes" of those who have gone before them and those who are currently responsible for the general spiritual welfare of the whole Christian community.

Teaching Notes 3

Text Pages 111–117

From Peak Times to Bleak Times

1. This period in Church history lends itself to an audiovisual presentation as an effective teaching device. Showing slides of the cathedrals, works of art, and architecture will communicate more than a written or spoken description.

Local libraries would probably have collections of slides on this period available. If your school has a Kodak Visualmaker, you could make your own collection of slides from pictures in magazines or books. Music of the Medieval Period should be included also.

2. Another suggestion would be to have the students prepare slides, filmstrips, posters, or models of cathedrals or feudal estates, etc. Research reports might also be done on the Crusades, and the culture of the East. The more work students do themselves, the more they will learn from the effort.

3. Asking the students to identify and describe the effects upon the Church should be the follow-up to the reports. Be sure to bring out the elements of decay that were beginning to corrupt Church leaders. Remind students about the human element that Jerry spoke about in the opening section of the chapter (text page 98). This is

essential for their understanding of the Avignon captivity, the selling of indulgences, the whole Reformation period, and also the East-West schism.

4. Have the students list the differences causing the East-West split in order to clarify the reasons behind this tragic situation:

- differences in language: Greek in the East, Latin in the West;
- cultural differences and differences in philosophical thinking;
- disputes over the law requiring priestly celibacy: the Eastern Church permitted priests to marry; the West did not;
- disagreements over the extent of the Pope's power: the Eastern Church refused to impose Western uniformity upon its people.

Unity between the two Churches had always been fragile. Point out to the students how minor differences can so often cloud the larger elements of unity. Another important lesson to be seen is how the struggle for power, whether to gain or to maintain it, can cause people to lose their perspective about essential matters (text page 112). Differences of thought and attitudes need not cause separation; they can bring about a healthy fullness for all concerned.

5. Imagine that the clock has been turned back a few centuries. You have been called in to a heated debate between representatives of the Eastern and Western Churches over the question of papal authority. You are asked to help them bring about a compromise situation. What would you say that would help them resolve their difficulties and accept the position of authority more peaceably? Be sure to include the positive effects that would result from the two Churches remaining united. Each student should explain his or her way of approaching this task.

6. As a conclusion to this section have students discuss the questions in the exercise (text page 112). Have them share their suggestions for fostering Christian unity.

Division: Wounds in Need of Healing

1. Have the students read the section on Martin Luther (text pages 112–113) and then hold a debate about whether or not Luther was doing the right thing in pulling away from the Church. Because the students' stage of development is probably, in Kohlberg terminology, on the law-and-order level, they will probably not be able to resolve the dilemma about Luther's position. Even so, it is good for them to think about both sides of an issue and to realize that some matters must remain unresolved. Remind students that God is the only reliable judge of human experiences. Be sure to comment on the good that resulted from Luther's actions. Reform was a very necessary task for the Church in this era. Out of the Protestant Revolt came an organized program for correcting abuses that had been growing within the Church community.

2. Another appropriate activity would be to have the students research and report on the personalities of saints of this era whose lives they might identify with as well as admire. Good examples are: Francis of Assisi, Catherine of Siena, Ignatius of Loyola, Thomas More, Joan of Arc, Thomas Aquinas. Be sure they include some explanation about what motivated each of the saints.

3. Point to the missionary movement as an outgrowth of the healing process that occurred after the Reformation. Here again, see to it that students notice the new type of religious group emerging, one which actively ministered to people's spiritual and intellectual needs. The Jesuits are a prime example (text page 114).

Another aspect to notice is the emergence and spread of women's religious communities. Showing a filmstrip on the life of St. Elizabeth Ann Seton would provide some insights into the women of that era. (See *Resources* for this Guide chapter.) Her response to God was initially one of inner conversion and then it became a vocation to start a new religious community. Since Elizabeth Seton typifies many of these women foundresses, spend time having students examine her life story. Ask students to react to her experience and to her understanding of God's call to educate the masses, especially the poor.

Many of the women who started religious orders in the 19th and 20th centuries were converts to Catholicism. It would be very worthwhile for the students to research the conversion experience of some of these individuals. Here are a few examples:

- Cornelia Connelly, foundress of the Society of the Holy Child Jesus; convert, married woman, and mother.
- Katharine Drexel, foundress of the Sisters of the Blessed Sacrament; dedicated to working among Native and Black Americans.
- Rose Hawthorne, foundress of Dominican Sisters of Hawthorne, Servants of Relief For Incurable Cancer; dedicated to this work.

Having seen conversion in the lives of various men and women, we see that the call to religious life is in a sense a "second conversion," a call to a deeper life with God in the service of his people.

4. After this introduction to some of the outstanding women in the Church, invite the students to complete *Worksheet #15.*

5. The end of the chapter briefly mentions the contributions of individuals in the 20th century. Each one of these people merits more coverage and all are also good examples for adolescents to know about. One way of introducing the life and work of Teilhard de Chardin and Pope John XXIII is by the use of filmstrips. *Images of the New Man* contains a ten-minute filmstrip about each of these men in its four-part set. (See *Resources* for this Guide chapter.) Reading excerpts from the writings of Merton, John XXIII, and Chardin is another way of presenting them. Students could be assigned to read and report on Merton's early autobiography, *The Seven Storey Mountain,* or John XXIII's *Journal of a Soul.* One value of

each book is the intimate sharing of each man's personal soul-searching and the subsequent discovery of God. Seeing Chardin's acceptance of his books being labelled as dangerous by his religious superiors is a great example of "large-mindedness" on his part. Ask students to suggest other examples of spiritual giants in the 20th century and assign them to research their lives.

6. A final point for inclusion is the changing and changed attitude of the 20th century Church. Spend time elaborating on the Second Vatican Council and its accomplishments. The students you are teaching were born after Vatican II ended and therefore they have experienced only its consequent results. See to it that they understand the kinds of changes this Council brought about and its effect on the life of the Church.

Point out to students the example shown by Pope John Paul I, the pope who ruled for only one month and died in 1978. At his coronation ceremony he made a dramatic break with tradition by eliminating the actual crowning with papal tiara. John Paul I's action illustrated his desire as pope to be more of a shepherd and spiritual leader of the Church. The significance of this change will be understood if students have clearly seen the power that had been exercised by popes in past centuries. See to it that students grasp the idea of decentralization of authority which has been an important result of Vatican II. This concept is a difficult one for high school students and will need careful handling.

7. In addition to the "Challenges" the final exercises should include the following:
   a. looking back to Jerry's story to compare students' experiences with Jerry's;
   b. re-reading students' paragraphs on "The Church As I See It" to see if there has been any change as a result of this study. If so, what is it and why?
   c. examining the cycle of events to see what the students were able to learn from analyzing this pattern in different eras.

Prayer and Worship Experiences

1. Have the students develop a prayer experience around the attributes of a saint. A banner could be made that says "A Willing Heart" and this could be the theme for the experience. A song from the *Wood Hath Hope* album, that speaks of commitment could be used, as could the song "Peace Prayer." This song lends itself to beautiful slides, which would intensify the prayer experience. Allow time for reflection and prayerful sharing about saintliness in today's world. Play quiet background music. Have the students end with spontaneous prayer using the "Prayer Reflection" at the end of the chapter (text page 117). As a conclusion, say the prayer of St. Ignatius Loyola together:
"Teach me, O Lord, to serve you as you deserve;
to give and not to count the cost,
to fight and not to heed the wounds,
to toil and not to seek for rest,
to labor and not to seek for any reward
except to know that I do your will,
O my God."

2. A monastic type of prayer service could be developed using either songs by the St. Louis Jesuits or the Benedictine Monks of Weston Priory. Most of the songs by the St. Louis Jesuits are actually psalms set to contemporary music. The album *Calm Is the Night* by the Weston Monks contains their morning prayer service on one side and the vesper service on the other. Short readings are also recorded in each service. Either of these two prayer services of the monks could be used as a framework for the students' prayer experience. Time could be provided for sharing of thoughts or prayers simply by stopping the record between bands on the album.

3. "Take, Lord, Receive" is a beautiful song put to movement. As part of a Eucharist celebration this addition would be quite beautiful and appropriate. Give each student a copy of Ignatius Loyola's prayer "Take, Lord, Receive" to say on their own.

Service Projects

1. One of the points of Church history covered was the mendicant orders who chose to live in poverty. Through your diocesan office find the nearest such order and volunteer your services over a weekend. These orders often run soup kitchens and thrift shops where student volunteers are always needed.

2. Consult *The Catholic Directory* to find the monastery closest to your area. Write a letter to the abbot or abbess asking if you can be of any service there. Be specific about ages, your interests, and ability to help. When you hear from them, fulfill the service asked of you promptly. Have the students report about this experience to the group.

3. The various religious orders have many elderly members. Make an appointment to see the appropriate person who works with the elderly and adopt members the students can get to know by visiting weekly.

Independent Study Projects

1. Choose a contemporary situation (e.g. abortion issues, arms race, racial prejudice) and ask: "If Peter (or Paul) were here today, how would he handle this problem?" Write a letter or a speech as Peter (or Paul) might express it. Where possible quote directly. Share with the whole group.

2. "Why does he have to learn the hard way?" We often hear ourselves saying this about someone's mistakes. The question could also be asked of the Church. In each age, the Church experienced itself in a different way depending on the cultural, political, and social circumstances of the day. Some of these experiences were *bad* but they taught the Church important lessons about its message and its mission in the world.

With this in mind, write a *thoughtful* and *thorough* essay on this theme:
What did the Church *learn* through the following experiences: 1) the barbarian invasions and the collapse of the Roman Empire, and 2) the Protestant Reformation?

Resources

Audiovisual

Francis of Assisi. Set of 3 filmstrips. TeleKETICS. Franciscan Communication Center, 1229 S. Santee St., Los Angeles, CA 90015.

St. Elizabeth Seton. A sound filmstrip. W.H. Sadlier, Inc., 11 Park Place, New York, NY 10007.

The Gift of Community. A filmstrip or slides with cassette recording. Weston Priory Productions, Weston, VT 05161.

Images of the New Man. A set of four filmstrips on Teilhard de Chardin, John XXIII, John Kennedy, and Martin Luther King, Jr. Thomas Klise, P.O. Box 3418, Peoria, IL 61614.

Catholic Americans. A set of 18 filmstrips. Paulist Press, 545 Island Rd., Ramsey, NJ 07446.

The Traveler. Set of 10 filmstrips on Church History. ROA, 1696 N. Astor St., Milwaukee, WI 53202.

Series of 8 session mini-course for students on motivation. Marilyn Vanderbur, Motivational Institute, Inc., 718 17th St., Suite 800, Denver, CO 80202.

Calm Is the Night, Listen, Go Up to the Mountain, Locusts and Wild Honey, That They May Have Bread. Albums by the Brothers of Weston Priory.

A Dwelling Place, Earthen Vessels, Wood Hath Hope. St. Louis Jesuits, North American Liturgy Resources, 2110 W. Peoria Ave., Phoenix, AZ.

Print

W.J. Bausch. *Pilgrim Church: A Popular History of Catholic Christianity.* Notre Dame, IN: Fides Press, 1973.

A. Boardman. *Such Love Is Seldom* (Life of Mary Walsh, O.P.). New York: Harper, 1950.

M.T. Brady. *Fruit of His Compassion.* (Life of Mary Caroline Dannat). New York: Pageant Press, 1962.

K. Burton. *Sorrow Built a Bridge.* (Life of Rose Hawthorne). New York: Longmans Green & Co., 1937.

M.L. Cozens. *A Handbook of Heresies.* New York: Sheed and Ward, 1947.

J.P. Dolan. *Catholicism: An Historical Survey.* Woodbury, NY: Barron's Educational Series, 1968.

M. Hellwig. *Tradition: The Catholic Story Today. The Christian Creeds.* Dayton, OH: Pflaum, 1974, 1975.

P. Hughes. *A Popular History of the Catholic Church* and *A Popular History of the Reformation.* New York: Doubleday, 1947, 1957.

John XXIII. *Journal of a Soul.* New York: McGraw Hill, 1964.

S. Kaye-Smith. *Quartet in Heaven.* (Excerpt on Cornelia Connelly). New York: Arno, 1952.

R. McBrien. *Catholicism.* Minneapolis, MN: Winston Press, 1980.

T. Merton. *The Seven Storey Mountain. Sign of Jonas.* New York: Doubleday, 1948, 1956.

H. Nouwen. *The Genesee Diary.* New York: Doubleday, 1976.

Sharing the Light of Faith: National Catechetical Directory for Catholics of the United States. Washington, D.C.: United States Catholic Conference, 1979.

7

Proclaiming Our Story

Objectives
Knowledge: To enable the students to identify the elements essential to proclaiming God's Word.
Attitude: To help the students to come to a more complete understanding of how their lives can proclaim the message of Jesus.
Practice: To have the students engage in an evangelization experience with a confused peer by writing a letter.

Orientation
This chapter gives the students an understanding of the call of Christians to evangelize, that is, to proclaim God's message with their lives.

The first section entitled "The Great Commission" (text page 118) presents a fantasy interview with Jesus about our methods of advertising and public relations today. Since it is an amusing vignette, students should relate to it easily. It becomes a good means of involving them in the topic of evangelization.

The scene is followed by an explanation of what the apostles were commissioned to do: to evangelize, to proclaim the Word of God as manifested in Jesus, what he taught as well as who he is and what he does.

This process was one the apostles were compelled to do after their Pentecost experience. From the *spoken* word the gospels were recorded to give *written* testimony to Jesus. Jesus' basic message was to proclaim the Kingdom of God. This explanation can be found in the section entitled "Jesus Proclaims the Kingdom" (text page 122). Here the students get an understanding of what Jesus meant by kingdom and what that kingdom could mean for us.

The Church's role (text page 122) in proclaiming the kingdom is clarified as both a sign pointing to the kingdom and a means of reaching the fullness of the kingdom. The meaning of kingdom is further developed by looking at the parables which serve as both explanation and challenge.

Once the source of the message of the kingdom is clear for the students, the next step is to see how the Church makes this an actuality in the world today. The section entitled "The Church Proclaiming Its Story" (text page 124) states that it is the Church that brings the kingdom to the world by the process of evangelization that has evolved over the course of time. The Church must constantly seek effective ways that can be heard by each generation. Since this is the case, the way in which the Word is proclaimed may take many special forms according to the people to whom it is proclaimed.

Regardless of how the message is proclaimed, the substance remains the same. The encounter with the living word can lead to a change of heart, a turning to God. The next point explained is the role of catechesis in the Church (text page 126), the instruction and deepening of faith that is the responsibility of every committed Christian. The avenues that are open for deepening one's faith are covered and encouraged. These components are then expressed in a life experience so that the students may understand more fully what the gospel message asks of committed Christians.

In the section "Shout the Gospel with Our Lives" (text page 130), the story of Charles de Foucauld is one in which they can readily identify the attributes of a truly committed Christian. From that experience the students are urged to live for Christ day by day—for to do that is to truly proclaim the gospel message.

The life experience that follows, the letter from the dissatisfied girl (text page 131), will give the students something to think about that involves them most profoundly because it is from a high school student. The students will have an opportunity to use the knowledge they gain in this chapter in discussing this girl's thoughts and feelings concerning the Church. This last section will provide a real testing ground for the students because it provides a firsthand experience of evangelization with someone their own age. By involving them in discussing, debating, and role playing the girl's situation students will have to draw upon their own beliefs and attitudes about the Church. Having them write a reply to the girl and offer her suggestions by which she could reconcile her relationship to the Church, students will have to clarify their own beliefs.

Life Experience Focus

The students have dealt with many of the elements that are involved in this chapter but they have probably not been exposed to much of the terminology as well as to the explicit purpose of the material. Because the chapter's purpose is to explain how a community shares its story, the students must get involved with the essential components of sharing the message. Each component is explained so that the student may have the opportunity of completely grasping its significance. The student moves from the experience of the early Church and how the apostles spread the good news through the experience of the message becoming more formalized, down through the ages to the contemporary situation. As the students get involved with the message in today's world they are challenged to live it day by day.

The call to be Christian is explained so that the students have the background and challenge they need to make a commitment. Along with the call, the students are given a life experience about a girl who is critical of the Christian commitment because of her own personal experience with the Church. With the knowledge the students have been exposed to in this chapter, this life experience can be an important learning experience for them.

Background on Content

This chapter, "Proclaiming Our Story,"
examines the need for spreading the
message of Jesus, the ways in which that
process evolved, and the demands it places on
those who call themselves Christians.

Sharing the Light of Faith maintains:
"Because Christ's revelation is
inexhaustible, we can always know more
about it and understand it better. We grow in
such knowledge and understanding when
we respond to God manifesting Himself
through creation, the events of daily life, the
triumphs and tragedies of history. God
speaks to us in a special manner in His
word—sacred scripture—and through
prayer, communicating His love and beauty
to us through the Holy Spirit. Above all He
communicates Himself through the
sacraments, through the witness of the
faithful, and through the full life and meaning
of the Church." (55)

These are the same basic assumptions which
the chapter is introducing to the student. In
our journey to faith we are continually
asked to respond and become more intimately
involved in relationship to God. As the
Spirit was given to the apostles to enable them
to proclaim the Word, so too are we called to
communicate his love. As the world
changes the ways in which we commuicate
may change—but the message is always
the same: God's love is alive and active in
our world. As the students respond to the
various life experiences presented in this
chapter they will grow in awareness of the
need to witness to this tremendous reality.

This is the challenge asked of all of us, a
challenge these students are just beginning
to understand, one they need to be
confronted with steadily and seriously if they
are to develop a truly committed mature
faith.

Teaching Notes 1

Text Pages 118–124

The Great Commission

1. The opening experience of this chapter is a scene between Jesus and a modern day advertising executive. Introduce the students to this chapter by having them read the scene, assigning them the parts of narrator, Jesus, and the Young Man. After the scene is read, discuss:

- What is the basic difference in approach between Jesus and the young man?
- What are the advantages and disadvantages of each?
- Do you think religion should make use of modern technologies in the spreading of the Word? Why or why not?

2. Brainstorm and list on the board the possible difficulties, obstacles, etc. faced by the followers of Jesus in fulfilling his command. (See text page 120.) What enormous advantage did they have? ("And I will be with you always . . . ")

3. Explain to the students what is meant by the "great commission" or ask them what they think it could mean. Direct them to Peter's first sermon in their *Good News Bible* (Acts 2:22–36). Have someone read the sermon aloud to the class and then discuss the question in the exercise that follows (text page 121).

This exercise will help the teacher to evaluate students' feelings concerning Jesus, and to see if any new insights have been gained from the last few chapters and also to determine the quality and depth of their insights.

The Message and the Person

1. In this section, students are introduced to the twofold task of ministry of the Word. Ask them for some examples of how each of these tasks might be accomplished today. Direct them to complete *Worksheet #16* which asks students to compare the ministry as exercised in the early Church, and as it is exercised today.

2. The next exercise (text page 121) asks the students to recall a favorite way of picturing or thinking about Jesus. In order to help them do this exercise, share your own favorite scene from the gospel. Invite a few students to share theirs as well. Hearing these recollections will inspire the rest of the students who may be timid.

Let them use the *Good News Bible* and also their journals. Each student should write a letter describing his or her favorite scene, as the exercise suggests. These might be kept in their journals.

Point out that letter writing is another way of proclaiming the Word, and recall that it was a means used repeatedly by St. Paul.

Jesus Proclaims the Kingdom

1. Have the students brainstorm what the concept of kingdom means. List their ideas on the board, and use them later when they are asked to work with parables.

2. Direct the students to the exercise on text pages 123–124. Since the students have already worked with parables, they should be able to do the exercises easily. As a review, however, it might be helpful to recall with them what they know about parables. Supply any needed information.

   a. Now ask the students to read the
introductory paragraph (text pages
123-124). Have the students in pairs go
through the two parables following the
instructions given.

   b. Once the students have completed the
exercise, have them look at their lists of
what they thought the kingdom meant.
After they have looked over their lists, give
them an opportunity to look back over
their notes on the parables also.

   c. Then ask the students to compare their
thoughts about the kingdom with those of
Jesus, giving reasons from the parables
as proof of their ideas. Initial the ones the
students listed on the board with the
parable that complements them.

   d. Circle any parables that were not
covered, and have the students comment
on why Jesus would not have used them
to describe the Kingdom of God. This should
help the students get a firm grasp of what
Jesus felt the kingdom is.

3. Have the students find in the parables as
many "kingdom metaphors" as they can
and create a visual interpretation of
these using drawings, photos, magazine
pictures, etc.

Teaching Notes 2

Text Pages
124–130

The Church Proclaiming Its Story

1. Summarize this section by outlining it on the chalkboard or a transparency.

   a. *Proclaiming the Word:*

- Spoken Tradition: To share their personal experience with Jesus.
- Gospel Writings: To accompany and reinforce preaching and to preserve it.
- Doctrines and Creeds: Formulated so that Christians could apply their beliefs to their lived experience.
- Hymns, songs, poetry.
- Symbols, Cathedrals: To proclaim the message through the ages.

   b. Once you have introduced all the various concepts, highlight some of them by first reviewing the concepts already covered, such as the gospels and doctrines. Then move to various ways through the ages of how the message was proclaimed. Some ideas might be:

- Have the students listen to a recording of Gregorian chant and possibly even learn to sing the chant. Give them a brief history of the chant and its use in the Church.
- Show the students a Celtic or Jerusalem cross explaining the history and the message of Jesus which each of these symbolized.
- Present a slide show of the cathedral of Notre Dame or Chartres with an accompanying script describing the times and the faith behind these monuments.
- Show the students pictures or slides of the works of great artists like Michelangelo, da Vinci, Fra Angelico, and explain how these express the faith vision of a certain period.

2. After this exposure to religious expressions of the past, have the students choose a modern symbol or medium which they feel carries a faith message for today. Have them explain its message to the group. *Jesus Christ Superstar* or *Godspell* are contemporary examples which students might immediately identify with and enjoy.

3. Follow this with the exercise on films, TV programs, and music (text page 125). This should be an enjoyable and interesting discussion. It will offer a good opportunity for discussing the values being communicated through TV and movies and clarifying the reasons why these values may or may not be positive ones. Adolescents are not always aware of influences that may be shaping their thinking. By allowing an open and free discussion, the students will gain a clearer understanding of what are considered to be Christian values and what are not, an invaluable message for adolescents.

Evangelization—Proclaiming the Message

Refer to Paul's letter to the Romans to clarify the meaning of the word "evangelization." In discussing the notion of conversion described in the text (page 126), ask students to give examples of "born-again Christians." Use these to illustrate the meaning of conversion. Here is an opportune time to introduce the *Rite of Christian Initiation of Adults* so that the concept is not entirely new to them. It will be treated indepth in Chapter 10.

Catechesis—Deepening the Message

1. Write the word "catechesis" on the board and next to it put the meaning, "to echo or resound the message." Ask the students to read the descriptions of people who are catechists (see text page 126). Discuss:

- Why do you think people like these become catechists?
- What characteristics do you feel would be essential to a good catechist?
- Is this something you might be interested in for yourself? Why or why not?

2. Have the students interview a catechist from their parish, asking for examples of:

- their preparation for this work
- their reasons for choosing to become a catechist
- how they feel about this ministry
- what it has done for their own faith life

Have the students share the results of these interviews with the group.

3. The next step is to present the students with what is needed in order to be a catechist. (See text page 128.) Direct the students to this section and discuss it with them.

4. The exercise which follows (text page 129) provides an opportunity for the students to do some personal reflection on the Bible. Provide some quiet background music and ample time in which to do this. Circulate among the students as they read, inviting possible discussion with individual students.

Shout the Gospel with Our Lives

1. Discuss the story of Charles de Foucauld, answering questions about his lifestyle, and elaborating on the life of extreme poverty which he inflicted on himself. Recall the notion of "counterculture" groups mentioned in Chapter 5 and point out de Foucauld as an example of this type.

Relate this life experience to the excerpts from Vatican II and from Pope John Paul II's address to youth.

2. A good follow-up exercise would be for the students to brainstorm how to "Shout the Gospel with Our Lives." This can be a reality for them as it was for Charles de Foucauld in his day and time. Write down all their ideas on the board and ask the students to choose one they can incorporate into their own lives on a day-to-day basis. Have students give reasons for their choice and how they will go about making their choice a reality.

Teaching Notes 3

**Text Pages
130–135**

A Story to Ponder

1. Ask the students to read the section (text page 130) and during the initial discussion begin to use *Worksheet #17.* This will be helpful in the debate that follows. The questions in the exercise (text page 133) should help the discussion.

2. Once the students are involved with the story ask for volunteers to role play various individuals mentioned and the reactions and response they might have to her story. For example:
- the girl's mother and father
- the parish priest
- the bishop
- a leader of a religious cult

Role play as many different situations as possible; for example, have one roleplay in which the people involved know who the letter writer is; have another situation where the author is anonymous and they are asked to make a response. Ask students to notice if there is any difference in the responses.

3. Whatever the reality the students role play, ask them to imagine the ideal. From this experience bring the students to an understanding of parish structure by listing those experiences that create community for all ages vs. those that destroy community. Relate it to the girl's experience by applying your findings to hers and deciding which she experienced.

4. Have the students choose sides:
- side one—the girl has enough experience of the Church and should leave with what she knows;
- side two—the girl has only experienced a small part of the Church community and should not let that experience be the deciding factor.

Each group should work together and plan their debate with existing facts and supportive reasons. The debate should be orderly and well executed by the students giving them the opportunity to sound out their feelings, both pro and con, concerning the girl's decision.

The debate should elicit many points of view that will help clarify the options open to the girl as well as those that the students have in their own experience of decision-making. The more the students have an opportunity to discover and discuss in a guided manner all the opinions and feelings concerning membership and commitment to the Church, the more enlightened and authentic their own response can truly become.

5. For the final activity, tell each student to write a reply to the girl in which they should use every reason they can think of to try and persuade the girl to reconsider her decision. Give them as much time as they need in order to formulate a convincing letter.

Call on a number of students to share their letters of persuasion, having the class vote on the best response that would surely have the girl reconsider her position on the Church. This should bring out some interesting insights.

As a reflection, ask the students to do the second part of the exercise (text page 133) in their journals. All the experiences that have been covered should be reflected if the students have been able to internalize the message.

Once there has been ample reflection time, have the students choose a review question they would like to discuss and answer in a group. When sufficient time has elapsed, have the students come together and discuss the questions as a class. This should further internalize the message of the chapter.

Prayer and Worship Experiences

1. A beautiful prayer reflection for the students could be the song, "I Don't Know How to Love Him" from *Jesus Christ Superstar*. Providing time and guidance for reflection on the humanness of the Church and our very real needs in the world today would be helpful as well as prayerful for the students.

2. The film *Martin the Cobbler* (see *Resources* for this Guide chapter) can help the students get in touch with the difference between having no place for God in their lives because God does nothing for them, and the discovery of God by reaching out to others and loving them. The sense of going out of self to find answers, rather than coming to conclusions because of the way things are, is strongly developed in this animated film. The film lends itself to a natural prayerful response.

3. A prayer service emphasizing the theme of the chapter, "Proclaiming Our Story," could begin with the song "All Good Gifts" from *Godspell*. Have the students read the closing "Prayer Reflection" from Ephesians 3:16–19 (text page 135) as well as the parable of the Lost Sheep. Have three or four students prepare petitions for a Prayer of the Faithful. Invite others to add their own petitions spontaneously about needs in their own parish and community. End with the song "Day By Day" from *Godspell*.

Service Projects

1. Suggest that some students volunteer to help the parish council research the needs of the parish community by setting up a study task force. From the parish membership have them choose a wide variety of individuals to interview on the ways in which the Church could become more of a community. From the interviews, compile the results and report to the parish council the findings and the recommendations of the study task force.

2. Those who have already received confirmation could offer to be of service in the confirmation program that is being planned for the year, in any capacity that is needed. Their presence can be a witness to those who are considering confirmation.

3. For those whose parish is involved with the Rite of Christian Initiation for Adults, there may be a great need for volunteer babysitting so that the adults can be free to attend the meetings. This could be an excellent way to show a supporting role of helping another on their journey of faith.

Independent Study Projects

1. Have the students research the response their parish has made to the needs of the community. This will help them to evaluate the inroads in recent years as well as to see what the possibilities of the future can truly be.

2. Have the students do a research report about Charles de Foucauld and the community that he founded. There are several biographies available. Include in the report some information on the prayer experiences called "desert days," which is a recent development in spirituality.

3. Have the students interview a catechumen (a person who is seeking full membership in the Catholic Church). The interview could cover why the person wants to become a part of the Catholic community as well as their own personal feelings about the Church and Catholicism. Report the interview to the entire group and plan a discussion based on the questions and reactions.

Resources

Audiovisual

"I Don't Know How to Love Him." Song from
    Jesus Christ Superstar. A rock opera.
"All Good Gifts," "Day By Day." Songs from
    the musical *Godspell.*
Martin the Cobbler. 28 min. animated film.
    Mass Media Industries, 2116 N. Charles
    Street, Baltimore, MD 21218.
*Evangelization: Reflections on Living the
    Word.* Set of 4 filmstrips. TeleKETICS.
    Franciscan Communications, 1229
    South Santee Street, Los Angeles, CA
    90015.

Print

M. Bruck, ed. *Parish Ministry Resources.*
    Ramsey, NJ: Paulist Press, 1979.
H. Kung. *On Being a Christian.* New York:
    Doubleday, 1976.
R. McBrien. *Catholicism.* Minneapolis, MN:
    Winston Press, 1980.
J. Wintz, "Small Groups: Today's Vehicle of
    Evangelization? An Interview with
    Archbishop Robert F. Sanchez." *St.
    Anthony Messenger.* August, 1979.
*Sharing the Light of Faith: National
    Catechetical Directory for Catholics of
    the United States.* Washington, D.C.:
    United States Catholic Conference, 1979.
Good News Bible, Catholic Study Edition, New
    York: Wm. H. Sadlier, 1979.

8

Celebrating Our Story

Text Pages
136–153

Objectives

Knowledge: To help the students to understand the meaning of celebration as it applies to their Christian life of worship.
Attitude: To help students see and accept their personal responsibility to be involved in community celebrations of Mass and the sacraments.
Practice: To have the students plan a meaningful celebration of the Liturgy for the entire group.

Orientation

The title of this chapter, "Celebrating Our Story," conveys the basic idea of the chapter just as the poem that begins the chapter speaks of the essence of celebration. The word "celebration" is one to which students need to have developed a personal approach. Then when it is applied in the community sense, they will be able to compare/contrast their feelings and grow in their understanding from this natural basis.

After the students are asked to think of reasons for celebrations that are part of everyday experiences, the roots of celebration found in the Scriptures are introduced. The parallel is drawn between the person who is open to celebrating life and a person who celebrates liturgy.

Liturgy is not a private celebration. The section on "Celebrating with Others" (text page 139) gives the students another insight into why we celebrate: to remember and be thankful as a community of believers. As an introduction to the evolution of community liturgy the student is given background information on the Passover experience in "Celebrating Our Story" (text page 140). The Last Supper was an event that celebrated two things: the Seder ritual recalling the Israelites' deliverance from slavery and the institution of the Eucharist, the memorial of Christ's passage from death to life.

The next section then brings to light the students' own considerations of meaningful liturgical celebrations. Here they are asked to be honest about their experiences of liturgy, whether and in what ways Mass is truly celebrative, so that they can begin to build in new possibilities and be part of change.

In order for this change to take place, the students are asked to take an "awareness walk" which should help them see the world around them in a new way and open them to the possibility that liturgical celebrations can also be looked at from a new, more exciting perspective.

Once the students are open to new ways of looking at celebration, they are given some more information that is important to understanding liturgy. The sections "The Meaning of the Eucharist" (text page 143) and "Celebrating the Story" (text page 144) bring out important explanations about liturgy and about the unique rhythm that is part of our liturgical year. The sacraments are presented as integral to this pattern so that the students see not only that liturgy celebrates the rhythm of life but also that our own personal life is blessed with "sacred signs" to help us grow in our Christian commitment.

The sacraments that are treated are Baptism, Reconciliation, Anointing of the Sick, and the Eucharist. An all-important task is for the students to acknowledge their personal feelings as well as to learn new forms in which to experience the sacraments.

Because the Mass can unite them so intimately to Christ, the students are asked to consider thoughtfully the meaning and the workings of the liturgy. Along with a growth in understanding the opportunity to experience this new way to look at liturgy should be an integral part of this chapter. The practices as well as the review questions will aid the students in their process of internalizing and updating liturgy as celebration in their own personal response to the Father.

Life Experience Focus

The content of this chapter is well related to an area of the adolescents' faith journey which is often problematic for them. There is a tendency among young people to reject formal religious practices, even though they may be developing in their personal relationships with Jesus Christ. They need help at this age to see the natural connection between our practices in worship and their relationship with Jesus. Adolescence is an age when they *can* be shown how each one reinforces the other. As *Sharing the Light of Faith* states: "For the most part, young people are searching for direction to help them become what God has created them to be." (200)

The text reveals how celebration is a basic part of our everyday human lives, and yet is at the same time a special aspect of life. Youthful enthusiasm should relate easily to this concept.

This paves the way for a study of liturgical celebration, of the Mass in particular. The exercise which invites their personal reactions to liturgy is a door-opener. Listen to the students' opinions, accept them nonjudgmentally, and the students will allow you to give them new insights into liturgy and sacraments which they might not have considered by themselves. The necessity of dealing with their honest feelings is imperative if they are to learn new ways of approaching, appreciating, and participating in the liturgy.

The challenge is one that can be tremendously fruitful because the students are seeking liturgy that is meaningful for them. To help them see and experience a good celebration of liturgy can open many doors for students' future life of worship and service in the Christian community.

Background on Content

The concept of celebration is a natural human point of interest. The need for the Church to be able to incorporate authentic celebration into its expressions of liturgy and sacrament is crucial.

Sharing the Light of Faith states: "Catechesis recognizes the Eucharist as the heart of Christian life. It helps people understand that celebration of the Eucharist nourishes the faithful with Christ, the Bread of Life, in order that, filled with the love of God and neighbor, they may become more and more a people acceptable to God and build up the Christian community with the works of charity, service, missionary activity, and witness." (121)

If Eucharist is truly the "heart of Christian life" and if the celebration of the Eucharist is a source of spiritual nourishment, then it is essential that the form this celebration takes has meaning to the Christian—that it calls forth a response to Christ, that it be significant, joyous, and celebrative.

Through the celebration of the Eucharist the faithful are nourished by Jesus to go forth to "build up the Christian community with the works of charity, service, missionary activity, and witness." Our unique response in celebration should be the catalyst propelling us to Christian works that express our devotion to Jesus. The signs of the kingdom have been given to us as gifts of what we can have now in sign, and what we will have in fullness when the kingdom is complete.

Teaching Notes 1

Text Pages 136–142

Celebrate!
Learning How to Celebrate

1. If possible, prepare a slide presentation to accompany the poem at the opening of the chapter. Have the poem narrated on an accompanying tape. Instrumental background music would add to the effectiveness. Adolescents can identify with and become a part of a visual interpretation without much effort and the follow-up life experience will blend well with the slides and poem.

2. Since this section (text page 136) calls for remembering personal experiences, allow ample time for reflection. Encourage students to share their images aloud, but do not coerce anyone to do so.

3. As students become engaged in the activity, move them beyond their own personal experiences. Have them stretch their imaginations to suggest as many ways as possible of celebrating each item in the exercise (text page 138). Point out to them that our present formal celebrations began by a similar process—of a group suggesting and deciding on the best ways of celebrating.

4. Discuss the many expressions of celebration mentioned in the text—music, art, and architecture. Here, too, visual examples would add to the effect.

5. The next section (text page 139) adds a scriptural basis to celebration giving the students a good sense of the roots of celebration, and also reinforcing the formal aspects of rituals.

6. Use *Worksheet #18* to help the students think about the components of a good celebration as they recall what made the time meaningful and worth remembering. If the students cannot recall such a celebration in their own lives have them pair up with someone who can and would like to share experiences.

7. At this point it would be effective to show the film *God's Grandeur* to expand the students' understanding of what it is we celebrate. The film is a visual interpretation of Gerard Manley Hopkins' poem and is done in such a way as to call our attention to the beauty and majesty of God in the ordinary things of the world. The film will help students understand the importance of celebrating our everyday existence, which is a basic Christian concept. (See *Resources* for this Guide chapter.)

Celebrating with Others

1. Invite the students to give examples of celebrations they have shared with family or friends, and give some examples of your own. This could be an enjoyable activity if some of the stories are like the example in the text of the "family that celebrates a disaster." (See text page 139.)

2. As students describe their experiences call attention to some common features of celebrations:
- usually involves eating and drinking;
- food is often special;
- certain actions in it become traditional and make the celebration complete.

Have students list these features in their journals, and also list the past, present, and future aspect of celebrations explained in the text (page 140).

3. After they have thoroughly examined the important characteristics of celebrations, have them move to the exercise asking them to recall a celebration that was special (text page 140). From all the previous discussion, they should be able to identify these points quickly.

Celebrating Our Story

1. Have the students recall the Exodus Passover event, perhaps even re-locating the event on the time line they created in Chapter 5.

The Passover meal, or "Seder Supper" as it may be called today, is a celebration that would interest the students and an important starting point for a study about liturgy. Showing students a filmstrip on the Passover ritual will give them a good visual understanding of the foundation of the Eucharist.

2. Once you have made the connection between the Passover Meal and the Last Supper, have students read the two other gospel accounts of the Last Supper, Luke 22:14–38 and Matthew 26:19–30, as well as the passage from Mark in the text (page 140). Have the students analyze the event according to the common features they listed previously in their journals, so that they see it as a celebration with friends. Ask:

- Why do you think Jesus chose that moment to single out as a significant event?
- Why did he choose to bless bread and wine in his own memory?

Bring out the significance of the Passover to Israel—a sign of God's saving love. Explain the ritual of blood and the meal of lamb in relation to Jesus' offering of his body and blood as food to his friends. Point out the words of the priest before he distributes the Eucharist—"Behold the Lamb of God . . ."

3. Have students examine closely Jesus' words at the Last Supper: "This is my body, which is given for you. Do this in memory of me" and "This is my blood which is poured out for many, my blood which seals God's covenant." Put the words of consecration on the board and make the connection between these words and the Last Supper.

Recall the blood offerings of the Israelites in Exodus 12 and the "scapegoat" ritual on the Day of Atonement (Leviticus 16:15-26). Explain to the students that Jesus was incorporating both of these rituals in his words at the Last Supper and in his act of dying on the cross. The "scapegoat" carried the sins of the Israelites upon his head and was then driven out into the desert to die.

Teaching Notes 2

Text Pages
142–148

What Is This Celebration About?

1. This section begins by giving the students the opportunity to talk about their experience of liturgy. The exercise (text page 142) that asks them to divide a piece of paper into three response columns and put the statements that follow in the appropriate columns will help the students articulate their feelings. Even though they can recall a memorable liturgical celebration that they really loved, their opinion of liturgy in an everyday sense might be more negative than positive.

Establish an accepting atmosphere during the discussion that follows. If you allow an honest venting of their feelings or complaints students will be more likely to listen to suggestions about more positive ways to experience the Mass.

If some students attempt to defend the Mass in response to others' complaints, let them have free rein. Students listen to their peers more than to adults!

2. Have the students act as if they are a liturgy planning committee and have them list in two columns: the things they want to see *improved* in liturgy and what things are *presently helpful.* On their list have them star (*) what are the most important elements

of a good celebration and add any they might have forgotten. Now ask them to explain how these elements achieve a good celebration. Tell the students to write down the points about meaningful celebrations and use these later when they are asked to plan a liturgical celebration.

3. The students are asked to take an awareness walk. Recall the film *God's Grandeur* to their minds. This will reinforce the film as well as open them even more to all that is worthy of celebration. Following the awareness walk, whether it is done at school or at home, tell the students to write a reflection in their journal.

The Meaning of the Eucharist

To illustrate what celebration can mean to us and to summarize for the students the meaning of the Eucharist, use an excellent short film called *Eucharist.* While the Mass is taking place, intercutting scenes from life show the need for God's nourishment in our life. The film would offer another chance for the students to deepen their understanding of the significance of the Eucharist. (See *Resources* for this Guide chapter.)

Celebrating the Story

1. This next section presents the liturgical year. Explaining the Church cycle will be both interesting and informative. Direct the students' attention to the chart on the Church year and as the explanation is given for the cycle, have certain symbols that are significant to each. Use, for instance, the various colors as well as significant symbols:

- Pentecost: the symbol of the tongues of fire;
- Advent: the wreath with an explanation of the candles and how they are used;
- Lent: the Way of the Cross that is a devotion for many Catholics at this time;
- Easter: the significance of the Easter candle;
- Christmas: the manger scene.

2. An excellent filmstrip is available called *The Liturgical Year.* (See *Resources* for this Guide chapter.) It links the seasons and celebrations of the Church year with the cycles and symbols of nature. It could be used as a follow-up meditation after the study of the text.

3. If the group represents diverse ethnic cultures, it would be interesting to depict certain celebrations that are unique to the various groups throughout the seasons.

The Sacraments
1. Begin with a brainstorming session on the meaning of sacraments. Clarify the meaning of the word *sacrament.* Once the students have listed all seven, single out three, Baptism, Reconciliation and Anointing of the Sick.

2. Write the word *Baptism* on the board and build from the students' present understandings into a deeper realization of the sacrament. Mention the *Rite of Christian Initiation of Adults* but save the details until Chapter 10. Introducing the concept now to the students will help the learning process later. Review the symbols of infant baptism with the students explaining their significance.

3. There are many fine audiovisual materials available which might help students appreciate the sacrament of baptism and even serve as a type of paraliturgical celebration of their own baptismal promises. Students could recommit themselves in a prayerful setting after the film or filmstrip is shown. Recommended materials are:
● *Baptism: Sacrament of Belonging,* a TeleKETICS film.
● *Water and Spirit,* a TeleKETICS film.
● *The Sacraments of Initiation:* "Baptism: Sacrament of Welcome" and "Confirmation: Sacrament of Courage," a filmstrip. (See *Resources* for this Guide chapter.)

4. Write the word *Reconciliation* on the board. Review and list the optional ways of experiencing this sacrament with your students. If possible visit a reconciliation room and explain the purpose of the change with the theology of the sacrament.

5. This review of the sacrament of Anointing of the Sick could provide a good chance for the students to become involved with the liturgy for elderly people that would be a good service project. Have the students look into the components of the sacrament, and prepare a liturgy that incorporates the sacrament of the sick. This is an opportunity for the students to experience a sacrament with which they are probably completely unfamiliar, and to witness the comfort it provides for elderly Catholics.

The students could arrange with some community action group to have the elderly of the parish brought to the Church to celebrate the liturgy after which the students could provide refreshments giving them an opportunity to socialize and get to know these parishioners. Allow opportunity for students to discuss the total experience afterwards.

Teaching Notes 3

Text Pages
148–153

Eucharistic Liturgy: The Mass

1. This next section (text page 148) gives the student some basic information on the composition of the liturgy. If the students can get a sense of the whole as well as the essential parts that make up the Mass, they can become more involved in the reason and purpose of what is done.

Write on the board the phrases: "Liturgy of the Word" and "Liturgy of the Eucharist." From their own experience have the students fill in the appropriate parts of the Mass that go under each phrase. Once they have included the majority of the parts, fill in the missing ones for them. Then ask the students to star (*) those that seem to be the most important ones and then number (#) those that are starred in order of importance.

Since there may be uncertainty during this exercise, it will provide a good opportunity for you to explain what are truly the more essential and important parts of the mass.

2. Call the students' attention to the diagram of the Mass in their text (pages 149–50). Once the students have taken a position concerning their personal understanding of the liturgy, use the diagram on a

transparency and compare what is on the board with this diagram for wording and for structure. Give the students a chance to make adjustments and ask questions concerning any confusion they might have with the concepts.

3. Direct the students to the exercise (text page 151) and see if they still agree that the central aspects of the Mass are the ones previously starred (*) and numbered (#). Follow up their decision by having them share their opinions about what part of the Mass has special significance and why they feel that way.

4. Before the students begin to plan a liturgical celebration, invite a liturgical specialist from the diocese to speak to the class about good liturgy. This should be someone who can help them see the best ways to plan a celebration and the elements that make a good liturgical celebration.

a. Once they have had good input, divide the class into groups according to their preference. Have them plan the various parts of the liturgy. For example, one group could focus on the Liturgy of the Word, and one on the Liturgy of the Eucharist, with special consulting groups that could work out ideas about music and about liturgical space. These four groups could take a basic theme and from it develop a celebration that incorporates the various ideas covered in the text. *Worksheets #18* and *#19* would be helpful to use during this activity.

b. Once the students have actually executed and experienced their liturgy, have them work on the review questions in groups, actually working on the projects mentioned and discussing their experiences with the whole group.

Prayer and Worship Experiences

1. The students saw a poem set to slides at the beginning of the chapter. Now have them build a prayer experience around slides that complement the prayer reflection at the end of the chapter.

2. The song, "Sing a New Song" from the album *Glory and Praise* could open a prayer service that would deal with the theme of celebration. The students could all contribute a "song" they want to sing to the Lord. Use the Magnificat (Luke 1:46–55) as the reading.

3. Arrange the students in groups of five. Have each group choose a popular song that says something they believe concerning celebration of life and use these songs in a prayer experience. Share the songs and reflect on their meaning.

Service Projects

1. Suggest that some students attend a parish liturgy planning committee and volunteer to work on the plans for a particular feast that is coming up in the liturgical calender.

2. If the school does not have a liturgy planning committee, suggest that the students propose the idea to the student council and provide names of persons interested in working on the committee.

3. Some interested students might check out the vestments at their parish church or school chapel. See if there is a need for new ones that a group could design and make in accordance with the liturgical colors.

Independent Study Projects

1. Some students might be interested in visiting various parishes to do a study of their liturgical celebration. Use the criteria of the chapter in evaluating the celebrations and write a report on your findings.

2. Some students might wish to attend a Passover celebration at a neighborhood synagogue. Have them identify common elements with our own traditions. Plan a similar or modified Seder Meal for the entire group and share your observations and conclusions with them in an oral report.

3. Have students conduct a survey interviewing people of all ages concerning their understanding of the liturgy, and what the Mass means to them. Have them compile and analyze the results and report their conclusions to the group.

Resources

Audiovisual

"Sing a New Song" by Dan Schutte S.J. on the *Glory and Praise Vol. 1* album, North American Liturgy Resources, 10802 No. 23rd Ave. Phoenix, AZ 85029.

Baptism: Sacrament of Belonging. 8 min. color film. TeleKETICS. Franciscan Communication Center, 1229 South Santee St., Los Angeles, CA 90015.

Water and the Spirit/Storyscape. 13 min. color film. TeleKETICS.

Eucharist. 8 min. color film. TeleKETICS.

Godparent Gussie/Storyscape. 20 min. color film. TeleKETICS.

Names of Sin/Reconciliation Storyscape. 20 min. color film. TeleKETICS.

God's Grandeur. 4 min. color film. TeleKETICS.

Celebrate the Mass! set of 4 filmstrips. TeleKETICS.

Of Sacraments and Symbols. Set of 8 filmstrips. TeleKETICS.

The Liturgical Year. Filmstrip. Paulist Press, 545 Island Road, Ramsey, N.J. 07446.

The Sacraments of Initiation. Set of 2 filmstrips. Winston Press, 430 Oak Grove, Minneapolis, MN 55403.

Print

K. Boyack. *A Parish Guide to Adult Initiation.* Ramsey, NJ: Paulist Press, 1979.

J. Champlin. *Sacraments in a World of Change.* Notre Dame, IN: Ave Maria Press.

L. Foley. *Signs of Love: The Sacraments of Christ.* Cincinnati, OH: St. Anthony Messenger Press, 1975.

Your Confession: Using the New Ritual. Cincinnati, OH: St. Anthony Messenger Press, 1976.

T. Guzie. *Jesus and the Eucharist.* Ramsey, NJ: Paulist Press, 1976.

B. Häring. *The Sacraments and Your Everyday Life.* Liquori, MO: Liguori Press, 1976.

M. Hellwig. *The Eucharist and the Hunger of the World.* Ramsey, NJ: Paulist Press, 1976.

The Meaning of the Sacraments. Dayton, OH: Pflaum-Standard, 1972.

K. Hurley, ed. *Why Sunday Mass?* Cincinnati, OH: St. Anthony Messenger Press, 1973.

P. Jones. *Rediscovering Ritual.* New York: Newman Press, 1973.

J. Jungmann. *The Mass.* Collegeville, MN: Liturgical Press, 1976.

A. Kavanaugh. "Christian Initiation for Those Baptized as Infants." *Living Light.* Fall, 1976.

N. Lohkamp. "A New Look at Mortal Sin." *St. Anthony's Messenger,* May, 1973.

G. McCauley. *Sacraments for a Secular Man.* New York: Herder and Herder, 1969.

R. McBrien. *Catholicism.* Minneapolis, MN: Winston Press, 1980.

C. Meyer. "Grace." *Chicago Studies.* Fall, 1973.

M. Newman. "Permanent Deacons." *St. Anthony's Messenger.* June, 1976.

J. Nolan. "Do We Still Need the Sacraments?" *U.S. Catholic.* June 1973.

R. Reichert. *A Learning Process for Religious Education.* Dayton, OH: Pflaum Press, 1977.

Teaching Sacraments to Youth. Ramsey, NJ: Paulist Press, 1975.

J. Wicks. "Sacraments." *Chicago Studies.* Fall, 1973.

A. Wilhem *Christ Among Us: A Modern Presentation of the Catholic Faith.* Ramsey, NJ: Paulist Press, 1975.

Good News Bible. Catholic Study Edition. New York: Wm. H. Sadlier 1979.

Sharing the Light of Faith: National Catechetical Directory for Catholics in the United States. Washington, D.C.: U.S. Catholic Conference, 1979.

Acting on Our Story

**Text Pages
154–171**

Objectives
Knowledge: To have the students understand the reason behind the need for social action in the Church today.
Attitude: To have the students see that some form of social action is an obligation for every Christian in response to the Gospel imperative to "love one another."
Practice: To find ways that the Christian response to social action can be a reality in the students' life.

Orientation
The description of Cathy's experience at the beginning of the chapter (text pages 154–155) helps the students understand the problem of hunger at the most basic level. The natural human response is one that calls us to responsible action. The message of Jesus as he washed the feet of the apostles gives us little room for doubt that one of our greatest Christian duties is to serve. The exercise of the hunger banquet (text page 157) gets the students immediately involved at one level, but to see themselves as part of the reality of hunger in the world may escape the adolescent. Because of this probability, a great deal of time will be required to help students see their own personal roles of responsibility.

In the "Social Values Auction" (text page 158) the students are asked to identify their own value system and get together with others who feel the same. Next they are asked to say in dollars and cents how much each value is worth to them. These exercises give the student an opportunity to sort out what they do value in the area of social justice and what they do not. This is a necessary beginning for any commitment. Once students have begun to get in touch with their value system, the next step is to take one value and study it in depth. This will take the students into a more profound understanding of the issue and add credibility to the value in their own estimation.

Finally the students are drawn to consider Jesus' values as stated in the Beatitudes. The students are asked to choose three Beatitudes which relate to specific problems and to suggest ways that might help solve that particular problem. This kind of exercise encourages the students to reflect upon the Word of God and the response we are called to give to that Word.

"The Good Samaritan—A Story of Love" (text page 162) moves the students from the task of *identifying* problems to the way in which a Christian should *react* to world problems. The choice that is given is obvious—to ignore the reality or to respond as Christ did.

Each of us must choose for ourselves. The courage and commitment of others can strengthen and inspire us, however, and this example is important, especially for adolescents. The students are asked to identify such models from their own experience. Then the students are asked to go to the Scriptures and find how Jesus served others.

This exercise gives them an opportunity to be involved with the life of Jesus and to witness his willingness to serve his neighbors. It is essential for us to serve as Jesus did—to be signs of his continuing presence in our world.

In the final sections of this chapter the students are introduced to different situations in which the Church today responds as Jesus did in the gospel. They are given insights into real needs in the world and presented with guidelines for aiding those in need. How to help people help themselves is the key to Christian response. The challenge of the Christian message is repeated in *Sharing the Light of Faith:* "One measure of a school's success is its ability to foster a sense of vocation, of eagerness to live out the basic baptismal commitment to service." (#232)

Whether to initiate a social service program or to join one that already exists, the challenge to encourage adolescents to move in this direction is one that cannot be taken lightly and will indeed help the adolescents reach beyond themselves to help others. This last response is the hopeful result of the chapter—for students to see the responsibility of being Christian and to respond as Jesus did in his lifetime and as the Church calls each of us to do in ours.

Life Experience Focus

Most adolescents have a great willingness to be of service but usually have difficulty putting their values in perspective. The task of the teacher is to encourage the students to examine and, where necessary, reorder their values. It is the teacher's task also constantly to challenge the students by having them confront the values of Jesus as an alternative to their own. The intent is not to threaten or to make them feel guilty—this must always be kept in mind. The intent is to develop an awareness of and a sensitivity to the compelling message of Jesus. As adolescents develop a healthy sense of themselves they begin to realize that there is more to life than having possessions. It is our important task to see that the values of Jesus have been properly communicated to them. Even if these values are rejected at the time, the seeds have been planted for future acceptance.

So the point is to recognize where the student is coming from, to respect that position, and at the same time to offer a different point of view concerning the essential values of life. The strength and example of Jesus is profound and with time will capture their interest. We must be patient and believe.

Background on Content

The foundation of Catholic social teaching derives from the words of the prophet Micah: "What he requires of us is this: to do what is just, to show constant love, and to live in humble fellowship with our God" (Micah 6:8). The reason social justice is a part of our Christian response is best described in *Sharing the Light of Faith:* "Catholic social teaching is based upon scripture, upon the development of moral doctrine in light of scripture, upon the centuries-old tradition of social teaching and practice, and upon efforts to work out the relationship of social ministry to the Church's overall mission. Catholic social teaching has also been enriched by the contributions of philosophers and thinkers of all ages, including some who pre-date Christianity itself. With regard to social ministry, the words of the Second Vatican Council should always be kept in mind: 'While helping the world and receiving many benefits from it, the Church has a single intention: That God's kingdom may come, and that the salvation of the whole human race may come to pass.'" (150)

In this chapter of the text the four points that are presented concerning Catholic social teaching—scripture, moral doctrine, tradition, and the Church's social ministry—are presented to the students and call for their response. If Christians are to be responsible, then they must be given sound reasoning that compels them to respond to the call to serve others.

As Christians we believe that the kingdom is both here with us now and yet to come in all its fullness. The call to social justice is one that challenges us to help create the kingdom to the extent that we can in our own time and place. We look to Jesus' example of ministry to others as a model for our response to others' needs.

In the world today, there is a great need for the loving service of Christians. Through this ministry we link ourselves to scripture, to tradition, and to Christ's promise of the kingdom. Our belief in the world as we know it and in the one that is to come reveals itself in our service to one another as brothers and sisters in the Lord Jesus. This noble task calls each of us to be Christlike and to give of ourselves, thereby making God's Kingdom present on our earth.

The fundamental basis for the social ministry is the dignity of the human person. It is to this dignity that we who are called to serve as Christians address ourselves. Each life is precious and the quality of existence on this planet is a challenge which no one in the world takes lightly today.

As we grow in our Christian understanding of what it means to serve, the Good Samaritan attitude becomes a reality that is manifested in the quality of life around us. As we learn to give of self, to value life, and to give each individual his or her dignity as a person, we become intimately involved with the mission of Jesus, following his way and his truth. It is ours to choose. Living this way *can* make a difference in the world.

Teaching Notes 1

Text Pages
154–158

Discovering Through Experience

1. The experience that Cathy has at the beginning of the chapter would be a good one for the students to have firsthand. The best way of doing it would be to follow the experience just as it happened to Cathy.

a. For the exercise, two rooms will be needed, one meeting room where the students gather initially and one where refreshments can be served. It might be good to read through this part of the text to get a sense of the whole experience.

b. The name tags are colored according to the refreshment tables, the red table has four chairs and four name tags, the blue table has eight chairs and name tags, and the rest of the name tags are green, with no chairs around the green table. If the majority of students do not get green name tags, the number at the blue and red tables needs to be decreased so that the effect of overcrowding at the green table is obvious.

c. The students receive the name tags as they enter the meeting room. Here they are given some information on social justice, either from a speaker, a film, or a filmstrip about social problems. Usually, the Catholic Relief Services, as well as area community organizations, have such services available. (See *Resources* for this Guide chapter.)

d. The presentation is for consciousness-raising but it is during the break for refreshments that the essential learning experience takes place. At the beginning of the break ask the students to go to the tables that correspond with the colors of their name tags.

e. Each table must be visible to everyone, the red having an abundance of appetizing snacks, the blue one an adequate amount, and the green one a plate of saltine crackers and a few cups with a pitcher of water.

f. Be sure to take note of whatever happens during this time; it will be useful in the discussion that follows. When everyone has had enough time for a break, bring them back to the meeting room and discuss the experience.

2. The discussion will deal with honest feelings which most students never considered. The teacher should observe these reactions to help the students internalize the experience. Once they have reached the point of wanting to become personally involved, ask them to consider the exercise (text page 157) and write a letter asking to sponsor such an experience for others in their parish.

3. Encourage the students to be specific about what can be learned by such an experience and what can be done by those who are motivated by such an experience. After they have thought of such concrete ways to help, show the film *Theirs Is the Kingdom*. (See *Resources* for this Guide chapter.) This film can give the students insight into the sensitivity needed in those who wish to help the poor as well as the necessity for the proper attitude in anyone who is willing to serve.

4. The students will want to discuss the film and perhaps refine their own initial plans to respond to the social problem. Have them bring in a copy of a daily newspaper, *Time,* or *Newsweek* magazines for their next assignment.

5. To raise the students' consciousness concerning the problem of hunger the teacher might want to present the following facts for student consideration and discussion.

- There are from 10–20 million people in the United States who are malnourished. What might be the reason for this? What could be done about it? What is the difference between malnourishment and undernourishment?

- An estimated 15,000 people somewhere in the world, mostly children, die *each day* from undernutrition and malnutrition. (Have a mathematics whiz in the group figure out what percentage of the class would die each day if those figures applied in their situation.)

- If we actually ate all the food we raised in the world today there would be enough for more than ten times the number of people now living. So why are people hungry? Is it a matter of distribution? economics? politics? greed?

6. Show one of the following films as a followup to these discussions (see *Resources* for this Guide chapter):

- *Depressed Area.* David Brinkley narrates the story of a West Virginia mining town. One of the men interviewed has five children suffering from malnutrition.

- *Who Shall Reap?* This film focuses on recent efforts to solve world problems.

- *Food or Famine.* This film asks for greater international cooperation in expanding food production internationally.

- *Tomorrow the Moon, but When Do We Get to Earth?* (filmstrip) This suggests some controversial solutions.

- *Bread for the World.* This is a 3-part filmstrip addressing the need for response to world hunger.

7. Following the viewing of one of the films ask the students to reflect quietly for a few minutes, no discussion—just thought. Then tell them that they are going to write a short letter. They must imagine they are starving; they are going to die. Ask:

- To whom will you write the letter?
- What will you say?
- There isn't much time; you are very weak; what are the most *important* things to say?

Where Do You Stand?

1. The text (page 158) presents for consideration five descriptive statements about the world. Have the students look through the magazines and newspapers they have brought in to find specific articles which correspond to or corroborate these descriptive statements. If possible, have these xeroxed so that each student has a copy of each example. Read the articles, share the information, list the facts under the appropriate statements on the board or on a transparency.

Have the students select and discuss the information they find to be most compelling.

2. Now ask the students to consider the questions in the exercise (text page 158) and prayerfully reflect on their answers. Once they have given some serious thought to the exercise, ask them to write these reflections in their journals.

Teaching Notes 2

Text Pages
158–166

Social Values Auction

1. The next section, "Social Values Auction" (text page 158), takes the students a step further in their understanding of service and the values of Christianity.

The steps in the student's text are clearly outlined and should be followed closely for optimum effectiveness.

● *Step 1:* Allow sufficient time for the students to separate their initial self-centered responses from their more altruistic long-range goals. Be prepared for the adolescent to be more ego-centered than other-oriented.

● *Step 2:* The opportunity to share in a group can serve as a kind of filter which sifts or reinforces values and opinions as they are combined with those of the peer group. Allow time for this discussion to develop.

● *Step 3:* This step involves the important stage of consensus. In arriving at consensus, further clarification evolves. It is vital to value development.

● *Step 4:* It is amazing what happens when recognizable money value is attached to a life value. Money, for most adolescents, is a very real, a very desired thing. Looking at priorities in terms of the dollar sign moves the

exercise from the abstract to the concrete. It might be helpful to have play money available for the bidding. The more authentic the auction the more enjoyable and productive the learning experience.

● *Step 5:* This is an important component of the exercise because it calls for evaluation. Do not omit it and allow the time required for the questions (text page 160) to be explored thoroughly.

2. The exercise (text page 160) moves the students from a values survey and evaluation to the much more specific task of realizing or putting into practice something they have identified as a priority. The exercise helps them to see the complexity involved in acting on decisions. The students will require a good deal of direction in gathering material for the research involved. Be sure to make available as much information as possible. (See *Resources* for this Guide chapter.)

3. Have the students complete *Worksheet #20* as a conclusion to this section.

Jesus the Servant
The Beatitudes—A Story of Hope

1. After reading the introductory paragraph of "Jesus the Servant" (text page 160) refer the students to the words Jesus read from the scroll in the synagogue (Luke 4:16-20). List on the board the elements of what Jesus sees as his mission.

● to bring good news to the poor
● to proclaim liberty to captives
● to restore sight to the blind
● to set free the oppressed
● to announce salvation

Ask the students to explore the following questions:

● What would be "good news" to the poor?
● Are there different ways of being "poor?" What are they?
● What about the different kinds of captivity: how are human beings held

captive? What is the liberty that Jesus promises?

● Is physical lack of sight the only kind of blindness? How else do we refuse to let in the light?

● Think of the many ways in which people are oppressed. How can the message of Jesus set them free?

2. After this discussion have a student read aloud quietly and prayerfully the words of Jesus from Matthew's Gospel (text page 160). These words have been put to music by the Monks of Weston Priory. Play the record "Come to Me" as both a reflection on the Scriptures and an introduction to service as Jesus proclaimed it.

3. The students are familiar with the Beatitudes—perhaps so familiar that the words have lost some significance for them. It is important and appropriate that the students *hear* them again at this point. The teacher and/or student volunteers might prepare in advance slides that they feel are interpretive of the Beatitudes. Show these slides as an accompaniment to a choral reading of the Beatitudes.

4. Allow time for the necessary questions and clarifications of this statement of the fundamental Christian message. Link the Beatitudes to the section Jesus selected from Isaiah to describe himself and his mission.

5. Show the filmstrip *The Beatitudes: Call to Discipleship.* (See *Resources* for this Guide chapter.) Draw the students to an understanding of the essential connection between Christianity and service. Try to do this in a way that is challenging but not threatening.

6. Direct the students to the exercise on text page 162. This activity provides them with an opportunity to relate the message of the Beatitudes to their own experience of the world. See to it that their suggestions are concrete and practical—there may be a tendency to be too idealistic and vague and solutions of this nature usually worsen a problem rather than solve it.

The Good Samaritan—A Story of Love

1. This section (text page 162) builds on the attitudes developed in the section on the Beatitudes. Begin it by having the students recall the two great commandments (Luke 10:27). Write these on the board and ask them to reflect on the meaning of the words before reading the story of the Good Samaritan in Luke 10:25–37 or its paraphrase in the text on pages 162–164.

2. Write the word "neighbor" on the board and ask the students to associate freely with the word. After a number of associations have been collected, ask someone for the dictionary derivation: "one who dwells near." Discuss with the students the relativity of the word "near"—the reality of our closeness to each other on planet earth, our dependence on each other whether we like it or not. It might be appropriate to provide the students with copies of "Who Is My Neighbor?" which can be found in *Social Issues: A Just World.* (See *Resources* for this Guide chapter.)

3. If you feel that your group is mature enough, have them read ee cummings' poem on the Samaritan. Elicit their reactions. Ask:

● How does the poet interpret the word "neighbor"?
● What are his emotions?
● Is the purpose of reaching out to others to make us feel good or do good?
● Explain the paradox expressed in the final two lines of the poem.

4. Direct the students to the exercise in the text (page 164) on local "good Samaritans." Have them answer the questions individually in writing and then in groups of three or four share their responses.

5. Have the students bring in items from the newspapers about people who have been "good Samaritans" and/or ask them to write their own contemporary version of this parable.

The Final Judgment—A Story of Challenge

1. Read to the students or have volunteer students prepare and present a dramatic reading of the poem "Abou Ben Adam." This is really the story of a judgment. Ask:

- Have you ever felt as Abou Ben Adam feels—that he doesn't know for sure if he loves God? Please explain.
- What is the one thing of which he is certain?
- What does the angel say is the criterion for loving God?
- Do you think the message in this poem is Christian? Why or why not?

2. Direct the students to the exercise in the text (page 166). Allow sufficient time for the students to do the research required and encourage them not simply to cite instances but also to reflect quietly on the words. Have the students write their reflections in their journals.

The Ministry of Service Today
Helping the Poor
In these sections of the chapter the students are introduced to concrete examples of service as well as guidelines from the Church that can assist them in this service of justice. The subsequent sections specify areas in which this service is being done, and where more is needed. Be sure that the students recognize that each example is a true story. This will help them to see that when just people act justice can become a reality.

Throughout the remainder of the chapter suggest that the group organize a display area. Have them collect and display photographs, articles, personal reflections, quotes, etc. which deal with the topics of justice being explored.

Helping Migrant Workers
1. If possible show one of the following films to the group. It is extremely difficult to portray the plight of the oppressed in words alone; the visual impact is important. (See *Resources* for this Guide chapter.)

- *Harvest of Shame*. This is Edward R. Murrow's report on migratory workers. It offers a discussion of the pros and cons of such labor and possible solutions.

Note: Conditions have improved somewhat since this film was produced in 1960.

- *The Harvester.* This is a shorter film depicting the condition of migrant workers in California.
- *Viva La Causa.* This is a filmstrip about Cesar Chavez, founder of the farm workers movement.

2. Prepare, or have student volunteers prepare, a brief history of the migrant workers in America. This report should be presented as factually and objectively as possible. The point to be made is the plight of these people and the need for Christians to be informed and to take positive steps to work for justice.

3. Discuss with the students the situation of the migrant worker. Ask them to speculate about what Jesus would have thought of their dilemma as well as of the solution of their problem. Help them find scriptural references which support their suggestions.

Aiding Health Care
Helping Communities

1. There is a great deal of interest in and attention given in our society to issues of life and death: euthanasia, abortion, prolonging life by artificial means, etc. This is important; it should be so. It is equally important, however, that the students' consciousness be raised concerning the justice of providing needy people with adequate medical care in the less extraordinary circumstances of daily life. Have student volunteers collect information regarding health care facilities in the area. Questions:

- Are these adequate?
- Are these available to the poor?
- Are these facilities self-help or government provided?

2. If possible, invite speakers into the group from local health care agencies. Have the students prepare questions for these occasions.

3. Have the students read "Helping Communities" (text page 168) and discuss the concept of community organizations.

4. Brainstorm for problem areas in a local community. List these on the board. Continue brainstorming for ways in which people working together might solve these problems. How could the local Church help in situations like these?

5. Divide the group into three sections. Assign each section one of the topics just presented and ask them to prepare a summary report.

- Migrant worker group: research the state of the worker today, find out what progress has been made, and discover how the Church has respnded to this need.
- Health care group: research the needs of the rural poor in the United States and see how the Church has responded to their plight.
- Community organizations group: research the ways in which the Church has helped people to organize in order to solve community problems. An extensive bibliography is given in *Resources* for this Guide chapter which could be helpful for students doing this project.

Working for Justice

1. As a conclusion to this section on service in the Church refer the students to the Scriptures—to Micah 6:8 and ask them to reflect on its implications for them:
. . . "the Lord has told us what is good. What he requires of us is this:
to do what is just,
to show constant love, and
to live in humble fellowship
with our God."

2. Direct the students to complete *Worksheet #21,* an exploration of the ways in which the Church must work for justice today.

Prayer and Worship Experiences

1. The students could create a liturgical celebration for the school on the theme of social justice. They could use scriptural readings from the chapter and songs that highlight social concerns, such as the "Cry of the Poor" by the St. Louis Jesuits and "That There May Be Bread" by the Weston Monks. If slides were used to illustrate the Beatitudes, the gospel would have a visual impact as well. The filmstrip *The Beatitudes: Call to Discipleship* might be used here also. (See *Resources* for this Guide chapter.)

2. Have the students use the "Prayer Reflection" at the end of the chapter for a silent meditation, using their journals to respond to the reflection.

3. Have the students listen to the song "He Ain't Heavy, He's My Brother," by Neil Diamond and reflect on the meaning of the words. Using slides that depict poverty and hunger can add to its effectiveness. . Conclude with an opportunity for spontaneous prayers and the recitation of the Our Father.

Service Projects

1. Have the students sponsor a hunger walk in which sponsors donate so much money for every mile that the students walk. Make sure that the walk is well planned and executed. Collect the money and give it to the committee that has taken the responsibility for the project. Use the donations for a good cause.

2. Have a fast day at school for consciousness-raising among the community. Offer a soup kitchen alternative in the school cafeteria and ask students to give their lunch money to the poor in exchange for a bowl of soup and a piece of bread. Give the money to the local soup kitchen in your town or to a national group such as Oxfam International, Bread for the World, or Catholic Relief Services.

3. Initiate the idea of a food closet that your school sponsors and in which all students and faculty members share responsibility. Be sure that the administration supports the idea and that only non-perishable food is given. Contact a social service department about your plans and offer to share your reserves with their needy.

Independent Study Projects

1. Have students choose a social problem of concern to them and find out its present status as well as any movements or plans to aid the concern. How can they be of service and what is needed to make the concern one which committed Christians choose to be aware of and help?

2. Have students conduct research about the United States Catholic Conference and its ability to be of service to those in need. What are the areas they choose to serve? Where have they been successful? How have they gone about helping? What has made their efforts effective?

3. Have students investigate your diocesan office and find out how it deals with problems of social justice in the local area. What does it see as the needs and what is it doing about them? Find out what opportunities are available for high school students to volunteer assistance.

Resources

Audiovisual

A World Hungry. 5-part filmstrip series. Southwest Film Center, 169 Franklyn Ave., San Gabriel, CA 91775.

Good Morning, Good People. 16 min., color film. Southwest Film Center.

Indian Viewpoints. 4-part filmstrip series. Southwest Film Center.

Living Simply. 5-part filmstrip series on world hunger. Franciscan.

Peacemaker. 7 min., color film. Franciscan. Communications Center, 1229 S. Santee St., Los Angeles, CA 90015.

Theirs Is the Kingdom. Film. Franciscan.

"They Are My People." 7 min. filmstrip about Mother Teresa.

"Viva La Causa." 7 min. color filmstrip about Chavez. Denoyer-Geppert Audiovisuals, 355 Lexington Ave., New York, NY 10017.

We Are Not Alone. 10 min. filmstrip on aging. TeleKETICS. 1229 S. Santee St., Los Angeles, CA 90015.

A Day in the Life of Bonnie Consuelo. 16-½ min., color film. Arthur Barr Productions, 3490 E. Foothill Blvd., Pasadena, CA 91107.

An Essay on War. 22 min., color film. Encyclopedia Brittannica Educational Corporation, 425 North Michigan Ave., Chicago, IL 60611.

The Way Home. 7 min., color film. Kent State University, Film Library, Kent, OH 44242.

The Eye of the Camel. 28 min. color film. Insight Films, Paulist Productions, PO Box 1057, Pacific Palisades, CA 90272.

The Beatitudes: Call to Discipleship. 20 min. color filmstrtip. Paulist.

Bread for the World. 3-part color filmstrip. 200 E. 16th St., New York, NY.

Mountain People. 24 min. color film. Film Rental Center of Syracuse University, 1455 E. Calvin St., Syracuse, NY 13210.

Depressed Area. 14 min., b/w film. Available for low service charge from AFL-CIO office.

The Harvester. 19 min. Franciscan Films. Available at low rental from local office of AFL-CIO.

Harvest of Shame. 54 min., b/w film. Available at low rental from local office of AFL-CIO.

Hunger in America (50 min.), *Poverty in Rural America* (28 min.), *Who Shall Reap?* (28 min.) all on free loan from U.S.D.A., Washington, D.C.

"Tomorrow the Moon, but When Do We Get to Earth?" 15 min. color filmstrip. Thomas Klise Co., P.O. Box 3418, Peoria, IL 61414.

Taproot Manuscript. Neil Diamond album. Universal City Records, Universal City, CA 91608.

Dwelling Place and *Wood Hath Hope.* St. Louis Jesuits, North American Liturgy Resources, Phoenix, AZ.

That There May Be Bread and *Locusts and Wild Honey.* Weston Priory Productions, Weston, VT 05161.

Food or Famine. 28 min., color film. Shell Oil Company, Houston, TX.

Print

F. Bockle. *The Social Message of the Gospels.* Ramsey, NJ: Concilium Series, Paulist Press: 1968.

D. Brown. *Bury My Heart at Wounded Knee.* New York: Bantam Books, 1970.

A. Cernera. *Social Issues: A Just World.* New York: W.H. Sadlier, 1981.

J. Gonzalez. *Two Blocks Apart.* New York: Holt, Rinehart and Winston, 1965.

Good News Bible. Catholic Study Edition. New York, Wm. H. Sadlier, Inc., 1979.

A. Greely. *A Future To Hope In.* Garden City, NY: Doubleday, 1969.

J. Haughey. *The Faith That Does Justice.* Woodstock Series. Paramus NJ: Paulist Press, 1978.

M. Hellwig. *The Eucharist and the Hungers of the World.* Paramus, NJ: Paulist Press, 1976.

M. Harrington. *The Other America.* Baltimore: Penguin, 1962.

S. Joseph. *The Me Nobody Knows: Children's Voices from the Ghetto.* New York: Avon.

A. Joseph. *Red Power: The American Indians' Fight for Freedom.* New York: Heritage Press, 1971.

K. Lorenz. *On Aggression.* New York: Bantam, 1970.

G. McKenzie. *Man and His Physical Environment.* Minneapolis: Burgess Publishing Co., 1975.

G. Mische. *Toward a Human World Order.* Ramsey, NJ: Paulist Press, 1976.

H. Fagan. *Empowerment: Skills for Social Action.* Ramsey, NJ: Paulist Press, 1980.

P. Riga. *The Church of the Poor.* Illinois: Divine Word Publishers, 1967.

A. Simon. *Bread For the World.* Paramus, NJ: Paulist Press, 1975.

R. Sider. *Rich Christians In an Age of Hunger.* A Biblical Stury. Paramus, NJ: Paulist Press, 1979.

Sharing the Light of Faith: National Catechetical Directory for Catholics in the United States. Washington, D.C.: US Catholic Conference, 1979.

Document on the Native American. Washington, D.C.: National Conference of Catholic Bishops, USCC, 1977.

Statement on American Indians. Washington, D.C.: USCC, 1977.

B. Ward. *The Rich Nations and The Poor Nations.* New York: Norton, 1962.

Kowalski, A. P. "Church and the Handicapped." *America,* May 27, 1978.

"Jobless Blacks." *U.S. News,* September 26, 1977.

Genovesi, Vincent J. "Birth Into Poverty." *America,* Dec. 24, 1977. "Human Right To A Job." *New-Republic,* Nov. 5 1977.

"Appalachia—Challenge and Vision." *National Catholic Reporter,* Feb. 28, 1975.

Savage, D. S., "Street Academies: Education Programs for High School Dropouts.' *'Education Digest,* Dec. 1976.

"Memo to Networks: Clean Up TV." *Christianity Today,* Dec. 30, 1977.

"TV Getting Gun Shy?" *Senior Scholastic,* Oct. 6, 1977.

Rossman & Everist (editors). "Church and The Coming Electronic Revolution." *Christian Century,* Dec. 14, 1977.

Taylor, J. A. "Violence: Media's Desperate Remedy." *Christian Century,* Oct. 5, 1977.

"Crisis in The Prisons: Not Enough Room For All The Criminals," *U.S. News,* Nov. 28, 1977.

10

Our Story Takes Shape

Text Pages
172–191

Objectives

Knowledge: To help the students identify and understand the various elements of the parish community and how they function.
Attitude: To see the reality of the parish today and be able to build toward greater understanding of and commitment to the parish in the future.
Practice: To be able to see and accept their own personal responsibility to the parish and the Church.

Orientation

In this last chapter the students are asked to implement their knowledge in an active way in their parishes. They are encouraged to feel responsible for helping their parish community to be alive and well.

"What's a Parish All About?" (text page 172) presents three life situations that depict young people's experiences of parish. These are typical reactions which the majority of students can most probably identify with and discuss. From there the students are asked to interview each other about their parish, which will help the students see similarities and differences among parishes. This realization will help them as they work through the chapter.

The next section, "Parish Is a Mosaic" (text page 174), invites students to look at their parish as a design. In this way the students can get a sense of the whole as well as the working parts of a parish community. They are asked to create a mosaic depicting their own parish, which helps personalize the design and also encourages them to think creatively about reshaping their parish in the future. The next section, "Story of the Parish/Story of The Church" (text page 175), develops the historical background of the parish and shows the students how it fits into the whole scheme of the Church—how the parish *is* the Church in microcosm.

In the section they are asked to be aware of leadership roles on the parish level that require special ministries, gifts, and talents to give to the community. In examining these various leadership roles the students can come to an understanding of each unique ministry and call to serve. The students are also encouraged to look for opportunities to become involved themselves in parish ministry.

In "Programs" (text page 179), the students are asked to examine and evaluate the existing parish programs and to suggest additional ones that may be necessary. This will help to broaden their understanding of the present and will help develop a future vision in them.

Each parish committee is responsible for an area of parish life. It is important that students begin to realize they have a share in this responsibility.

Once the students get a sense of what is expected, they are asked to compare these areas with their concept of an ideal parish. This gives the students the opportunity to work with the various components and see how they fit into their own ideal design. As they come to an understanding of what the ideal would be for them, the next step is to compare their ideal pictures with the reality of their own parish. Here the similarities and differences are clearly outlined and students are challenged to suggest ways in which their parish could be improved.

In order for the students to be able to understand how a community is truly improved, the next section (text page 182) introduces them to the *Rite of Christian Initiation for Adults* and gives them an opportunity to experience how community can truly be evangelized and recommitted to the work of Jesus Christ.

Once the students come to a fuller understanding of the rite as well as of their role in the process of evangelization, they are asked to consider what the future challenges are for the parish community. When students look at the priorities that are listed (text page 188) they are challenge to stop and think about the changing needs in today's world and to realize that the future holds unlimited other possibilities calling for a Christian response.

The students are asked to explore these possibilities because they will be the future leaders of the Church. It is to them that we owe an understanding of the past and the present so that the possibilities of the future can be a reality.

Life Experience Focus

The students' experiences of parish and Church will be a mixture of both positive and negative primarily, perhaps, because of their age. For most students the parish and Church appear as other authority figures and it is natural for them to examine these with a critical eye. This "sizing-up" is a healthy and normal thing for adolescents because what they are ultimately doing is trying to choose whether they want to be a part of the structure as an adult. When they step back to take a critical look at what they have been taught, they begin to make it their own. That is necessary if they are to develop a mature faith.

This chapter can aid that process of critical assessment because we ask the students to see the parish in the ideal as well as the real situation. They are asked to look at themselves and to question their commitment to this Church.

These challenges are not easily recognized or accepted by the students but once involved they naturally begin to see how they can become a part of and make a difference in the Church. Whether or not they choose to be a part of the Church in any significant manner has a great deal to do both with their perceptions of it and their level of maturity. It may be too soon for them to take any significant steps but the fact that the alternative to be an active vibrant member of the Church and of the parish is there for the choosing gives them the option, whether it's used now or later. The challenge before the teacher is a great one!

The explanation of the *Rite of Christian Initiation of Adults* makes this challenge very immediate. It should raise the question in their minds about what it means to be Catholic right now for them. As they experience the components of the rite, they should see themselves as the representatives of the believing community. What does it mean to be a believer? To represent that belief to others? What does it mean to belong to this community?

A study of this rite for adults helps the students see how questioning, searching, mature people have found strength and support in the Church. Through this example they can see the Church as the alternative they need to make sense out of their lives, and that it is possible to experience in the parish community fulfillment and nourishment they are seeking.

Background on Content

As we have seen, this chapter deals with our understanding of and commitment to the Church as to the parish and also introduces the *Rite of Christian Initiation of Adults.* These aspects are important for many reasons, but for the purpose of this book, their importance lies in how these particular points give meaning and purpose to our total understanding of the Church.

The document *Sharing the Light of Faith* says: "The parish is the basic structure within which most Catholics express and experience faith." If this is indeed true, we must take our understanding and commitment to the parish most seriously. The document goes on to say: "Catholics have a right to look at their parishes to carry out Christ's mission by being centers of worship, preaching, witness, community, and service."

These are the key areas that each parish should be involved in and committed to. These are the areas that the students are asked to examine and consider as areas in which they too might serve. Just as the parish has a responsibility to our faith life so are we responsible for the quality of the life of that community through our own personal commitment to the parish.

Teaching Notes 1

Text Pages
172–177

What's a Parish All About?

1. The three vignettes opening this chapter will engage the students immediately since the sketches involve three typical adolescents experiencing different parish situations: Chris is bored; Beth is involved and interested; Brian doesn't understand it all, but the liturgy makes him feel close to God and his family.

Be prepared for a rousing discussion about parish life. The discussion should give you much insight about the students' attitudes towards their parish. As they identify with one or another of the young persons in the three sketches, the students will begin to speak comparatively about *their* parish experience. Be attuned to their concerns which may be cloaked behind criticisms, complaints, mockery, and/or rejection of the discussion.

2. In the exercise that follows (text page 174), having the students interview each other should expose them to a different experience from their own in real life as well as encouraging positive reactions in their suggestions of ways to improve the parish. Plan your follow-up to the interviews with extreme care.

Parish Is a Mosaic

1. Spend a few minutes talking about mosaics or bring one to the classroom, if possible, so that the idea can truly be appreciated. Seeing the parish roles as a mosaic made up of varied parts—all sizes and shapes, all colors—which add up to a beautiful whole will bring out St. Paul's concept of the Church as the Body of Christ very effectively. Make the connection between the two in your opening remarks.

2. In order to further develop this concept, have the students read 1 Corinthians 12:12–31, Paul's analogy of the Body. Ask them to compare this text with the mosaic idea.

3. The exercise that follows can allow for a great deal of creativity if you choose to expand on the project of sketching individual mosaics. Remind them to include ideas that may have surfaced during their previous interviews about parish life. You may want this creation to be saved and reexamined after completing the study of this chapter.

Story of the Parish/Story of the Church

1. Diagramming the relationship of the parish to the larger Church will help the students get a sense of the whole picture of leadership in the Church, from parish to diocese to universal See in Rome. Explain how each of those persons in leadership positions are called to serve and to carry out the works of Jesus.

2. If possible, show the students a picture of the present Pope, as well as one of the bishop of their diocese, and explain how that diocese came to be. If your bishop or a parish priest could come to school and share his understanding of leadership in the Church, the students would have an even greater understanding of this aspect of Church.

3. Be sure to clarify the meaning of infallibility for the students. Give them a number of examples to identify as infallible truth or not, such as:

- the Pope citing one baseball team to be better than another;
- the Pope condemning courses in assertiveness training;
- the Pope balancing his checkbook;
- the Pope praising the space shuttle program.

All of these are clearly not matters in which the gift of truth is guarded by papal infallibility. See that you stress the point that the search for truth and the expression of truth is a task for *all* persons, not only the Pope (text page 177), and also that we are *guaranteed* of having the Spirit with us in all our decisions. Read aloud John 14:16–17 and John 16:13 (Jesus' promise of the Spirit). The following exercise allows the students to draw on their grasp of Church history studied in previous chapters. They should be able to recall significant individuals from the past who have functioned in a teaching capacity in the Church. Have them share these reports with the rest of the group.

Teaching Notes 2

Parish: Persons, Programs, and Priorities

As you begin this section of the chapter, tell the students to reserve a special section in their journals which will serve as a log of their parish. In it they should record as much data about their parish as possible under the categories of persons, programs, and priorities.

Persons

1. The first section deals with eight different roles in a parish. There are many ways for the students to reinforce their understanding of these particular roles.

a. One would be to have the students interview each category of person in their parish and compare their explanation of their role with the one in the book. Each time they conducted an interview, the students could bring their information back to the group and discuss it. Their understanding of each role should become more enlightened and real as they interview.

b. Before they interview, the students need to have a good understanding of what each role involves. Assign all eight roles to various groups and ask them to give an explanation of that person's role with visual aids such as symbols that are connected with each role. Have the students share their person with the rest of the group and give them an opportunity to discuss and clarify the various roles. Once they have a good understanding of what responsibilities these persons have, then an interview will make more sense to the students.

c. If all the students belong to one parish, it might be more feasible to assign a group of two or three to each leadership person. The person being interviewed will be thankful for the consideration and the task will not seem so tremendous to the student.

2. From this task, direct the students to the exercise (text page 178) which asks the students to expand their knowledge of significant leadership roles in the parish. From the interview as well as their knowledge of the parish they should be able to do this exercise.

Programs

1. The next section introduces the students to the important parish committees. Again divide the students into groups that represent committees. Have each group research one committee and find out its purpose and responsibilities.

It might be helpful for each group to experience an actual committee of a parish during a meeting. What are their concerns and how do they go about making those concerns felt in the parish community?

They should return to the class and explain how their committee works, what their major concerns are, and how they plan to make those concerns a reality in their parish. The students should again have time for discussion and clarification during this exercise.

2. The exercise that follows (text page 182) concerns the ideal parish. It is one which allows the students to put all this information together and to see it take shape in their imaginations. Enough time should be given to the students to create the type of parish that is truly ideal and one they want to share with others. *Worksheet #22* can help the students with their ideal parish.

3. Now have the students recreate a parish council meeting. Each student has a role to play and each committee is represented by a member. Fix an agenda for the meeting and have the students follow parliamentary rule. As the meeting progresses each leadership person and committee member should have the opportunity to comment on the agenda of the meeting in terms of their particular responsibility.

4. The remaining students should react as concerned parishioners who want their leadership people and committee members to truly represent their concerns. At the end of the meeting these students should be able to evaluate the meeting for the ones involved, giving insights and criticism about the final outcome.

This process can help the students get involved with the actual process that occurs in a parish and how each role works according to the process.

Teaching Notes 3

Text Pages
182–191

A New, Yet Old, Part of the Story

1. For the students actually to experience the *Rite of Christian Initiation of Adults* in some form would be a tremendous way to catechize as well as recommit them to their baptismal promises.

There are three stages of this Rite which the students need to be involved in. An adaptation of these for catechetical purposes can be a useful tool. Have the class choose roles that include the priest, the catechumens, a family member to each catechumen, and the parish community who support these groups.

2. In the first stage the catechumens indicate their acceptance of faith in Jesus Christ, and the faithful of the parish are asked to share their faith with the catechumens. Have the students who are in the role of the parish community share their faith story—why they believe along with the catechumens.

3. The next stage is the rite of election, which is done in ritual form. Have each godparent or catechist to the catechumen witness to the faith of that person. A celebration follows, with the catechumens giving their names in response to the call of God. The witnesses should have a formal written document that can be read by them at the proper time.

4. Once the catechumens are past the rite of election, there is time for spiritual purification. For the class, this could be done in the form of a silent guided retreat, where the students are asked to look at their own faith commitment and their relationship to God.

5. At this point it might be good for the class to discuss what is happening and to do the exercise (text page 186) and discuss the question. They should be able to draw on others' understanding of Christian life and help deepen the experience of faith for everyone.

6. Now continue with the third stage, where the catechumens receive the sacraments of initiation. It would be helpful actually to go through these sacraments for the students, giving them the theology and ritual explanations as each sacrament is treated.

7. Lastly the students are asked to continue to learn more profoundly about Jesus and the Christian way of life. Allow the students the opportunity to ask questions about faith that they might have. A review of all doctrines of the faith at this time might be helpful for the students.

8. After they have experienced the rite, ask the class to talk about the possibilities that this rite can have in the Church today. Then direct them to the exercise (text page 188). When they reflect on their particular roles, these reflections would be a good addition to their journal.

9. As a conclusion to this section, have the students complete *Worksheet #23.*

Priorities

1. The last section in the chapter (text page 188) talks about the future of the Church, a subject the students should think about and discuss seriously. Remind them that they are in fact the future Church. List on the board some concerns the Church is now addressing and ask the students to offer suggestions on how the Church can reach out to these areas particularly through the parish structure. Do a second brainstorming on suggestions for other areas which the parish should look to in future years.

2. The review questions (text page 190) provide excellent opportunities for group discussion. They are intended to help the students to internalize the focal points of the chapter. Have the students choose the the one they are most interested in and work on sharing their findings with the group.

3. *Worksheet #24* challenges the student with a specific look at the parish as mosaic.

Prayer and Worship Experiences

1. Have the students plan a prayer service that is centered on the theme of leadership in the Church. The song "For You Are My God" can be a good reflection on leadership roles. In the prayer of the faithful have the students address the concerns that face people in leadership roles. Readings from the Scriptures should include Jesus' washing of the feet of the apostles in order to link the idea of leadership with service.

2. Use the reflection at the end of the chapter to encourage the students' private reflection. Ask them to reread their journals, looking for significant changes in their thinking from the beginning of the course up to now. Play some quiet music in the background. Encourage them to get a sense of where they are now. End with spontaneous prayer and recitation of the Our Father.

Service Projects

1. Now that they have gained an understanding of the workings of the parish, encourage the students to run for the parish council if membership on it is open to them. If not, have them propose the idea to the council for consideration.

2. Have the students choose one committee in the parish and volunteer to serve on it. Tell them to record all of the concerns and efforts of the committee for future sharing with the group.

3. Have the students decide what commitment they personally want to work toward, writing a paper on why they chose that particular commitment and what you foresee as their ability to give to the parish in that capacity.

Independent Study Projects

1. Have the students investigate those areas that are priorities for the diocese and to which it has committed itself. Have them compare this reality to the points suggested in the "Ideal Parish" worksheet. Have the students share their reports with the group.

2. Have the students research the history of their parish from its beginnings. Find out what concerns were important in each decade and how the people of the parish responded to each concern.

3. Research the structure of the Vatican Offices in Rome. Find out the role of each Office and what contribution it is making to the universal Church at present. Explain how the pope works with them to guide the universal Church. Illustrate this by means of a poster-size diagram.

Resources

Audiovisual

"For You Are My God." Song by John Foley.
Neither Silver Nor Gold. North
American Liturgy Resources, 2110
West Peoria Avenue, Phoenix, AZ 85029.

Print

C. Davis. *Sacrament of Initiation: Baptism and
Confirmation.* New York: Sheed and
Ward, 1964.

A. Dulles. *Models of the Church.* New York:
Doubleday, 1974.

A. Kavanaugh. *The Shape of Baptism: The Rite
of Christian Initiation.* New York:
Pueblo Publishing, 1978.

R. McBrien. *Catholicism.* Minneapolis:
Winston Press, 1980.

_____. *Church: The Continuing Quest.* New
York: Newman Press, 1970.

Made Not Born. New Perspectives on
Christian Initiation and the
Catechumenate. Notre Dame. IN:
University of Notre Dame Press, 1976.

Good News Bible. Catholic Study Edition, New
York: Wm. H. Sadlier, 1979.

*Sharing the Light of Faith: National
Catechetical Directory for Catholics in
the United States.* Washington D.C.:
United States Catholic Conference, 1979.

132

A set of twenty-five worksheets is an important component of each Guide of the *Journey in Faith Series*. These worksheets include an attitudinal and informational survey to be used at the beginning of the course and at least two worksheets per chapter. These resources are designed as alternative ways of teaching to encourage reflection and dialogue about the themes of the chapter and as a more dynamic way of facilitating the student's journey in faith.

These worksheets are reproduced in individual form here for the teacher's use. They are available as a *Spirit Master Pak* in reproducible form for student use from William H. Sadlier, Inc., 11 Park Place, New York, NY 10007.

Name: _____

Survey

1. Each of us is a story.
   List six words that you would use to tell your story. Then circle the one word that best tells your story. _____

2. Think about the story of Jesus as you know it, and then write six words that best describe him. _____ _____

3. Imagine for a moment that it is 2000 years ago and you are one of the apostles. Jesus has just been crucified. The man you believed and hoped in is dead. Describe your feelings.

   Now, you have just heard that he is not dead but risen from the dead and you have experienced his presence. How will this change your life? What will you do now?

4. The word *Church* can mean different things to different people. From your experience of Church, write a description of what it means to you.

5. The story of the Church and its Jewish ancestors is told in the Bible. List 5 important people that you remember from the Bible.

6. From your knowledge of the history of the Church, mention three of its major strengths or accomplishments.

   Mention three of its weaknesses or failings.

7. How would you summarize the basic message of Jesus Christ in a way that the Church could proclaim today?

8. Mention an injustice that you see in your community, our country, or throughout the world. Then describe what action you might take to help.

9. List two things that you like about your parish.

10. List two things about your parish that you would like to change.

_____

Name: _____

Being and Belonging

Directions:
Special people and special groups help us to become ourselves—they give us a sense of belonging. Fill out the chart below on these special ones in your life.

Special People: Help us to be ourselves

Name of Person | Outstanding Characteristics

1. _____ _____ because _____

2. _____ _____ because _____

3. _____ _____ because _____

4. _____ _____ because _____

5. _____ _____ because _____

Special Groups: Help us to belong

Name of Groups | Outstanding Characteristics

1. _____ _____ because _____

2. _____ _____ because _____

3. _____ _____ because _____

4. _____ _____ because _____

5. _____ _____ because _____

Name: _____

Stories

Directions:
Stories have universal appeal—whether they come to us in books, or films, or are told to us by others. From the list below circle *three* of your favorite types of stories.

Fiction *(tales, romance, etc.)* Non-fiction

Mystery   Novels

History   Biography

Humor   Science Fiction

Spy Stories   Fantasy

Explain why you like these kinds of stories.

_____

_____

What kind of character appeals to you? Circle one.

unfortunate   heroic   tragic

dramatic   humorous   aggressive

handicapped   clever   courageous

romantic   macho   mysterious

other _____

Why do you like this type of character?

_____

_____

What stories do you remember as childhood favorites?

_____

_____

Think of your story in the Church. Go back to the first part of this exercise and decide what type of story yours has been; which adjective describes your role? How do you think your story will develop in the future?

_____

_____

Worksheet #4

Name: _____

The Mission of Jesus

Directions:
Write three examples for each area in which Jesus showed his special purpose in life.

Proclaiming and teaching about the Father's will and ways in the world:

1. _____
2. _____
3. _____

Calling people to worship and prayer:

1. _____
2. _____
3. _____

Insisting upon works of service to all those persons who are in need:

1. _____
2. _____
3. _____

My understanding of the mission of Jesus is:

_____
_____
_____

Worksheet #3

Name: _____

Who Is This Jesus?
Mark 8.27

Directions:
Take time to do the following activity slowly and thoughtfully.

Then Jesus and his disciples went away to the villages near Caesarea Philippi. On the way he asked them, "Tell me, who do people say I am?" (Mark 8:27). The disciples gave several answers.

Reflect for a moment. Now write down *ten* words or phrases that people might use when referring to Jesus.

_____
_____
_____
_____
_____

Jesus listened to the disciples. "What about you?" he asked them. "Who do you say I am?"

Reflect again. Now write *three* words or phrases that say who Jesus is for you.

_____
_____
_____

Worksheet #6

Name: _____

The Early Church
Acts 5:1–11; 15:1–21

Directions:
Read Acts 5:1–11 or 15:1–21 where some of the problems faced by the early Church are described. Choose one and analyze it in the following chart.

The Problem

1. The setting: _____

2. Groups involved: _____

3. Basic Differences: _____

4. Basic Complaint: _____

5. Problematic Point (cannot agree): _____

The Solution

1. Did the leaders of the early Christians pray and ask guidance from the Spirit? (Circle)   **Yes**   **No**

2. What process did they use to decide?
   Discussion   Debate   Prayer   Other

3. What exactly did they decide to do and why? _____

4. How did the members of the community react to their decision? _____

5. Do you think they made the right decision? (Circle)   **Yes**   **No**
   Explain your answer: _____

From *Spirit Master Pak for Church: Our Faith Story.*
Copyright © 1981 by W.H. Sadlier, Inc.

Worksheet #5

Name: _____

Parables

Directions:
Choose a favorite parable and complete the following outline.

The parable I chose can be found in _____

The setting for the parable is _____

The people to whom Jesus was speaking were: (circle)
Jews   Apostles   Outcasts   Other
Gentiles   Friends   Leaders of
                                   the people

Jesus' parable was: (circle one)
something they could understand   confusing to them

Explain: _____

Describe how Jesus' message was received. _____

The point of this parable was: _____

This is what the parable means in my own life. _____

From *Spirit Master Pak for Church: Our Faith Story.*
Copyright © 1981 by W.H. Sadlier, Inc.

Worksheet #7

Name: _____

Continuing Jesus' Ministry

Directions:
The ministry of Jesus was one of Word, Celebration, Service, and Healing. The members of the Church continue the ministry of Jesus. Describe how each of those listed below can participate in the ministry of Jesus.

	Word	Celebration	Service and Healing
Doctor			
Actor/Actress			
Student			
Artist			
Parent			
Lawyer			
Waitress			
Teacher			
Priest			

Worksheet #8

Name: _____

Models of the Church

Directions:
Follow the instructions given to you by your teacher.

	Harry	June	Mickey	Joe	Sara
Point of View:					
Model:					
Features:					
Needs:					
Graffiti:					

Name: _____

Today's Church

Directions:
How do you think each of the following persons might view the Church?

1. A migrant worker in California _____
2. A teenager hooked on drugs _____
3. A member of a cloistered religious community _____
4. The archbishop of a large city _____
5. A member of the Jesus movement _____
6. An American Indian _____
7. A Protestant minister _____
8. A conservative, white, middle-class, middle-aged American _____
9. A pastor of a small parish _____
10. An atheist _____
11. An activist in the Women's Liberation Movement _____
12. Mother Theresa of Calcutta _____
13. A high school religion teacher _____

a. Why might each person stress one particular aspect or another?

b. Choose five of the above opinions and explain if you agree/disagree with each of them and why.

From Spirit Master Pak for Church: Our Faith Story,
Copyright © 1981 by W.H. Sadlier, Inc.

Name: _____

Tell Me About Me

Directions:
We must depend on others to tell us about our first days and years. Conduct an interview with your parents or someone who will remember your beginnings. The following questions will guide your interview.

Name of Interviewer: _____
Person(s) to be interviewed: _____

Pertinent Information

Date of Birth: _____   Day of the Week: _____
Place of Birth: _____   Weight: _____
Length: _____   Color of eyes: _____
Color of hair: _____

Special moments to recall: _____

Any significant circumstances or events relating to the birth: _____

How Others Felt About My Birth:
My Mother said that she felt: _____

My Father said he felt: _____

My grandparents' reaction was: _____

My sister(s) and/or brother(s)' thought: _____

From Spirit Master Pak for Church: Our Faith Story,
Copyright © 1981 by W.H. Sadlier, Inc.

Name: _____

Worksheet #12

Personalities in Scripture

Directions:
From what you know of the following great persons in Scripture, characterize their call and their response.

God's Chosen: Call: Response:

Abraham: _____

Jacob: _____

Moses: _____

Amos: _____

Hosea: _____

Jeremiah: _____

Ezekiel: _____

Jesus: _____

Mary: _____

Paul: _____

Stephen: _____

From *Spirit Master Pak for Church: Our Faith Story.*
Copyright © 1981 by W.H. Sadlier, Inc.

Name: _____

Worksheet #11

After the Interview

Directions:
This worksheet will give you the opportunity to reflect on the interview you conducted with someone who remembers your earliest days.

What I learned from the interview:

What impressed me most about the interview:

How I felt about myself after the interview:

How I felt towards my parents after the interview:

From *Spirit Master Pak for Church: Our Faith Story.*
Copyright © 1981 by W.H. Sadlier, Inc.

Name: _____

Worksheet #14

Monastic Life

Directions:
During the Dark Ages civilization had reached an all time low except for a spark of life quietly growing in the monasteries.

- Monasteries were centers of learning.
- Peasants came there to learn farming and other trades.
- The illiterate came to learn to read and write.
- Scribes translated manuscripts in the Libraries.
- A spirit of hospitality and prayer filled the atmosphere.

Draw a representation of one of these monasteries.
Give it a name.
Appoint an abbot.
Make a time schedule.
Show the specific places where work would be done.

Explain how this monastery was the center of the life of the surrounding countryside.

From *Spirit Master Pak for Church: Our Faith Story.*
Copyright © 1981 by W.H. Sadlier, Inc.

Name: _____

Worksheet #13

A Character Study: Peter and Paul

Directions:
The Church Jesus founded is a human Church. From the beginning the human gifts, faults, successes, and mistakes of its members have been significant in history. Jesus worked with the personalities of Sts. Peter and Paul in building the foundation of the Church as he works with ours today to continue its history.

Make a character sketch of Sts. Peter and Paul by finding scriptural quotations to illustrate their personalities.

Peter   *References*

- Impulsive
- Headstrong
- Often says the wrong thing
- Misses the point
- Quick to say, "I'm sorry"
- Weak when confronted
- Deeply repentant

Paul

- Arrogant firebrand
- Enthusiastic
- Not afraid to say what he believes
- Unlimited energy
- Persuasive speaker
- Extremely impatient

For Peter, Jesus was _____

For Paul, Jesus was _____

From *Spirit Master Pak for Church: Our Faith Story.*
Copyright © 1981 by W.H. Sadlier, Inc.

140

Worksheet #15

Name: _____

Women in the History of the Church

Directions:
Study the synopsis given for the following women who had great influence on the life of the Church. Choose one or more of the issues listed below and write a newspaper statement signed by one of the women.

_____

St. Monica
Her habits of prayer and charity annoyed her husband; her married life was unhappy. Her son Augustine was wayward and lazy but later in his life he was converted and became a saint.

St. Catherine of Siena
Was distinguished for her great love of the Church. Her letters are as wise and practical today as they were when they were written in the 14th century. During the Great Schism she went boldly to Avignon and persuaded the Pope to return to Rome.

Cornelia Connelly
Convert, wife, mother, foundress of an order which began schools to provide quality education for women.

St. Elizabeth Seton
Wife, mother, and foundress of a religious community dedicated to education for all, and the care of the poor and orphans.

Rose Hawthorne
Foundress of the Dominican Sisters for Relief of Incurable Cancer.

Mary Caroline Starr
Convert, divorcee, foundress of an order dedicated to the work of helping homeless and wayward girls.

Issues
Quality Education for women	Teenage pregnancies
Second careers for women	One-parent families
Greater leadership roles for women in the Church	Ministry to divorced women
	The Hospice movement

Worksheet #16

Name: _____

The Message and the Person

Directions:
The Ministry of the Word proclaims the Good News in a twofold way:

a. to proclaim the *message* of Jesus, the things taught during his years on earth.

b. to proclaim the *person* of Jesus, who he is and what he does.

Give three examples of how the early Christians proclaimed the message and person of Jesus, and three examples of how we can continue to do so today.

The early Christians proclaimed the message and person of Jesus by:

1. _____

2. _____

3. _____

We can proclaim the message and person of Jesus today by:

1. _____

2. _____

3. _____

Name: _____

Worksheet #17

A Story to Ponder

Directions:
Follow the instructions of your teacher as you complete this outline.

_____

Brief description of girl: _____
_____
_____

Basic reason for leaving the Church: _____
_____

Reasons to support her arguments against Church: _____
_____

Areas where her reasons are not valid: _____
_____

Suggestions to help make her sure the decision was right: _____
_____
_____
_____
_____

From *Spirit Master Pak for Church: Our Faith Story.*
Copyright © 1981 by W.H. Sadlier, Inc.

Worksheet #18

Liturgy

Directions:
Use the following two worksheets as you organize your liturgical celebration.

Theme: _____

Date and Time: _____

Celebrant: _____

Introductory Rite

Entrance Procession: _____

Song: _____

Penitential Rite: _____

Gloria: _____

Liturgy of the Word

First Reading: _____ Reader: _____

Responsorial Psalm: _____ Reader: _____

Second Reading: _____ Reader: _____

Gospel Acclamation: _____

Gospel: _____ Homilist: _____

Petitions for the Prayer of
the Faithful: # _____ Reader: _____

Responsibilities of the Group:

1. Contact a celebrant, inform him of day and time, of themes with readings. Be sure Sacramentary and Lectionary are there for use.
2. Choose readers and rehearse.
3. Rehearse songs.
4. Choose people for the procession and decide what each will carry.
5. Write petitions and decide on how they will be presented.
6. Decide which parts will be spoken or sung and tell both celebrant and students.

From *Spirit Master Pak for Church: Our Faith Story.*
Copyright © 1981 by W.H. Sadlier, Inc.

142

Name: _____

Liturgy (part II)

Liturgy of the Eucharist

Preparation of Gifts: Procession: _____

                        Songs: _____

Eucharistic Prayer: Holy Holy Holy: _____

                        Acclamation: _____

                        Great Amen: _____

Communal Rite: Lord's Prayer: _____

                        Sign of Peace: _____

                        Song: _____

                        Meditation: _____

Concluding Rite: Dismissal Song: _____

Responsibilities of the Group

1. Have all the necessary Mass equipment on hand. Choose people to carry gifts and fix altar.

2. Rehearse songs.

3. Choose the Eucharistic Prayer to be used and indicate whether parts will be spoken or sung.

4. Decide whether the Lord's Prayer will be spoken or sung and how the sign of peace will be done.

5. Choose an appropriate communion meditation and a reader and rehearse beforehand.

6. Be sure all borrowed items are returned and place returned to normal setting.

From *Spirit Master Pak for Church: Our Faith Story.*
Copyright © 1981 by W.H. Sadlier, Inc.

Name: _____

Values to Consider

Directions:
Choose five of the following and list them in order of importance to you.

A job for every family that would be adequate to provide basic needs of food, clothing, and shelter. _____

Freedom from violent and criminal action such as theft, mugging, murder, rape. _____

The elimination of racial and sexual discrimination in employment, housing, and educational opportunities. _____

Appropriate respect, care, and service for handicapped or mentally or physically retarded. _____

Elimination of civil and international wars. _____

Freedom from worry, plus good physical and emotional health for you for the rest of your life. _____

Equal opportunity for a meaningful education for all people. _____

A guaranteed job and a yearly income of $50,000 for life. _____

The elimination of all pollution from the air and water. _____

Briefly explain your selection for most important.

_____

_____

_____

From *Spirit Master Pak for Church: Our Faith Story.*
Copyright © 1981 by W.H. Sadlier, Inc.

Name: _____

Our Ideal Parish

Directions:
Think of this: You are involved in starting a completely new parish. How would you organize it?

The responsibility for this parish belongs to: _____

The way in which our parish will divide up responsibility is by identifying areas of concern. These areas are as follows:

_____

_____

_____

These areas will be given the following to help them become an integral part of our parish. (Check each one your select.)

___ Leadership role	___ Parish support and
___ Budget	encouragement
___ Parish facilities	___ Study and reflection
___ Committee	opportunities
___ (other)	___ (other)

Evaluation of the success of our parish will be done in the following manner:

_____

_____

From *Spirit Master Pak for Church. Our Faith Story.*
Copyright © 1981 by W.H. Sadlier, Inc.

Name: _____

Human Rights

Directions:
On December 10, 1948 the United Nations issued The Universal Declaration of Human Rights from which the statements below are taken. Reflect on each of these and then find a scriptural quote to illustrate it. List in the third column the ways the Church works for these rights today.

	Scriptural Text	The Church works for this right today by:
All human beings are born free and equal in dignity. (art. 1)		
Everyone has the right to life, liberty, and security of person. (art. 3)		
Everyone has the right to freedom of thought, conscience, and religion. (art. 18)		
Everyone has the right to a standard of living adequate for the health and well being of him/herself and of his/her family, including food, clothing, housing, and necessary social services. (art. 25)		
Everyone has the right to education. . . (art. 26)		
Everyone has the right freely to participate in the cultural life of the community, to enjoy the arts, and to share in scientific advancement and its benefits . . . (art. 27)		

From *Spirit Master Pak for Church. Our Faith Story.*
Copyright © 1981 by W.H. Sadlier, Inc.

143

Worksheet #24

Name: _____

The Parish Is a Mosaic

Directions:
Imagine that you have been asked to help plan the organizational services of a new parish. At present you are working with the pastor and three sisters. The budget will allow you to hire two full-time parish workers. Many generous parishioners have volunteered to help in any way they can. You need: a Director of Religious Education, a Minister of Music, a Parish Council President, committees on Religious Education, Ecumenism, Worship, Social Justice, Finances, Building and Grounds.

1. For which position will you hire full-time workers? Why have you chosen these?

   a) _____

   b) _____

2. Indicate on a chart how all of these people and committees will work with the pastor. What will be the role of the sisters?

From *Spirit Master Pak for Church: Our Faith Story.*
Copyright © 1981 by W.H. Sadlier, Inc.

Worksheet #23

Name: _____

Becoming a Christian

Directions:
Your friend has begun instructions to become a member of the Catholic Church. The instructions are following the Rite of the Christian Initiation of Adults. In the spaces corresponding to the Rite, indicate how you can help your friend and grow in your own faith life in each of the stages:

Stages	What can you do?
1. *Rite of Becoming a Catechumen* During this stage the baptized share their faith stories with the catechumens. This stage should be marked by hospitality and friendship.	1.
2. *Rite of election* The catechumen receives catechetical instruction; asks to be received into the Church and is accepted. This time has the spirit of a retreat.	2.
3. *Celebration of the sacraments of Initiation* The new member of the Church receives Baptism, Confirmation, and Eucharist. This is a time of rejoicing and celebration.	3.

Following the sacramental celebration, the new member learns more about the story of Jesus and the Church. This period, called *mystagogia*, is a time marked by sharing, service, and joy. What can you do to help during this period?

From *Spirit Master Pak for Church: Our Faith Story.*
Copyright © 1981 by W.H. Sadlier, Inc.

*Journey
in Faith
Series*

Church

Our Faith Story

**by
Rev. James T. Mahoney, Ph.D.
Sr. Mary E. Dennison, r.c.**

Contributing Author
John Roberto

General Editors
John S. Nelson, Ph.D
Catherine Zates Nelson

Special Consultants
Rev. Peter Mann
Sr. Ruth McDonell, I.H.M.
Rev. Samuel Natale, S.J., Ph.D.
Sr. Marie Paul, O.P.
Sr. Dominga M. Zapata, S.H.

Contributors
Elinor R. Ford, Ed.D.
Eileen E. Anderson
Eleanor Ann Brownell
Joyce A. Crider
Mary Ellen McCarthy
William M. McDonald
Joan McGinnis-Knorr
William J. Reedy
Joseph F. Sweeney

The content of this program
reflects the goals of *Sharing
the Light of Faith* (NCD).

Sadlier
A Division of
William H. Sadlier, Inc.
New York
Chicago
Los Angeles

Contents

Nihil Obstat
Raymond J. Kupke
Censor Librorum

Imprimatur
✠ Frank J. Rodimer, D.D.
Bishop of Paterson
September 2, 1980

The nihil obstat and imprimatur are
official declarations that a book or
pamphlet is free of doctrinal or
moral error. No implication is contained
therein that those who have
granted the nihil obstat and imprimatur
agree with the contents, opinions, or
statements expressed.

Printed in the United States of America.
Home Office:
11 Park Place,
New York, NY 10007
ISBN: 0-8215-2900-5
ISBN: 0-8215-2910-2
123456789/987654321

Project Director: William M. McDonald
Project Editors: Gerard F. Baumbach
         Sr. Jane Keegan
Managing Editor: Gerald A. Johannsen
Design Director: Willi Kunz
Designer: Grace Kao
Photo Editor: Lenore Weber
Photo Researcher: Mary Brandimarte
Photo Coordinator: Martha Hill Newell

Introduction

The *Journey in Faith Series* is offered to contemporary Catholic youth and to those who minister with them as they work through faith questions together and share faith experiences as a Christian community. The team of authors, consultants, and editors for this Series believe that they have put together fresh and useful materials to respond to these needs.

The team hopes that this Series will serve as a useful instrument for such wider goals as these:
● That those who use it come to know more and more that they are a ministering community, that is, people who help each other along the way.
● That in this shared journey all of us find our own way of believing, praying, serving, becoming our own best self.
● That all of us become more literate and at home with the community's symbols, doctrines, values, and great persons.

The *Journey in Faith Series* reflects the spirit and goals of *Sharing the Light of Faith*. The Series' catechetical team members have welcomed the Directory as normative for their catechetical thinking. They are confident that this Series applies practically the wisdom of *Sharing the Light of Faith*.

This book explores the questions of why people belong to a Church, what membership in a Church community really means, and what, among world religions, is distinctive of Catholic Christianity. Reflections on the Church in the Christian Scriptures, the Church in human history, and the influence of certain Church personalities are interwoven throughout the text.

After clarifying the secular, biblical, and etymological meanings of Church, the text encourages you to develop your own sense of Church—of what it means to *belong* to a Church. Each of us is a part of the ongoing story and history of the Church. You are asked to reflect on the questions: "What has been my story, my journey of discovery so far?" "Who am I discovering Jesus to be?" "Who am I discovering myself to be because of him?"

The book closes with a consideration of the educational, missionary, and social mission of the Church.

3

1 Writing Your Story

"Each of us is a story. It is not that we have a story; we are an ongoing story."

What's In a Story
Welcome to a book about stories. People like many different kinds of stories: mysteries, adventures, even romances. Some people like stories about history, famous people, or even ordinary people who remind them of people they have met. Some of us may tend to take our stories for granted.

When we were very young, fairy tales and nursery rhymes became a part of our lives. As we grew older, we chose what to read and also told stories to others. We learned about each other through the stories that we shared.

This book is about a story we are familiar with and that we can share with others. It is the story of the Church. The book will present the exciting stories that make up the life of the Church today. It will also tell the stories of God's people and stories about the life of Jesus and ways in which the Church began. As we discover the meaning of the Church, we will explore what a parish can be like, what our life

in the Church can be like. We will learn how the story of our own life is very much connected with the story of the Church.

Events from our own lives have an impact on the values we develop and on the relationships we share. They affect the way we grow as Christian people. Here is a story of how such an event helped to shape the life—and the ongoing story—of one individual.

A young man, Bill Robinson, tells an interesting story of his high school days. As we can see, its details are still vivid and meaningful to him. As a high school student, Bill loved sports, especially basketball. He tried out for the CYO team in his parish. Bill was thrilled when he made the team, but soon became aware that talent had nothing to do with the choice. Ten players were needed, and only ten tried out. In the two years that he was on the team, they won only four games out of forty. That was not important to him. What was significant was that he remembered never playing a full game, and usually only playing after the game was a hopeless loss. Bill was a bench-warmer. The team

could not have done worse even if he had played, yet the message of the coach was crystal clear: you're not good enough.

What made matters even more difficult was the fact that the team members did not seem to know how to work together. Petty arguments, unwillingness to share the ball, and poor team morale only added to Bill's dissatisfaction. Today Bill has strong feelings about the need for cooperation, supporting another person's feelings of self-worth, and competition for fun instead of points. His values have been shaped by his experience. What a team they would have had if they had played together, working to build each other's feelings of self-worth and to discover each other's gifts and talents, whatever they might have been. The CYO basketball story had a great impact on Bill's life, on his adult values, and on his actions and relationships. He carried that event with him as part of his story. It became a part of who he is.

■   What is the most important event that has shaped the story of your life up until now? Why was this event so important in your life? What values did this event bring to your life that you have found important to hold onto during your time in high school? How is it possible for other persons to learn from this event?

Families are complicated—sometimes easy to understand, sometimes hard to understand. Families can give us a sense of belonging when the members share the stories of their past dreams, successes, and even hardships.

When a parent shares with us childhood memories about our grandparents or other relatives, we discover more about our own story and where we have come from. The simple sharing of words begins to bind us to their past, which is ours too, and we begin to build a foundation for the future. The more we are told, the clearer the picture of our history becomes. As we identify with and share our history with other family members, a sense of community and intimacy develops.

It is natural for a group of people who share this way to try to care for each other. When a child is sick, parents quickly sacrifice sleep or leisure to help the child. When a parent needs care, a child responds in a similar way. When family members share their happiness or sorrow together, they learn to celebrate their uniqueness and love for each other. In fact, the most important family bonds may come through celebration of both good times and of bad.

■ Can you think of the times when you have felt the closest to the members of your family? What caused you to feel like this? When did you feel the furthest away from your family? What caused you to feel far away from your family?

Family Stories

There are many other parts of our lives that affect us in some way. Think for a moment about your family, the way you live, and the story that you share. Often a family's stories lie behind the scenes, backstage, in places we never see unless we do some exploring. For example, a young newly-married couple often discovers family stories around holiday times when two different, accepted ways of celebrating the holiday must be blended into a common way, a single style of celebration.

Special People

The people who love us teach us how to love. Sometimes groups outside of our own families become special to us. A special club, a team, a unique group of friends, the family of a friend—any one or all of these may help us feel especially welcome.

We know that when we are with them we can be ourselves without hesitation. We might say that it is like being able to enter a room without knocking. The group becomes part of our special story as we become part of the special story of the group. We feel a sense of belonging when we share common experiences. This group has many of the characteristics of the family for us.

We possess the special ability to choose to be part of this type of extended family. That ability calls for something extra—some extra effort to be part of this family because the only part of the story we share with this group is the story that we have made together.

■ Take a few minutes to consider important groups that you have been part of in your life. Develop a list of the characteristics of these groups that made you want to be part of them. With the other members of your group, can you find any common experiences in the various groups that you have wanted to join?

The Christian Community's Story

Many groups play an important part in shaping a person's values, choices, and story. Like any other important group of people, the Christian community, the Church, has a story to share. It is a story that has been passed on through the values that its members have shared and through the words they have written, through the prayers its members speak, and through their experience of the presence of Jesus Christ in their lives.

Many parts of the story are familiar to us, as is the primary person in the story, Jesus. As often as we hear about Jesus, his life and story become important to us only when they become part of our own. The stories of Jesus enable us to participate in the special history of the community, to listen to the values and traditions that shaped it in the past and continue to shape it today. These stories give us a reason to relate not only with other people, but also with God.

One of the most compelling stories told by Jesus was the parable about two sons; one remained home to be with his father, the other went away, squandered all of his money, and even had to live with pigs in order to survive. When the second son returned home, the father welcomed him, causing the seemingly faithful son to be jealous. He was jealous because his father seemed so eager to welcome back the son who had wasted all his money. It was difficult for this son to experience the

genuine joy that the father felt when his son returned. The father said to him:

"My son, . . . you are always here with me, and everything I have is yours. But we had to celebrate and be happy, because your brother was dead, but now he is alive; he was lost, but now he has been found."

Luke 15:31—32

This account of the two sons and the forgiving father was a parable told by Jesus, a story that communicated some significant truths about God. Jesus used concrete examples that his listeners could identify with, stories that allowed the listeners to see themselves as they were and as they could be.

We have all probably felt like the characters in the above story. At times, we have really needed to be forgiven. At other times, we felt that we were not appreciated enough. And still at other times, we were the one who quickly forgave those persons that we loved.

Stories are full of power. Jesus constantly used the power of stories to tell us about his Father, and at the same time to tell his listeners about himself. As we hear his stories and find ourselves in them, we can discover new truths about who we really are. The early Christian community recognized this and passed on to us an exciting collection of stories that help us to grow in our relationship with God. These stories tell us how important we are since God's Son came to show us how to live, and how necessary it is to live in community with all those who have heard and understood the stories of God's people.

■ Our Christian community values stories about Jesus and the things he did, as well as the stories Jesus told. Make a brief list of reasons why you feel both types of stories are important. Is there one reason that is particularly meaningful to you? Please explain.

Our Story Is Ongoing

The Christian community, the Church, is not a simple story to learn about. It is a complex and exciting story for us to hear and to participate in. The story of the Christian community is the kind of story that can make you aware of the important meaning that the Church has had for almost 2000 years. This is a story that tells us about time: about the past times, present times, and what God has in store for us in the future. This story is about life lived to the fullest, about persons unafraid to forgive, and even unafraid to die if it means dying for values and a person who is absolutely important to them, Jesus Christ.

In the story of the Christian community, we become part of an experience that continues to change the world: to make persons aware of the need to celebrate the goodness of God in our lives and to be clear signs of the power and force of goodness in the world. We are not alone in this work. *Sharing the Light of Faith,* an important document with guidelines for Catholics of the United States, states:

"The Spirit helps believers perceive the divine presence in history and interpret human experiences in the light of faith. As the word of the Lord helped the prophets see the divine plan in the signs of these times, so today the Spirit helps the people of the Church interpret the signs of these times and carry out their prophetic tasks." (#54)

In this book, we will discover the many different dimensions of the story of the Christian community. Why is it so important to understand the story of the Church, the Christian community? Quite simply, because the story of the Church is our story. We all have had a chance to shape our own stories by the choices we make; at the same time, our story, as we live it, shapes who we are. The story of the Church has shaped our families and friends and will even shape our own experiences in the future. It is an exciting story. It is a way to understand ourselves—whether we be alone, working with someone else, or even with large groups of people.

One author explains the importance of using stories to understand our lives and important forces in our lives this way:

"When we forget this (that our life is an ongoing story), our life becomes a series of unconnected events, connected only in the sense that they all happened to *us*. But when each of us gets a sense of our own history, there is a whole different quality to the events of our lives. Things that happen to us cease to be just 'stupid' and they become instead filled with possibilities, because we have a sense that we have come from somewhere and are going somewhere in life. We find a sense of direction."

This sense of direction gives us the chance to learn about the direction of those things that have influenced the life of the Christian community. That is why this is important for us in learning about the story of the Church. The direction of the Church is something exciting to consider, especially when we realize how important the Church has been and how important the Church can be in our own life. In this course we will be considering aspects of Church that give direction even in your own parish. We will deal with those things that you find helpful and even things that may change and grow as your future and the future of the Christian community unfolds.

My Own Sense of Direction

This would appear to be a good point to identify our past story, with all of its goodness as well as its disappointments. A good way to do this is by developing a lifeline. This will help you to reflect on meaningful events and the direction of your own life.

Begin by drawing a line which represents your life from birth to the present moment. Using slash marks, divide that line into three periods: Childhood; Junior High Years; High School Years. The following directions will help you to identify significant parts of your story during those times:

1. *Above* your lifeline, indicate where you lived during each period of your life. Include as many places as necessary.

2. *On* your lifeline use the symbols listed below to show important times in your life. Before you begin think for a moment about the events and/or people which stand out in your mind during each of the three periods. Think about why and how these people/events were important in your life.

Symbols

}   When a crisis occurred in your life

★   When you were recognized for an outstanding achievement

x   When you were humiliated or failed at something

+   When God became more than just a name to you

)   When you grew in your relationship to God

(When you slipped back in your relationship to God

!   For any happy surprises

?   For a time of doubt and disillusionment

Create your own symbols for others you wish to add.

3. *Beneath* each symbol indicate the significant event or person (people) connected with that symbol.

Our lifeline provides us with an outline of the things in our life story which are significant. These are the people, events, and the experiences which have influenced who we are and who we will become. All are woven into a whole story which then becomes our ongoing story that makes us special.

14

Still, making a lifeline is not enough. Translating our lifeline into an actual story is important because it allows us to add details, color, and depth to our story. We can describe the importance of our significant people, events, and places. And although we often invent stories, we never invent our *own* stories. Instead we *discover* more about ourselves as we begin to identify what makes us who we are. The blending of our story into the story of the Church begins with our own life.

One way to describe your life—to put your lifeline into story form—is to prepare your own "book of life." Imagine now that your life is a book. Choose chapters to represent important stages in your growth as a person. How many chapters will you need to describe your life from birth to the present moment? What names will you choose to identify each of your chapters?

Each chapter will have important people and events. Each will have a setting, the place or places where it happens. Perhaps a major event or decision will begin each chapter or bring it to a close. For example, your first chapter may begin with this important event—"I was born!" It may end when you moved to a new home, or changed schools, or met a new special friend. Before you begin, identify the chapters in your book of life. Each chapter should cover a certain period of time in your life. Try to put yourself back at those times and ask yourself the questions that appear below. Then bring your book up-to-date by asking these questions about your present life. You may have two or three chapters, or you may have more, depending on how you see to divide your story; your lifeline should be a help with this.

Model for *The Book of Life*
Name of Chapter:
Opening Event or Decision:
Significant Person or People:
Who are the people in your chapter who are so important that you have to know them to be who you are?
Who stirs the greatest feeling in you? *
Who is the person who most challenges you to be better than you are?

Significant Events:
What significant events make your chapter special?
Who are the people associated with these events?
Do you make any choices, or are any choices made for you that make a real difference in your life?
What are they?

Significant Places:
Where does your chapter take place?
Where do you meet people?
At this time in your life, where are you most comfortable?
Where do you feel the greatest warmth and peace?

Faith Experiences:
At this stage of your life,
Who is God for you?
Who is Jesus Christ for you?
What does the Church mean to you?
What does it mean for you to be a Catholic Christian?
What concerns or questions do you have about your Church?
Are there any people who help you identify your beliefs, questions, feelings about your faith?
Who are they?

Who Are You?
At this stage in your life, describe yourself by completing this sentence: "I am . . ."
(feel free to use a series of words, phases, or sentences).

Concluding Event or Decision:
How is your chapter brought to a close?

Reflecting on Our Story

We have completed the first stage of our journey. We have begun to discover the story that each of us is. As we said before, we do not invent our own story. Rather, we live it. When we learn to appreciate our own story, with its happiness, struggles, and growth, we can move closer to an understanding of our participation in the story and life of the Church. This participation can actually help us to grow in understanding who we are, in learning more about others, and even in learning more about Jesus Christ and his place in our own story.

As one writer has said:

"When we know someone's story, it is a key step in being able to love that person. It allows other persons to become new to us. Knowing their (other persons') stories is often the clue to allowing them to be original and special to us."

The story that we explore in this course is one that links the story of our lives with the story of the Christian community. In this chapter, we have taken the time together to develop our own story so that we will know exactly where it begins. Later we will develop further its relationship with the Church's story.

For the moment, we can begin to appreciate the importance of our story in the Church by considering this statement of St. Paul:

You are the people of God; he loved you and chose you for his own. So then,

you must clothe yourselves with compassion, kindness, humility, gentleness, and patience. Be tolerant with one another and forgive one another whenever any of you has a complaint against someone else. . . . And to all these qualities add love, which binds all things together in perfect unity. The peace that Christ gives is to guide you in the decisions you make; for it is to this peace that God has called you together in one body. . . .

Colossians 3:12–15

Why was it important to begin with our story? Simply speaking, that is how we link our lives with the story of the Christian community. Your story is important. But the story of Jesus can make it more important and even more exciting in many different ways. It is exciting because it is a story of people learning about their roots, of celebrating their love, and even demonstrating to the world how important that love is and how it can change people's lives. It is a story of adventure in the history of the Church, of forgiveness on the part of those who call themselves Christian, and a story of continuous patience in the presence of mistakes and hardship.

As we discover ways in which your story is joined with the story of Jesus and the Church, it is hoped you will come to understand how much your own life is part of the life of the Church community. This discovery is not an easy task, but one that persons over the centuries have found to be both meaningful and hope-filled. Of course, you are bound to have a variety of feelings about the Church. Everyone looks at the Church from several points of view. And other persons' stories are important in helping your story to become clearer. But the story of your own life and the story of the Christian community are what this course is all about.

■ One underlying theme of this chapter has been the idea that you are important—to God, to family and friends, and to the Christian community. Your lifeline and book of life are important records of your own growth. A further question, however, is this one: Are you now able to view *others'* stories with a new outlook? Have other people become more important to you? If so, why?

Challenges

The first sentence of this chapter begins with a quote about "story." Now that you have read the chapter and prepared your own story, what does this quote mean to you? How do you feel about the statement that your story never ends? Do you see any signs of the way your story may develop in the future?

Belonging to groups can help us identify who we are and what is meaningful to us. Are there characteristics of your family or some other group you belong to that you also find in the community of the Church?

What are they? Do they help you see the story of the Church and your own story as part of a single ongoing story?

As your personal story blends with the story of the Church it helps to shape the story of the Christian community. What do you think is the main part of the story of the Christian community? Why do you think Jesus used stories when talking with his followers?

Prayer
Reflection

It would be good for us to take time now to
pray about our own story and the story of
the Church. This can be a time not only
to think about how our own story has been
developed in this chapter, but also a time
to place ourselves in the story of Jesus and
those who have followed him throughout
history.

God, our loving and forgiving Father,
we write the story of our lives together
with the story of the people who follow
your Son Jesus in the Christian
community, the Church. His life was one of
love, hope, challenges, and service. May his
story speak to our story—to help us in our
dreams, to focus our vision, and to give
new life to our relationships with each other
and with you. May we never stop reading
and writing the story of goodness that is
found in the lives of all your people. May
we always be unafraid to grow, to look
back, to go forward, to seek constantly the
meaning of the story that lasts always,
the story of your Son, Jesus, who is our
Lord and Brother. Amen.

2 Jesus: The Father's Story

Our Rediscovery

Each of our lives has been greatly influenced by people who are significant to us. Sometimes these persons have been famous, such as sports figures or well-known celebrities. However, for most of us, the persons who have influenced us have been people of quiet influence, rather than worldwide acclaim.

It is probably difficult for us to recognize how it would be possible for one person to affect the lives of millions of persons not just today, but for nearly 2000 years. Yet, this is precisely what has happened with the life of Jesus. Jesus is the Father's story to us. He is the person who has influenced, shaped, and inspired the Christian community by his story, his words, and his actions.

It is impossible to learn about the Church without learning about Jesus Christ. Yet, it is quite possible that you might be tired of hearing about Jesus Christ. This is why we shall change the approach for a little while. It seems to be true that the best way to learn about someone or something is to put ourselves in that person's shoes. It is also true that each of us can approach a new thought or problem from perspectives quite different from those of other people. Because of this quality (one that actually makes us unique), it seems time to look at the story of Jesus not from anyone else's point of view, but rather from our own point of view.

Every generation since the beginning of the Church in the first century has looked at the story of Jesus in ways that showed the presence of God in their lives. We are going to do that too, but in such a way that the story of Jesus will actually be part of our own story. That is what is fascinating about studying the

Church. We may not realize it at first, but the mystery of the Church is going to be part of our lives in strong and lasting ways. This is because Jesus is becoming more and more a part of our lives. He invites us to share our lives with him.

It would be helpful for you to rediscover the most interesting things that you already remember about the story of Jesus. You can use these ideas to develop your own story of Jesus:

Step 1—What We Remember
● Write down as many brief statements as possible that tell the memories or beliefs about Jesus that are important to you. There is no preferred list. You can write down your own experience and memories. Hint: to stimulate your writing, try to remember things Jesus did and said, and beliefs that you have about him.
● Look at all your statements. Select the *ten* most important things about Jesus that you want to share with other people.

Step 2—Receive Statements from Others
● Share your list of the ten most important statements with a small group of three or four people.

Step 4—Reflecting on Your Story

● Now that you have completed your story of Jesus, you can use it to consider some special questions about why your story was written the way that it was. You might take the time to exchange your story of Jesus with other persons in your group to see if you had similar ideas.

● Here are some questions that will help you to think about the experience of writing your own story of Jesus:

1. What were the easiest parts of the story to write? Are there any reasons why they were easy for you to write?

2. What were the hardest parts of the story to write? Are there any reasons why they were hard for you to write?

3. What personal feelings do you have about the story you have written?

4. Describe the kinds of feelings that other persons might have about Jesus after reading your story.

5. What kinds of things did you learn about Jesus after writing your story?

The experience we have just completed is actually an experience of writing our own gospel about Jesus Christ. In studying about the Church, we must begin the story with what happened in the life of Jesus. We cannot learn about the excitement of being in the Church unless we first understand the forces that made the Church what it is today, and what it can become. On a much smaller scale, the same thing is true if we want to understand more things about each other. We would have to study each person's background, beliefs, and even customs, in order to figure out why they act the way that they do. This is how we are going to learn about the Church. We will study the mission of Jesus and learn how it shaped the way we believe and the way that we should live.

● After sharing, select from the other persons' lists one or more statements to add to their own list.

Step 3—Writing Your Own Story of Jesus

● Using your ten statements and the statements you have received from others, begin to write your own story about Jesus. Think in terms of several major chapters with each chapter containing about ten verses. Try to have one major theme or event in each of the chapters.

● Be sure to write your story so that it reads in your own words.

The Mission of Jesus

The word "mission" can be understood in several different ways. For some, the word means the type of settlement where Christians came to preach about Jesus Christ to persons who had never heard of him. To others, the word may mean a special purpose that one has in life. The mission of Jesus is related to this second description. The mission of Jesus was really concentrated on three major areas of his own life and purpose:

● to proclaim and teach about God's will and ways in the world;
● to call people to worship and to pray;
● to insist upon works of service to all those persons who are in need.

Sharing the Light of Faith has a brief but important statement about the mission of the Church. It states in part:

"The Church continues the mission of Jesus, prophet, priest, and servant king. Its mission, like His, is essentially one—to bring about God's kingdom—but this mission has three aspects: proclaiming and teaching God's word, celebrating the sacred mysteries, and serving the people of the world." (#30)

As members of the Church, we directly share in this mission of Jesus to the world. Jesus gave us the basis for acting in a responsible and caring way toward others. We are able to continue the mission of Jesus in the total life of the Church. Later we will probe different dimensions of this mission as we continue to learn about the Christian community and our role in it. We will learn about what Jesus said. We will discover why it is important to celebrate through worship in the life of the Church. We will even learn what types of service are required for those who are trying to follow Jesus in the world.

A passage from the beginning of Luke's Gospel will help us to understand the mission of Jesus. Luke describes what happened to Jesus after his baptism. Jesus had just entered the synagogue in Nazareth and spoke to his friends:

He stood up to read the Scriptures and was handed the book of the prophet Isaiah. He unrolled the scroll and found the place where it is written,

"The Spirit of the Lord is upon me,
because he has chosen me to bring good news to the poor.
He has sent me to proclaim liberty to the captives and recovery of sight to the blind,
to set free the oppressed and announce that the time has come when the Lord will save his people."

Jesus rolled up the scroll, gave it back to the attendant, and sat down. All the people in the synagogue had their eyes fixed on him, as he said to them, "This passage of scripture has come true today, as you heard it being read."

Luke 4:16–21

This crucial passage announced the beginning of Jesus' ministry and provides us with several insights into Jesus' mission:

● First, the time has now come when God will offer his people new hope and new life.

● Second, Jesus has been chosen, blessed, and sent by the Father to announce God's offer of new life. This offer of new life is called "good news." Jesus is sent to show the Father's love for his people and to invite all persons to share in his love.

● Third, Jesus shows his Father's love by proclaiming this good news in his teaching, preaching, healing, serving, celebrating, and even in his relationships with people. Jesus' entire life shows the Father's love.

One special way of understanding God and experiencing his love can come from understanding and experiencing the life of Jesus. What is it about Jesus that you find most appealing right now? Can you identify other characteristics that you would like to know more about? List them on a piece of paper.

The Ministry of Jesus

The mission of Jesus was essentially one of showing the good news of God's love to all people. When we describe the way in which Jesus brought this love to others we use the word "ministry." Ministry means people helping people. When Jesus ministered to people, God's love reached out to them and changed them.

The story of the Samaritan woman, found in John 4:5–42, shows the way in which Jesus ministered to people. Jesus met the Samaritan woman at Jacob's well and quickly turned a request for a drink of water into an offer of the life-giving water of God's love. As the woman accepted Jesus' offer, he proceeded to tell her everything she had ever done. The woman began to feel total love and acceptance.

This experience of God's love opened the Samaritan woman to accept the special mission of Jesus as the Messiah, the Savior of all people. She returned home to her townspeople and told them that she had met a man who told her everything she had ever done. She told them that he might even be the Messiah, the person that they had been awaiting for centuries. Many of the Samaritans in the town believed in Jesus because of the woman's story. In fact, many of those persons came to hear Jesus' message and then believed in him.

So far in this chapter, we have considered the mission of Jesus and even had time to develop our own stories of Jesus. The importance of understanding the story of Jesus in order to understand the Church cannot be overemphasized. It is good, then, to stop briefly and try to reflect upon this story.

What parts of Jesus' story seem to be like your own life? Can you find it easy to understand why Jesus has been so important in the history of the world? Can you think of some reasons why the Church continues to grow because of his life? Can you even stop and think about ways in which Jesus' mission can become your own mission in life? Does it sound strange to think of your life being connected with Jesus' life? It might be to some. But if you take the time to think about it, this could be a wonderful way to live: meeting the needs of those who are searching for meaning, of those who are alone, and of people wherever they may be found.

Different Ways to Minister

The four gospels include many examples of the various ways in which Jesus invited people to experience the love of God. These are the main ways in which Jesus ministered to people:

- Ministry of the Word—Jesus preaching and teaching.
- Ministry of Community Building— Jesus calling people into new relationships.
- Ministry of Serving and Healing— Jesus responding to the needs of the poor, the outcast, the sick, and the hungry.
- Ministry of Celebration—Jesus giving praise and thanks for God's love and offer of new life.

In the next four sections, we will try to discover more about these ways in which Jesus ministered to people.

Ministry of the Word

Words are powerful. They communicate meaning. They inform us. They shape the way we think. Jesus used words in such a special way that they could change the direction of people's lives:

After John had been put in prison, Jesus went to Galilee and preached the Good News from God. "The right time has come," he said, "and the Kingdom of God is near! Turn away from your sins and believe the Good News!"

Mark 1:14–15

Jesus was a master of the spoken word, both in his preaching and his teaching. Something about his style and his message compelled his listeners, and affirmed what they believed. Jesus proclaimed this special Word not only in his preaching, but throughout all of the actions of his life. The ministry of the Word is Jesus telling us that he is the Father's story. He calls us to hear and to believe in this story.

Jesus was a masterful storyteller. He could use words that caused people to change the way that they looked at things. He showed people that the truest Word was the Word of God, a Word that gives us life and calls us to greater life and love. Jesus' words showed that our God is even a God of surprises. He does things that are unexpected. He takes care of the poor; he heals those who are sick; he is even able to show that death is not the final answer. Rather, it is life that has the final victory.

■ The story form that Jesus used most frequently was the parable. Here are several different parables that will show how we might understand more fully the impact of Jesus' stories. For each of these parables, try to identify the main theme and purpose. How can people learn about the life and love of God from reading these particular parables? Can you figure out the meaning that Jesus intended to communicate by these parables?

Luke 8:4—15	The Parable of the Sower
Luke 10:25—37	The Parable of the Good Samaritan
Luke 16:19—31	The Rich Man and Lazarus
Luke 18:9—14	The Parable of the Pharisee and the Tax Collector
Matthew 20:1—16	The Workers in the Vineyard

The Ministry of Community Building

It is hard to be alone, feeling that there is no one who cares about us. It is hard to believe that there is no way anyone could love us. For nearly 2000 years, the people in the Church have been trying to spread Jesus' message that we are not alone in this world. He has promised to be with us always. In fact, the best way that we can experience Jesus is with other people, especially people that we love and enjoy.

Jesus developed his followers into a community that became the Church. The community of believers who listened to him and shared with him included people with a wide variety of personalities and

characteristics. Although they came from all walks of life, they were able to grow and live in community with one another.

The Acts of the Apostles is filled with startling accounts of the ways in which the Church began to develop, at times slowly and at times quickly. The persons who followed Jesus were very excited about being called by him. This was because Jesus had called them to lead lives that were based on his mission: lives of the Word, of prayer, and of service.

Other parts of the New Testament also provide us with a good understanding of community building in the Church. For example, in Paul's letter to the Romans we read:

Love must be completely sincere. Hate what is evil, hold on to what is good. Love one another warmly as Christian brothers, and be eager to show respect for one another. Work hard and do not be lazy. Serve the Lord with a heart full of devotion. Let your hope keep you joyful, be patient in your troubles, and pray at all times. Share your belongings with your needy fellow Christians, and open your homes to strangers.

Romans 12:9–13

■ Read the second chapter of the Acts of the apostles to recall what happened to the apostles after Pentecost. This should be a very familiar reading to you. Yet, now that you have started probing the story of Jesus and his mission, does it seem the same to you as when you first read or heard this chapter? Would you want to add the reactions of the apostles to your story of Jesus? Please explain.

33

Ministry of Serving and Healing

It is not enough to think about the power of words and the necessity to build community. Where would your life be going if no one took the time to see what your needs were and how they might be met? Jesus took time to meet not only the spiritual needs of people, but also their physical needs. It was a way of showing all those who would follow him that to truly change people, one must deal with all the aspects of their lives.

One of the ways in which members of the Church continue the mission of Jesus is by meeting the needs of persons who are poor, sick, and alone. Jesus has called each of us to live the type of life that will change people's lives for the better. Jesus tells us that what we have done to the hungry, thirsty, the strangers, the naked, the sick, and the prisoners are the actions by which we will be judged.

We are called to minister as Jesus did. When asked by a disciple of John the Baptist if he was the one who John had said was going to come, Jesus replied:

"Go back and tell John what you have seen and heard: the blind can see, the lame can walk, those who suffer from dreaded skin diseases are made clean, the deaf can hear, the dead are raised to life, and the Good News is preached to the poor. How happy are those who have no doubts about me!"
Luke 7:22–23

When we accept the story of Jesus and reach out like him, we are part of his ministry of serving and healing. Each time Jesus healed a person, he not only cured the physical illness, he also set the person free to live a new life in relationship to God. As in the other ministries of Jesus, this ministry of healing and serving is aimed at allowing people to experience his Father's mercy and love and to enter into a new relationship with God.

■   There are several sections of the gospels which show quite dramatically Jesus' ministry of healing and serving. Read some of these passages, and then develop the reflections that follow:

Matthew 8:14–17   Mark 10:46–52
Matthew 9:1–7   Luke 10:25–37
Matthew 20:29–34

●   How did Jesus identify the needs of people? Can you apply these passages to needs of our society today?
●   As a member of the Church, what do you think the Church can do to meet the needs of persons in the world today? How?

Ministry of Celebration

There are many reasons we can have to celebrate. We might just want to have a good time. There might be some special event that is really worth celebrating, like a birthday or some special time in a person's life. At certain times in the year, we have special celebrations that are pretty similar from year to year. Even though they are similar, we enjoy doing them because they remind us of special things or they are times for families and friends to gather together.

Jesus called people together in thanksgiving for the love of his Father. Although his basic message of love and forgiveness was a serious one, it nonetheless provided a reason for joyful celebration. Many of the stories that Jesus told, in fact, centered upon celebrations of various kinds: a lost sheep that was found, a wayward son that had returned home, the holding of a great banquet.

Jesus calls us all to celebrate with him whenever God offers new life to people who have suffered. He reminds us to constantly celebrate his relationship with his Father and with all people. Jesus celebrated his relationship with the Father at meals, at parties, at meetings with people, and at prayer. The gospels give a number of examples where Jesus withdrew from the crowds and his apostles to pray to his Father. He prayed for strength, insight, and understanding. He prayed by giving thanks to his Father for all that the Father had given to him. He prayed that he might grow in the Father's love. He also taught his apostles to pray and give thanks to God (Matthew 6:9–13, 7:7–11; Luke 11:1–13).

At the Last Supper, Jesus offered the apostles a lasting celebration of his presence in the world. The Last Supper was a celebration of God's love for his people.

• ■ Think for a moment about the celebration you are able to share in at Mass. What is your attitude about celebrating this way? Can you suggest anything that might help to make your parish Mass more of a celebration?

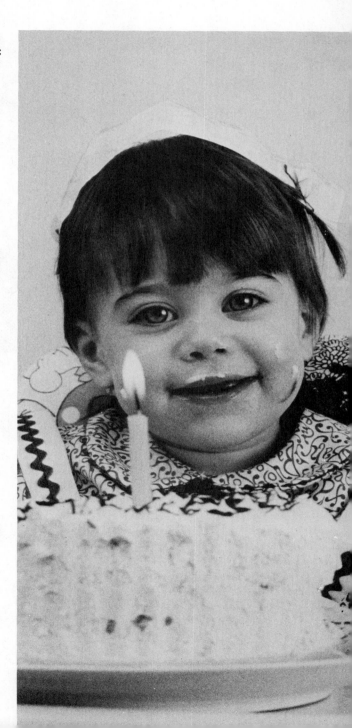

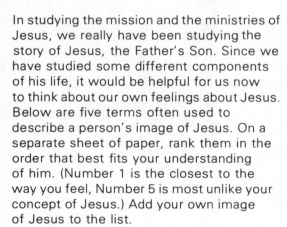

In studying the mission and the ministries of Jesus, we really have been studying the story of Jesus, the Father's Son. Since we have studied some different components of his life, it would be helpful for us now to think about our own feelings about Jesus. Below are five terms often used to describe a person's image of Jesus. On a separate sheet of paper, rank them in the order that best fits your understanding of him. (Number 1 is the closest to the way you feel, Number 5 is most unlike your concept of Jesus.) Add your own image of Jesus to the list.

Supreme Being	Friend
Son of God	Spirit
Judge	

What are the reasons for your first choice? Do they have anything at all to do with the mission of Jesus that you have studied in this chapter? What are your reasons for your fifth choice? Do they have anything to do with your past memories of the story of Jesus?

Moving On
The study of Jesus' mission and ministry is very important to being able to understand the role of the Church in the world today. For the last 2000 years, the Church has considered as the foundation of its own story the story of Jesus that we find in the Scriptures. Whenever the Church is puzzled about the correct road to take in

dealing with the difficulties of our world, the first place the Christians look to is the Scriptures and the story of Jesus.

In Jesus we see the life of one giving what he has received. Jesus, the man on a mission of giving as God gives, continually passes on to others the gifts he has received from God. Jesus' whole life and mission center around the love of the Father and bringing that love to his people.

Anything that the story of Jesus teaches us is something that is of lasting value. If the Church is faithful to Jesus, the Father's story, then the Church's story will continue to be discovered by good people throughout history. If the Church is faithful to Jesus, then each of us should be able to discover the excitement of learning about his story, a story that has become our story in the life of the Church.

Challenges

The story of Jesus is a story for all time. It is as meaningful today as it was centuries ago. What effect do you think the story of Jesus can have on your life? How has this chapter helped you to know Jesus better?

In his ministry to others Jesus showed his love for all people. What can you do to minister to the needs of others? Do you ever feel a sense of "mission" in the Church? Explain your response.

Earlier in this chapter it was stated that it is impossible to learn about the Church without learning about Jesus Christ. What do you think of this statement? Have you discovered anything about Jesus that has helped you understand the meaning of Church in your life? What is it?

Prayer Reflection

When we think of the story of Jesus, we are inclined to think of the Father as well. The following scriptural passage and prayer should help us to focus our lives on the Father's gift of Jesus to us and on the ministry Jesus shares with us:

Out of the fullness of his grace he has blessed us all, giving us one blessing after another. God gave the Law through Moses, but grace and truth came through Jesus Christ. No one has ever seen God. The only Son, who is the same as God and is at the Father's side, he has made him known.

John 1:16—18

Father, we pray to you today that we might more fully understand the impact of the story of your Son, Jesus. May we hear his Word in our lives. May we grow in the community that he asks us to be part of in the world. May we heal and serve all those persons who are in need. May we celebrate the goodness of his life and warmth of his presence. May our participation in the Church lead us faithfully into lives of total goodness, sharing, and love. We ask this in Jesus' name. Amen.

3 The Father's Story in the Church

To Be Continued . . .

Imagine that we are watching a TV show. We are caught up in the action unfolding before our eyes:

A two-year old has wandered away from his home into a nearby field. He falls into an old abandoned well. A search crew is organized and finally locates the boy, but the well is too narrow to permit any of the men to get down, and the toddler is too young and too frightened to be able to fasten a rope around himself. The well is very deep. Digging a tunnel to the child could take hours! A slim, teenaged girl comes forward and offers to be lowered into the well on a rope. The rescuers hesitate; the sides of the well may not be strong enough to take any jostling. Finally they agree to accept the girl's offer. Slowly and carefully she is lowered into the well. She reaches the child, and secures him. Cautiously he is lifted from the well shaft. As his head appears, a cry of jubilation goes up from the waiting crowd. The toddler is handed to his parents. Relief is on everyone's face. But it changes to horror as a rumble under the earth signals that the well is caving in. The girl is buried before she can be lifted.

We are all stunned by the action on the screen. What will happen now? Just then the announcer comes on. The program will be continued tomorrow evening at the same time. We are left with a sense of emptiness, a feeling of tragedy. Will the girl die in her rescue attempt? Or will she be rescued too? How will the story end? Will the outcome surprise us? How wonderful if the seeming tragedy should end in another rescue, a victory.

■   Stories such as this one sometimes have little effect on people because they are "only" television stories. In other words, some people are unable to see "real life" in this type of story. How do you feel about this?

The Father's Story Continues Too
Something similar happened with the Jesus story. What looked like darkness and failure when Jesus died became joy and victory when the apostles discovered that he was alive! But the Jesus story did not end with the resurrection either. It continued in the lives of Jesus' followers, in their understanding of his message, and in what they did about it.

Try to imagine the feelings of Jesus' followers as they witnessed the final days of Jesus' life among them. How hard it must have been to believe with every ounce of their being that they had found the Messiah, the one who would restore God's Kingdom, only to see him be arrested, tried, and finally die by crucifixion. How easy it was for them to sink into despair, feeling that their hopes in Jesus must have been misplaced. Yet Jesus had promised that he would return. That thread of hope is the beginning of the Christian community's story.

Luke in Chapter 24 of his Gospel tells us of the experience of the women who went to the tomb to anoint Jesus' body early on the third day. When they found the tomb empty they looked around for Jesus' body. Suddenly two men in shining clothes appeared, saying to them:

"Why are you looking among the dead for one who is alive? He is not here; he has been raised. Remember what he said to you while he was in Galilee: 'The Son of Man must be handed over to sinful men, be crucified, and three days later rise to life.' "

Luke 24:5–7

The turning point came when Jesus finally appeared to his apostles. Their panic and fear were obvious. They thought they were seeing a ghost. But Jesus calmed them. He assured them that it was he, and that everything that had happened was in fulfillment of the Scriptures. After Jesus left, the apostles were filled with wonder and a new hope. The Jesus story, which seemed to have ended with death on the cross, continued on. It would continue even after he ascended into heaven.

In the Acts of the Apostles, the sequel to Luke's Gospel, Luke weaves together a unified story of the early followers of Jesus as they continued his story and his work. Although the apostles were still not sure what God had in store for them, they were ready to accept the challenge after they experienced the strength of the Holy Spirit on Pentecost. The apostles, no longer afraid, went out into the streets and began to preach about Jesus. Luke gives this account of Peter's remarks to the crowd:

"God has raised this very Jesus from death, and we are all witnesses to this fact. He has been raised to the right side of God, his Father, and has received from him the Holy Spirit, as he had promised. What you now see and hear is his gift that he has poured out on us."

Many of them believed his message and were baptized, and about three thousand people were added to the group that day.

Acts 2:32–33, 41

The women rushed back to the apostles and reported what had happened. Peter went to check out the women's story. When he found the tomb empty, he was filled with happiness.

Behind Luke's account of this resurrection experience, we can feel the questions and even apprehensions that must have been present when Jesus died. Jesus' followers had had such hope in him. Was it all over now? Was Jesus *really* God's prophet? If not, why did they struggle to follow his teachings? To whom could they turn now? What would the future hold?

44 ■ Many people have the experience of feeling strong before they accept a challenge. They feel very confident about what they are setting out to do. Have you had a personal experience like this? How did it help you to discover more about yourself?

The Challenge to Continue the Story
It may be difficult for us to appreciate the challenge that Jesus gave to his apostles:

"Go, then, to all peoples everywhere and make them my disciples: baptize them in the name of the Father, the Son, and the Holy Spirit, and teach them to obey everything I have commanded you. . . ."
Matthew 28:19–20

It is hard to imagine what we might have done in their place. Perhaps an example will help. Suppose we are playing on a soccer team. Today is the play-off game for the league championship and the coach is sick and unable to be with us. Each of us on the team tries to carry on, attempting to remember everything that the coach has taught us. We try our best to win the game for our coach.

Another example might be this one: Sons and daughters of a couple who had died in a tragic accident take over the family business. They try to run it in the same manner as their parents had. In the situations which arise, they think about how their mother and father would have handled the transaction, and then make the best decision they can. As the new owners, they try to do what their parents would have done so that the business will continue in the family tradition.

Now imagine that we are Jesus' followers in the days of the early Christians. We have been with him for more that two years. In the past weeks we have watched as Jesus was arrested, tried, and put to death. These events seem to block out the rest of life. We now realize that the resurrection is a reality—and the ascension, too. Jesus has left us with a command to wait until we have received strength to be witnesses for him.

Now the strength has come. The Holy Spirit has filled us with joy and a tremendous energy to do what Jesus commanded. But what are we to do first? Where will we begin?

■ Below are some possible courses of action. We must decide which of the options below, or any others we might think of, seem right for us. We need to think this through clearly, and be ready to give reasons for our choices.

● Go out to the streets and into the synagogues and proclaim that Jesus was the Messiah. Tell people to repent, believe in him, and be baptized.
● Go out to those that are poor and afflicted and help them in whatever way we can.
● Get together with other people who feel like we do and organize into communities to consider action.
● Get some of Jesus' followers together to celebrate our joy in his life and resurrection.
● Go alone to an isolated place to pray about the meaning of these last two years.
● Return to our families and our old jobs and try to live as we did before.
● Try to recall and write down as much of the life of Jesus and his teachings as we can.
● Any other options? Record and discuss them.

Decide on what to do first. After a decision has been made, join a group with others who have made the same decision. Together list on newsprint or the chalkboard all the reasons your group can think of for making this choice.

Sharing these with groups who may have made different choices for perhaps different reasons can broaden our thinking about the apostles and the courses of action which they chose.

The same alternatives we were given were also open to the apostles. In one way or another the followers of Jesus did all of these things in the years which were ahead. But the manner in which they did them, and the priority which they gave to each, grew out of their understanding of the story of Jesus and of themselves as his followers.

Continuing What Jesus Had Begun

In Chapter 2 we discussed the ministry and mission of Jesus. The apostles knew that they were to continue what Jesus had begun. But Jesus did not leave them any detailed plan for doing this. The Acts of the Apostles, which might be called the ''Early Church in Action,'' tells us the story of the early community of Jesus' followers as they attempted to answer the same questions that we just did: What are we to do first? Where will we begin?

Let us examine briefly just what this early Church did.

Jesus' Ministry: Building Community

The early Christians made building community one of their main concerns. Immediately after Pentecost, Acts 2:42 tells us that the early believers:

. . . spent their time in learning from the apostles, taking part in the fellowship, and sharing in the fellowship meals and the prayers.

In the Jerusalem community resources were pooled:

All the believers continued together in close fellowship and shared their belongings with one another. They would sell their property and possessions, and distribute the money among all, according to what each one needed.
Acts 2:44—45

Some other communities did not follow this practice. However, Christians not only assisted one another, but also gave to other Christian communities who were in

need. They believed that in Christ all persons were to be as one, Jew and Gentile, slave and free, men and women. Christ had died and risen for everyone. Though this meant quite a change in their thinking, Christians tried to live out the implications of what they believed. In general, they formed welcoming communities that were open to all new believers and believers who had come from other communities.

Today, in parishes where the new *Rite of Christian Initiation of Adults* is being used, parishioners are becoming aware of their need to be a welcoming community for those persons who might be interested in sharing their beliefs. This *Rite of Christian Initiation of Adults* is a means for each parish to provide a comprehensive approach of discovering and experiencing the story of good news of Jesus Christ in his Church. We will look at this rite in more detail in Chapter 10.

■ It is as important today for Christians to actively share in building community as it was nearly two thousand years ago. Some would say it is even more important today—and more necessary. What do you think?

Jesus' Ministry: The Word

Jesus himself taught and preached about the good news of God's love for people. Even while he was on earth, he sent his disciples on preaching missions. His final words challenged his followers to make disciples of everyone (Matthew 28:19).

Jesus' early followers took this challenge seriously. Though we do not have extensive documented material, we do know that there were Christian communities in every province of the Roman Empire by the end of the second century. This was no small feat considering the difficulties of travel at that time.

Wherever the disciples went they established small communities of believers leaving a responsible person from the area to care for their local church. Paul's first letter to Timothy, Chapter 3, gives us the qualities for a church leader or helper: they must be of good character, able to preach, and be clear examples of humility. They must hold to the faith clearly and without hesitation.

■ Christians today also need certain qualities to help them in their ministries. Using the summary given above from Paul's first letter to Timothy as a start, what other qualities do you feel are needed by Christian leaders and helpers in a modern world?

Jesus' Ministry: Celebration

Jesus had celebrated Jewish feasts with his disciples. He had also celebrated the breaking of the bread at the Last Supper. From the earliest days of the Church his followers continued what he began, meeting regularly to celebrate the breaking of the bread. Paul gives us their understanding of what this meant:

. . . every time you eat this bread and drink from this cup you proclaim the Lord's death until he comes.

1 Corinthians 11:26

When Christian worship began to evolve apart from the synagogue, and the weekly celebration was moved from the Sabbath to Sunday in honor of the Lord's resurrection, each Sunday celebration was viewed as a little Easter. A spirit of joy characterized the group as they celebrated the Lord's rising, and looked forward to his coming again.

■ Our weekly celebration of the Eucharist should be for us a sign of our community's decision to share together in the ministry of Jesus Christ. Is there any other special meaning this celebration has for you? What is it?

48

Jesus' Ministry: Service and Healing

The early Christians continued this ministry in their care for the poor in their midst, and in their desire to make love the distinguishing sign of Jesus' discipleship. Jesus said to his followers:

"And now I give you a new commandment: love one another. As I have loved you, so you must love one another. If you have love for one another, then everyone will know that you are my disciples."

John 13:34—35

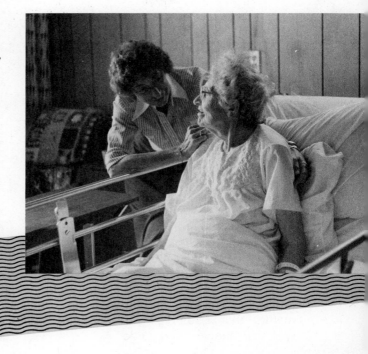

The early Christians did all they could to make this love for all visible among the community. Many persons were first attracted to Christianity because of the love and warmth evident among Christians.

■ A central mission of the early community of faith was loving service to those in need. They knew they were called to treat others as Jesus had treated them. What can you do to continue this spirit of Christian service and healing in your home, school, or parish?

The above picture might give us the idea that the early Christian community was a perfect one. Though some passages of the Acts of the Apostles seem to paint an idyllic picture of the early Church, other passages tell us of dissension and problems. The story is not always a perfect one. Jesus' followers were human beings. Then, as now, the story is one of saints and sinners, of good times and bad, of triumphs and failures.

Problems! Problems! or
One Headache After Another

The early followers of Jesus encountered many problems and obstacles. They dealt with the situation as best they could under the guidance of the Holy Spirit. They were aware that they were to continue Christ's presence and work in the world. They tried to handle situations in the manner that Jesus did. The Holy Spirit was their teacher and guide.

The Catholic Church today has its roots in these early Christian communities. Their responses and solutions helped to form the Church we know and experience today. They helped shape the story of our Christian community.

In the paragraphs below we will examine some of the problem situations which challenged the early followers of Jesus. It will be helpful for us to look for how they responded under the prayerful guidance of the Holy Spirit.

Example: Jesus' early followers in Jerusalem pool their resources, each receiving what he or she needs from the common purse. A description is given in Acts 4:32–37. But very soon problems arise. There is an argument about the way the goods are distributed. Within the community are two factions, native Jews and Jews who speak Greek. The Greek-speaking Jews feel that they are not being treated fairly. They contend that the native Jews are receiving more than they are. To resolve this problem, the apostles propose choosing seven men to assist them in this task. Seven men from the Greek-speaking group, called Hellenists, are selected to take care of the distribution of goods. Acts 6:1–6 outlines the problem for us and shows how the group of believers dealt with it.

The Problem: Factions and disagreement over seeming unfair treatment when goods are distributed in the community.

The Response or Solution: To appoint more helpers from the dissatisfied group which feels it is being treated unfairly.

In the following situations, try to name and describe the problem and show how the followers of Jesus responded:

● The apostles continue to preach about Jesus. Daily they come to the Temple to pray. Many signs and wonders are being done by them in Jesus' name. A lame man is healed. Other people bring their sick for healing. Day after day more persons come to believe in Jesus. This disturbs the leaders of the Jews. They had hoped that Jesus would be forgotten. The Council and the High Priest call in the apostles and forbid them to preach in Jesus' name.

■ The whole story is given in Acts 5:27−32. What is the problem situation? How did the apostles respond? And why?

● At first all who come to believe in Jesus are Jews. But now some non-Jews or Gentiles are beginning to get interested. The apostles are not quite sure whether these Gentiles are to be received among Jesus' followers. Jews did not normally associate with Gentiles. How are they to handle these potential new believers? Acts 10:1–8 tells us about one such person, a captain in the Roman army named Cornelius. Cornelius is a good and loving man. He is told in a vision to send for Peter. At the same time, Peter has a vision (Acts 10:9–17) which helps him to understand that the Gentiles also are pleasing to God, and open to the gospel. Peter goes to Cornelius' house and begins to teach about Jesus.

While Peter was still speaking, the Holy Spirit came down on all those who were listening to his message. The Jewish believers who had come from Joppa with Peter were amazed that God had poured out his gift of the Spirit on the Gentiles also. . . . Peter spoke up: "These people have received the Holy Spirit, just as we also did. Can anyone, then, stop them from being baptized with water?" So he ordered them to be baptized in the name of Jesus Christ. . . .

Acts 10:44–48

■ How do you see the problem situation here? How did Peter respond to the problem?

● As the years pass, more and more Gentiles are coming to believe in Jesus. This is especially true in places where the great apostle Paul preached. Many within the Christian community feel that all Gentiles should be circumcised like Jews are, and should keep the Mosaic Law. Others disagree with this position. One of these latter is Paul. He does not require that his Gentile converts be circumcised. A fierce argument about this breaks out in Antioch. Paul and Barnabas are sent to Jerusalem to see the apostles and elders for a decision in the matter. They are welcomed by the Jerusalem community and a debate over the issue follows. Acts 15:6–21 tells us about the debate.

The result is a letter which is sent from the Jerusalem Church to the Gentile believers. It contains the solution to the problem (Acts 15:23–29).

■ What do you see here as the problem situation? How did the Church of Jerusalem respond?

In describing its decision in its letter to the Gentile converts, the Jerusalem Council begins with the words "The Holy Spirit and we. . ." to show how conscious they are of the guidance of the Spirit among them. This same Spirit is present in the Church today and in the lives of individual Christians, calling them to respond to situations in the way Christ would.

There are many parallels between the problems which the early Christians encountered and those we face today. The responses of those early Christians can give us insights into what our own Christian response could be. For example, there may be groups in a parish who feel that they are being treated unfairly, just as the Greek-speaking Jews in the early Church felt. Consider this type of situation:

The youth group at St. Henry's Parish felt that their needs were not sufficiently considered in the overall parish planning. They began to make themselves of more service within the parish. They volunteered to help maintain the grounds. They offered their services in the nursery. They ran errands for the elderly. They asked for and received representation on the Parish Council where decisions were made. Their own decision to be more visibly a part of parish life resulted in greater consideration of their needs in future planning in the parish.

■ The story of the Church is not without problems. Neither is it without solutions. What are some problems that are facing the Christian community today? What are some solutions? How might the early Church's response to problem situations provide us with a direction for solution?

It would be helpful for us to reflect on these words about Church as given to us by the American bishops. They tell us something rich and meaningful about the growth of the Church:

"There is no 'coming great Church'
that is not already present in the world,
having come to us across the
*   centuries*
from the first Pentecost and the
*   primitive Christian community;*
the Church as it yet may be,
*   however different its style*
*   or developed its structures,*
*   will be the tree*
*   essentially present*
when the first mustard seed
*   began to sprout;*
*   the Church*
in every stage of its maturity
*   was present*
*   in that tiny seed."*

A Look Ahead

Like the early followers of Jesus, we in the Church today are aware that our mission and ministry is to continue the mission and ministry of Jesus in our world.

In the coming chapters we will look closely at the Church as a sign of God's presence and love in our world. We will explore some ways of understanding Church in Chapter 4. Then, as part of our Church, we will look at our own mission and ministry in greater detail as we:

● invite people to a new vision of community and fellowship, open to all races and peoples;

● tell the story of Jesus to all peoples;
● celebrate the story of the good news of God's call to friendship with him;
● reach out in service to the needs of the peoples of the world.

Our personal story—who I am in the Christian community, why I serve—is not simply linked to the story of the Church. Rather, it is a very real and necessary part of that story. Our stories come together as one as we share in the various ministries of the Christian community.

Challenges

The Father's story continues in the Church. What does this statement mean to you in light of this chapter?

The ministry of the Church is closely united to the ministry of Jesus. What do you think the Church can do today to minister more effectively to others the way Jesus did? Is there something especially appealing to you about Jesus' ministry? What is it?

Although when he left them, Jesus had not given his apostles a worked-out plan, he had given them direction to insure that the Father's story would continue through them. Explain.

Prayer
Reflection

To Make Jesus Present . . .
One day a missionary priest had travelled
to a remote mission outpost in Africa.
Because it was so far away, he was able to
get there only once a year. He relied on
catechists to teach the people and conduct
Bible services with them during the rest of
the months.

Of course, the arrival of their priest was a
great event. They came from many miles
to celebrate the Eucharist with him. After
Mass, the missionary gathered the
children around him for a lesson. He began
to speak very simply about Jesus and about
his love for people. As he spoke, a tiny girl
in the front began to get more and more
excited. Finally she could contain herself no
longer. She jumped up and cried, "I
know that man you are talking about! He's
the catechist in our village!"

Dear Jesus,
when I think about the story of this
missionary,
I feel very small and very big at the
same time. . .
small, because I am so often far from
the ideal;
big, because I, too, am meant to be
another Christ.
No one would ever mistake me for you.
Yet, I would like to make you more
present
in the world of my family,
my school,
my parish,
through my being there.
You know how to accomplish this
better than I do.
But I will try to do my part,
and count on your help. Amen.

4 Understanding Our Story

The Experience of Church

For many of us as Catholics, Church has been part of our everyday experience. Perhaps when we were quite young, we were taken to church with our families. Church was a place different from home or the store. It was quieter; it smelled different. People came to church to pray. Later, we began to think of Church as the worship, or the people, or even the activities that went on around the church building.

On a piece of paper write the word Church in the center. Around it, write as many words as you can that you associate with the term "Church." Call this paper a "graffiti" board.

■ Think about these questions for a few minutes before you answer them. What is your most positive experience of Church? When did you most feel that you belonged in the Church? What is it you do not like about Church?

As we work through these exercises and think about Church in a personal way, we realize that there are many ways to think about Church. Different people understand Church in different ways. No one way seems sufficient to express all the Church is or can be. Pope Paul VI provided one meaning of Church in his opening address at the second session of the Second Vatican Council. He said:

"The Church is a mystery. It is a reality imbued with the hidden presence of God. It lies, therefore, within the very nature of the Church to be always open to new and greater exploration."

The American Church has also spoken of the Church as a mystery. In *Sharing the Light of Faith,* we read:

"Born of the Father's love, Christ's redeeming act, and the outpouring of the Holy Spirit, it reflects the very mystery of God." (#63)

Since the Church is so much a part of the mystery of God's love for all people in Christ, it is described as mystery. It is like a hidden plan of God which is gradually being shown to us.

This mystery is something like a deep and beautiful canyon. The further we explore into it, the more beauty we discover. This is somewhat like what we do when we "look at ourselves." We may see ourselves as mystery, with each new day, each new relationship helping us to explore and unfold who we are. We are challenged by each new discovery to go on and on in our explorations. The mystery that is our Church can challenge us in the same way.

More Than One View

One way that can help our understanding of Church is through models. When an architect has drawn a design for a building, a scale model is made so that people can get an idea of what the real structure will look like. It gives us a chance to view the building from different sides. It helps us to understand the reality of the building better. In much the same way, there are "idea models" of Church which can help us to understand the reality of Church better. The Jesuit theologian, Father Avery Dulles, has grouped people's understandings of Church into five models. All of the models are present in the Church, each in its own way. Any one of the

Harry, a member of the Student Council, took the floor. "I think the first step we should take is to decide our purpose. Then we should elect officers and make a few rules. This way we'll have a group to see that what we want to do gets done. We'll know what we want from our members, and our members will know what's expected."

"Well," said June thoughtfully, "I think we should first talk about what makes St. Mark's special to us. Maybe then we'll know just what we want to pass along to the new students."

"That sounds like a good idea," said Mickey. "Maybe if we could get T-shirts printed with 'Welcome to St. Mark's' on the back and a catchy slogan of what the school means to us on the front we'd attract attention and at the same time remind the new students and ourselves of who we are and what we are doing. Maybe we could even plan a celebration for the first day . . ."

"Hold it!" interjected Joe. "Before we get into T-shirts I think we should talk about *how* we'd help new students. Can you remember what it was like the first day you came here? Everything was new, the place, the people, the classes—and it was all so big! Maybe a guide system . . ."

"Yes, I remember," said Sara, "but most important to me was a feeling of belonging, of knowing that I was a part of this group of people now. How do you think we can help new freshmen feel that they belong?"

Each of the above students approached the task from a different viewpoint. Probably, before they were finished, all the viewpoints would be blended together in order to accomplish their task.

models can become a focus for us as we ask ourselves what the Church is.

To help us understand, we might shift the scene for a few moments. Consider the following story about a group of high school students and their efforts to help others get used to their school:

A group of students from St. Mark's High School was talking about working together to help incoming students feel at home at the school next fall. They were just beginning to work out their ideas.

Harry thought primarily of the group as an organization. He talked in terms of purpose, organization, structure. June thought of the message and spirit to be handed on to new students; Mickey, of some visible way of symbolizing the message and maybe even of celebrating it. Joe spoke in terms of the help new students need and of how to supply it. Sara talked of ways to make newcomers feel at home with older students.

We might say that Harry thought of the group as an *institution;* June, as the bearer of a message, or *herald;* Mickey, as a sign or *sacrament;* Joe, as a helper or *servant;* and Sara, as people joined in *community.* Fr. Dulles' five ways of thinking about the Church are similar to these students' ways of thinking about their group.

■   As we can see, there are several different, yet related, ways to view groups. What do you think are some things that hold groups together? Is there any single most important factor?

Taking a Closer Look

Imagine for a moment that these same five students have ideas about our Church similar to their ideas about their group. Let us consider the various models from the perspective of the Church.

Model 1—Church as Institution

Harry would think of our Church primarily as an organization or a society. When he told someone about Church he might talk about the visible structures of our Church, the organization, our creeds, and our worship as ways of expressing our common beliefs.

This way of thinking about Church puts emphasis on the way the Church is organized and the way it expresses its beliefs as a group. Being small, the early Church community had little need for detailed organization. Peter was the recognized leader of the group. The rest of the apostles held special places in the community because of their close association with Jesus. As the Church grew, there was need for more structure and offices. The organization of the Catholic Church today, with pope, bishops, priests, religious, and laity, came into being only gradually.

Expression of belief was also simple in the early Church. One of the earliest expressions was "Jesus is Lord." Later, slightly longer statements of the Church's beliefs were written as summaries for people to learn and use in their worship. Our Profession of Faith that we pray on Sunday at Mass is an example of such a statement of belief. Structure, organization, and creeds are important so that our Church can fulfill the mission given us by Christ. The institution has a special responsibility to always serve the mission and the people who are the Church.

■   Why do you think it is helpful to have an institution that can help serve the needs of the Church? What do you see as some of those needs for the Church of the 1980s?

Model 2—Church as Community

Sara would be more likely to talk about a Church with emphasis on its membership. She would think of our Church as a "we," a group of persons joined together in fellowship with God and one another.

"People of God" was the primary image for our Church used by the bishops at the Second Vatican Council. Our bishops said:

"It has pleased God . . . to make men holy and save them not merely as individuals . . . but my making them into a single people, a people which acknowledges Him in truth and serves Him in holiness."

In this model, people within the Church are the focus. The people are the Church, old and young, rich and poor, laity and priests—all called together by their belief in Jesus and their common ways of expressing and celebrating this belief. Viewed from this model, a parish would be a family or a community of persons.

■ Sharing in community with others is something we may have heard much about during the past few years. What might happen if 500 persons in a parish took seriously the phrase: We are the community of the Church? What might change in the life of the parish?

Model 3—Church as Sacrament

Mickey might think of our Church as a symbol of our invisible sharing in the life of God. He might speak of Church as a kind of sacred sign or sacrament which points to and makes present this inner reality.

Like Jesus, the Church is to be a sign pointing out and displaying God's love for all people. The bishops at the Second Vatican Council called the Church "the visible sacrament of saving unity."

They meant that our Church, though a visible society, also points to an invisible inner reality: the presence of Jesus Christ in our midst. Our closeness to Jesus Christ and to each other calls us as Catholics to live lives that will remind the world of his presence. It also calls us to celebrate his presence in our worship. In this way the Church is a sign pointing toward Jesus, and at the same time, making him present. Jesus said:

"You are like light for the whole world. A city built on a hill cannot be hid. No one lights a lamp and puts it under a bowl; instead he puts it on the lampstand, where it gives light for everyone in the house. In the same way your light must shine before people, so that they will see the good things you do and praise your Father in heaven."
Matthew 5:14—16

This model refers to the Church as a whole. As Church, we are meant to be a holy sign for the world.

■ Each time we celebrate in a sacramental way we are reminded of who we are and what we are called to be. What part can the celebration of the sacraments play in your own story as a growing Christian?

Model 4—Church as Herald

June might think of our Church in relation to the message entrusted to it by Jesus. She might speak of the Church as a people formed by the gospel who want to share it with others. This good news or gospel makes us what we are—a people conscious of God's love. It is also a message to be shared with all people. Sara might understand our Church best in the role of preaching and teaching. The Church has an official message to be passed on. The Church is like the herald of a king who comes bringing the king's message and proclaiming it to the people in the public square. We call this the ministry of the Word.

■ If you were asked to select the primary message of the good news of Jesus Christ, what would you choose? Why?

Model 5—Church as Servant

Joe might think of our Church first in the role of helping or serving people. Jesus gives us the example for this. At the Last Supper Jesus rises from the table, girds himself, and begins to wash the apostles' feet. After he finishes, he turns to his astonished friends and astonishes them more by telling them to do the same thing for each other. The message is clear. He had just performed the task assigned to the lowest servant. They are also to be servants (John 13:4—17).

This scene sums up the whole life of Jesus, a life lived and given in service of others. Service is the ideal he passes on to his followers:

"If one of you wants to be great, he must be the servant of the rest; and if one of you wants to be first, he must be your slave—like the Son of Man, who did not come to be served, but to serve and to give his life to redeem many people."
Matthew 20:26—28

To view our Church from this perspective is to focus on the tasks of service which a parish community does. It would understand working for justice, for minority groups, the operating of an emergency food pantry, ministering to the sick and elderly and counseling of youth as vital to the identity and mission of our Church.

■ The Church also commits itself to the global struggle against injustice, racism, and poverty. What do you think you can do as a start to become more aware of these global matters? Do you see your service in a parish or school or family as part of a larger mission—the mission of the Church and of Jesus? Explain.

Your View of the Church

Each of the five models gives us some understanding about our Church. No single one of them tells everything about our Church. In fact, most people have combinations of these models in their idea of Church, though they might give more importance to one aspect than the others.

What is your concept of Church? Take a sheet of paper and write these terms on it in whatever pattern you prefer: Herald, Sacrament, Institution, Community, Servant. Be sure to have enough room for writing under each term. Now go back to the graffiti board you did at the beginning of this chapter. Take each of the words you wrote and put it under the heading where it fits best. For example, words like "preaching" or "homily" would go under Herald; "parish family" or "fellowship" would go under Community; "bishop" or "organization" might go under Institution.

Have you any words that do not seem to fit under these models? Fr. Dulles did not see his models as the only ones, but considered them to be the most important ones for understanding our Church today. In later chapters we will take a more detailed look at our Church in trying to understand who we are and what we are called to do. The models can help us as we explore our specific way of continuing the story of the Father's love.

Identifying Our Church

What identifies a person? Think for a moment of some of the things by which a person is identified: name, address, school, birthday, dental work, library card. These and other characteristics help to tell something about an individual.

What identifies our Church? Traditionally the Catholic Church has four marks or signs by which it is identified. We recall them each Sunday at Mass in our Profession of Faith when we say we believe in the *one holy catholic* and *apostolic* Church.

What many Catholics do not often think about is that these distinguishing marks of the Church are both a gift and a task. They are a gift given to us with our membership in our Church. But they are also a task—they challenge us, since *we are Church* to make these marks of oneness, holiness, catholicity, and apostolicity visible for others to see. To accept this challenge, we need to understand the meaning behind each mark.

70

To Be One

Today oneness is a problem for many people. Often we feel alienated, alone, cut off, and lonely. To feel oneness with things, oneself, others, and God—these are needs we experience frequently.

At the Last Supper Jesus prayed to his Father for his followers:

"... that they may be one just as you and I are one. ... I in them and you in me, so that they may be completely one, ..."

John 17:11, 23

Unity among Jesus' followers is one of the ways the Church can be recognized. Jesus gave us the eucharist as both a sign and a means to unity. What a symbol of oneness! Many grains of wheat are ground into one flour and baked into one bread; many grapes are crushed to make one wine. Even as food and drink become one with us, receiving the eucharist makes us one with Jesus and the others who receive him. We will discuss the sacrament of the Eucharist in some detail in Chapter 8.

But unity does not mean that we all must do exactly the same thing. For instance, at the Eucharistic liturgy we celebrate Christ's death and resurrection. But the style of worship may differ. Think of a folk Mass, a choir-led Mass, a Mass in Africa accompanied by drums, a mariachi Mass in San Antonio, or a jazz Mass in New Orleans. There is unity in the action and the meaning, but differences in the style because the people worshiping are different. A Church like ours, made up of people from all cultures, has a real challenge to express its unity and yet respect differences.

72

A parish can show unity in tangible ways when its people work together on joint projects, or play together at a parish picnic. We are a people drawn together by what we believe and we can show this in many ways. Our bishops and our pope are visible expressions of our oneness in the Church. *Sharing the Light of Faith* reminds us that, "while the Holy Spirit is the Church's principle of unity, the pope . . . and bishops embody that principle in a special way." (#72)

Real oneness does not happen unless we work at it continually. When we work for unity in our own lives, in our parish families, in our communities, we become signs of oneness.

■ Some people have the idea that unity means the same thing as uniformity. Does it mean this to you? How do you think the Church still shows unity even though people in the Church minister to one another in many different ways?

To Be Holy

Today some persons seem to be fascinated with evil and the powers of evil. God calls us to a fascination with the exact opposite. He invites us to separate ourselves from sin and to live lives of holiness and goodness with him. Jesus said:

"You must be perfect—just as your Father in heaven is perfect."
Matthew 5:48

Jesus himself was holy. His very presence was a threat to the powers of evil. Because the Church is to be a continuation of Jesus in the world, the Church is holy, and offers us holiness. The sacraments are sources of holiness, as are prayer and the Bible. They place us in contact with holiness and goodness.

Holiness, then, is a gift the Church offers, but each individual has the task of responding freely. Only we can make the Church a holy sign for the world. Only we can make the Church stand in opposition to evil in our world.

The call to holiness is for all, but not everyone responds to its demands. The lives of the saints remind us that the Church is holy and offers the means of holiness to all who will say "yes" to the call of God.

Story of a "Yes"

Bernard was 22 when God touched his life. A young French nobleman who could have had any career he wanted, he chose instead to enter a poor monastery at Citeaux. He was such a leader that thirty of his friends and relatives came along to enter with him!

A few years later Bernard was sent to found a new monastery at Clairvaux. Soon its reputation for holiness was known throughout the country. Bernard's own reputation made him one of the most influential men in the Church of his time. Rich and poor alike came to him for help.

Today we call him St. Bernard of Clairvaux, and though he died in 1153, many persons today still find his writings a help to them in their own journey to God.

■ Holiness may strike us as one of those words that we seem to understand, but have a hard time defining. Because of this, we often use examples to understand what holiness means. What examples of holiness can you think of?

To Be Catholic

Today, thanks to electronic communication and the use of satellites, people all over the world are more conscious than any other generation of the things we have in common with other people. But there is still a tendency to think of "us," those whom we perceive to be like ourselves, and "them," those whom we perceive to be unlike ourselves. Jesus came to break down the walls which separate people. His story and our story in the Church is that God's love is for all people.

Catholic really means universal. The gospel is for all people. People in different cultures make the gospel message real in their lives in ways that may be different from our own. Within our Church there is room for all these expressions. St. Paul tells us:

. . . there is no difference between Jews and Gentiles; God is the same Lord of all and richly blesses all who call to him.
Romans 10:12

Each person in the Church shares in the call to invite and welcome others to join us in sharing the good news. We make the gospel real in our lives, but we accept others as they make the gospel real in their lives, too.

■ If you were asked why you call yourself a "Catholic," how do you think you would respond? In your opinion what is it about being Roman Catholic that helps you to identify with your Church community?

To Be Apostolic
Today, because so many people move so often, persons often feel a lack of rootedness. This can make us more private, less willing to share with others.

This mark of our Church has a twofold meaning. First, it means that the Church can trace its roots back to Jesus and his apostles. Secondly, it means that the mission given to the apostles to preach the gospel is the mission of the whole Church, shared in by each of us. From earliest times the Church understood itself this way. In fact, the rapid early spread of Christianity was helped by the spreading of the gospel by laity as well as clergy. If the gospel is good news for us, we feel compelled to share it. This is the task of an apostolic Church.

■   You may not think of yourself as one who spreads the good news of Christ to others. But that is exactly what you do when you act caringly toward others or speak a kind word to someone who is lonely or discouraged. Are there examples from your own life of how you have acted in ways like this? What are they? How do they help you grow in your love for Christ and his Church community?

Challenges

Several models of Church have been presented in this chapter. Which would you identify as the most prominent in the life of your parish? How do you think a balance can be maintained among the various models of the Church?

One of the models of the Church presented here deals with building community. How might your school group strengthen relationships, not only among its own members, but also within the surrounding community? What do you think can be done to build community without isolating your group from other groups?

How do you think you would explain the marks of the Church to a person who knows little or nothing about the Catholic Christian community? What examples from your own story of being a Catholic Christian would you choose to help in your explanation?

Prayer Reflection

Jesus is the focus for our own lives and for the life of the Christian community that we have discussed in this chapter. No matter what model or mark of the Church we choose to consider, Jesus is surely with us. Let us prayerfully read these words of our American bishops, and then the prayer that follows:

"Christ once stood in our midst. The Church is a sign to all the world that Jesus Christ still stands in our midst. A Catholic . . . well knows that . . . Christ must always be found in the holy, visible Catholic Church."

Dear God,
I'm beginning to see that it does make a difference the way I think of and understand Church. I really believe that we are the Church—that I am Church. This means that I have to accept the responsibility to make our Church be what you intended. What a job! But what a challenge, too! Help me live up to it.
Amen.

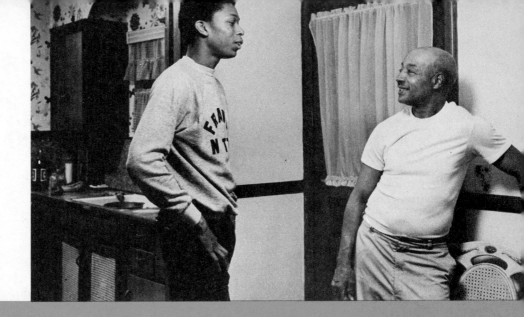

5 Living the Story Together

A Surprise Ending

The droning bell signaled the end of class. Jerry yawned as he climbed out of his desk and ambled out of the room. Another boring course, he thought as he sauntered down the hall. His thoughts sagged again as he recalled that the pleasant pace of summer vacation had ended a few days ago, and the long hard stretch of the school year had begun. He had been looking forward to this new course, and had heard some good things about this teacher. Neither one had caught his interest today. In fact, he really felt disturbed.

Jerry's pace began to quicken the more he thought about it. He thought their first assignment was really dumb. What a waste of time to interview your parents! What could be learned? Who cared to know how much you weighed, what time you were born, and all that stuff about your first days, and how your parents felt?

He had looked around the room to see if he was the only one who felt this way. No, he was not alone. He noticed a lot of strange expressions and questioning looks. Jerry did not know the answers to these questions, and he did not care to. He could hardly think of any questions to ask his parents.

As Jane came along and interrupted his thoughts, he recalled that her expression in class had not seemed so negative. He was curious to know what she thought. So he began to talk to her about his annoyance. The more he complained, the more she tried to change his mind about it. In the end, all she could say to him was to wait and see. He said he would; he had no other choice.

That evening at supper, Jerry avoided all mention of school. He put off the dreaded interview as long as he could. Finally, later that evening he approached his parents and began.

The next day in school, a very sheepish Jerry approached Jane in the corridor after class. After admitting his prejudice of the day before, he told her about the terrific night he had spent with his parents. Jerry said the more he talked with his parents, the more questions he wanted to ask, and the more fascinated he had become. Jerry recalled that he never knew any of these things. He said he asked them why they had not told him before.

There was so much more about his family that he wanted to know. Somehow, he reflected, he felt much closer to his parents now. Jerry felt good about himself as he shared his experience with Jane.

Jerry's realization is not an unusual one. Searching the past for a clearer picture of our identity has challenged individuals down through the ages. In the 1970s, attention was drawn to this quest by the painstaking efforts of Alex Haley, the author of the now famous book, *Roots.*

Since then, Alex Haley's efforts have stimulated many other people to search for and discover their roots. Knowing the story of our past can help us to understand ourselves better. We can gain a deeper appreciation for who and what we are. This is an invaluable asset for helping us to shape what we become in the future.

The Bishops of Vatican II knew the importance of understanding our heritage in the Church for understanding Church today. One of the major images they used to describe the Church was that of the People of God. When we read through the Old Testament and find again the story of the

The Story of Our Religious Roots

The Bible is, in many ways, our family story. Because it covers such a broad span of time, we shall treat only some of the major highlights of our religious history.

Our story begins with a prologue, or introduction, to it. In Greek theatre, the prologue sets the stage and gives the audience a perspective on what is to follow. The opening phrase of the prologue in the Book of Genesis, "In the beginning," is as familiar to our Jewish ancestors, and to us, as the phrase "once upon a time" which signals a child to sit and listen. Hearing that phrase was a cue to the listener that a special story was to be told or retold.

What follows in this prologue is not history, but a series of symbolic stories which establish the setting and the background. We are introduced to the main characters in this story, God and ourselves, and we gain a sense of the theme which is that of relationship.

As the stories unfold, we begin to understand our relationship with God, ourselves, and one another. Our roots begin in the Lord God, and as brothers and sisters to one another, we share a common experience of the profound mysteries of life and death, pain and suffering, of God. Our Hebrew ancestors set down in symbolic stories those deeper questions of life that challenge all of us. Whether we read or listen to these familiar stories in Genesis—of a Paradise lost, of the serpent tempter, of brother pitted against brother, of the destroying flood, of the good person saved—we know this is our common story. We can sit back and marvel at the incredible relationship that this prologue presents. It introduces a God who loves us and desires to share the fullness of life with us. For example, the story of Abraham . . .

people of God, we can come to a fresh understanding of Church, and ourselves as members, and of what it means to live this story together.

■ Why do you think it is important to people to search for their past? What do you think may be gained from doing this? In what ways are we shaped by our past?

● Abraham, Founding Father

As our story unfolds in history, about 4000 years ago in the moon-worshiping city of Ur, a person named Abram experienced this call from God:

"Leave your country . . .
      and your father's home,
and go to a land I am going to
      show you."

Genesis 12:1

Abram left the security of home and family to risk the unknown. As he trusted God, a more promising message came:

"Your name will no longer be Abram, but Abraham, because I am making you the ancestor of many nations. . . .
I will keep my promise to you and to your descendants . . . as an everlasting covenant. I will be your God and the God of your descendants."

Genesis 17:5–7

The promise was inherited by Abraham and Sarah's child ISAAC, then by Isaac and Rebecca's child JACOB.

"Your name is Jacob, but from now on it will be Israel." So God named him Israel. And God said to him, "I am Almighty God. Have many children. Nations will be descended from you, and you will be the ancestor of kings. I will give you the land which I gave to Abraham and to Isaac, and I will also give it to your descendants after you."

Genesis 35:10–12

The family grew and moved to EGYPT, first for food, and plenty—then came a change in the political scene, and they became a people ENSLAVED!

● From Slavery to Freedom

Years later, in the thirteenth century B.C., another call came to a young Israelite named MOSES and a trusting response:

"Moses! Moses!"
. . . "Yes, here I am." . . .

"I am the God of your ancestors, the God of Abraham, Isaac, and Jacob. . . .
I have . . . heard the cry of my people,
. . . Now I am sending you to the king of Egypt so that you can lead my people out of his country."

Exodus 3:4–10

Despite his own natural fears, Moses trusted in this God and led his people through the desert to the foot of Mt. Sinai. There God made a covenant with them saying:

"Now, if you will obey me and keep my covenant, you will be my own people. The whole earth is mine, but you will be my chosen people, a people dedicated to me alone, . . ."

Exodus 19:5–6

In the mutual agreement of this covenant with God the people promised to do all that the Lord wanted.

Read all about it in the Book of EXODUS, perhaps the most important book of the Hebrew Scriptures.

■ Read Exodus 19 and 20, as well as Deuteronomy 6 and 7, for a fuller treatment of the covenant and its terms.

● Chosen But Not Perfect

If Israel remained true to the covenant with the Lord, Israel prospered; if not, disaster came. When other nations asked why, the answer was:

"It is because the LORD's people broke the covenant they had made with him, the God of their ancestors, . . ."

Deuteronomy 29:25

Israel was a chosen covenant people of God, but not a perfect people.

THEY CRIED FOR A KING LIKE OTHER NATIONS!

● **David, King After God's Own Heart**

The shepherd boy from Bethlehem's hill,
    Jesse's youngest son
The courageous slayer of the giant
    Philistine, Goliath
The musician-singer whose music
     soothed
    the turbulent King Saul
David—young man called to be king!

The LORD said to Samuel, . . . "I have rejected him [Saul] as king of Israel. . . . Samuel . . . anointed David in front of his brothers. Immediately the spirit of the Lord took control of David and was with him from that day on.
                1 Samuel 16:1, 13

KING DAVID—
    beloved by his people,
    repentant sinner,
    faithful worshiper of God.
Under King David,
    a KINGDOM UNITED
    religiously and politically.

King David . . . addressed them: "My countrymen, . . . the LORD . . . chose me and my descendants to rule Israel forever. He chose the tribe of Judah to provide leadership, and out of Judah he chose my father's family. . . . The LORD said to me: 'Your son Solomon is the one who will build my Temple. I have chosen him to be my son, and I will be his father. I will make his kingdom last forever. . . .' "
             1 Chronicles 28:2, 4, 6, 7

From this time on, the promise to Abraham was passed down through David's family line.

The Kingdom of Israel divided into two after Solomon's death, yet the covenant continued to be kept by faithful persons in both Northern and Southern Kingdoms.

PROBLEMS KEPT CROPPING UP
    idolatry,
    social injustice,
    religious formalism

The meaning of trust in God and of relationship with him grew as the history of God's people was marked by a continuous cycle of faithfulness and prosperity, followed by infidelity, disaster, suffering.

● **God Called Forth Prophets . . .**
to call his people back to fidelity to the covenant, to worship him alone.

AMOS
Rugged shepherd from Judah who spoke stern warnings to the people of the north, who courageously challenged the social injustices. . .

Hate what is evil, love what is right, and see that justice prevails in the courts.
             Amos 5:15

HOSEA
Wounded lover of an unfaithful wife, who spoke so movingly of God's forgiving love because of his own experience. . .

How can I give you up, Israel?
How can I abandon you? . . .
My heart will not let me do it!
My love for you is too strong.
Hosea 11:8

Who could understand such great love? One could only try . . .

Many people did not listen to their prophets. Both kingdoms were destroyed, first the northern kingdom, Israel, by Assyria, then the southern kingdom, Judah, by Babylon.

A REMNANT, a few of them, were taken into captivity to Babylon.

■ Read Amos 5:7–13 and Hosea 11:1–7. Briefly explain the message that each prophet was expressing. Think of one or two situations today that might benefit from hearing each of these messages.

• Prophets in Exile

Again, the prophets spoke for God, warning of disaster, comforting his people, calling forth hope.

JEREMIAH

Sensitive man who warned the people of Judah that Jerusalem would fall if they did not mend their ways and turn back to God . . . They did not listen!

"So Jeremiah, you will speak all these words to my people, but they will not listen to you; you will call them, but they will not answer."

Jeremiah 7:27

EZEKIEL

A visionary prophet who spoke his message of hope symbolically to the people in exile . . .

"Tell them that, I, the Sovereign LORD, am saying to them: I am going to put breath into you and bring you back to life. . . . I have promised that I would do this—and I will."

Ezekiel 37:5, 14

"The new covenant that I will make with the people of Israel will be this: I will put my law within them and write it on their hearts. I will be their God, and they will be my people."

Jeremiah 31:33

"I will give you a new heart and mind. I will take away your stubborn heart of stone and give you an obedient heart. . . . You will be my people and I will be your God."

Ezekiel 36:26, 28

A NEW COVENANT,
A NEW HEART,
A NEW SPIRIT.

In a foreign land without their Temple for worship, God's people turned to the work of preserving and adding to their Scriptures. They began to use them for prayer in synagogue services. Their story, in written word, renewed their life and hope and strength.

■   When we read and pray with the Scriptures today, we too can be renewed in hope and confidence. Read through some of the following psalms:

Psalm 34, 46, 61, 63, 130, 131, 139.

Choose one or two that appeal to you most. Think about what the psalm says to you about your life. Then spend a few quiet moments saying the words of the psalm slowly and making it your own prayer to God.

● Freedom from Exile

When the Jews returned to Jerusalem, their homeland, they began the long hard task of REBUILDING a new community, not the old one repeated, and a new sense of the covenant, born of changed hearts. Under Ezra and Nehemiah, the covenant was renewed, and the Temple was rebuilt.

The people asked Ezra, the priest and scholar of the Law, to read the Law to them from dawn until noon, and the people all listened.

When the people heard what the Law required, they were so moved that they began to cry. . . .

Nehemiah 8:9

From this point on, a weaving of experiences began in the life of God's people . . .
 hardships, oppression,
 strength, captivity, victory,
 all shaping . . .
GOD'S PEOPLE REBORN—
 Jews, separate,
 chosen, repentant,
 waiting in fidelity
 for the promise of the MESSIAH!

Time Out to Think

So ends the first part of the story of our religious roots. Before we move on, let's take some time to think about God's call to people over the ages and to people today. We can then reflect on the meaning of God's call to each of us.

In every family history, similar patterns are often repeated in later generations. This is noticeable in the history of God's people, as well. We notice that circumstances change, but we see also that some basic experiences remain the same.

One such experience that is repeated in our scriptural story is that of call and response. Abraham, Moses, David, Jeremiah, to name but a few persons, were all ordinary people like ourselves. Each one experienced God's call to serve, and each responded in a unique way. Because they put aside their natural uncertainties and trusted God, each of these ordinary persons became extraordinary.

The experience of God's call to individuals continues today, initially in baptism, with a fuller response being lived out in life.

Cathy Woods is one example. Her story began about 12 years ago when Cathy graduated from high school and began college. During her college years, she became a volunteer in the Big Sister program with disadvantaged children. In spite of many other activities Cathy's interest in this work never ceased. When she finished college, Cathy left her comfortable home to teach in a poor, inner-city school. Cathy hates to miss a day of teaching because "Those kids really need me!"

This is Cathy's response to God's call and her way of living out her baptismal commitment.

Tony Perratta is another example of a person who heard God's call, and said "yes" in response. Tony works as a high school teacher by day. At night he does volunteer work for world hunger programs. Tony, too, is living out his baptismal call to serve God's people.

■ How do you think people today recognize God's call? What might be some other ways in which people try to live out God's call today?

The Story of Our Roots Continues

Now let us pick up the threads of our story in the New Testament: ROME . . . a new empire overpowered the world. Fears and factions divided the religious leaders of the Jews, creating tensions and groups.

Into a turbulent culture he came,
    the promised one, the Messiah,
JESUS, the little known carpenter's son,
    from Nazareth.
Was he the promised Messiah?
    the Christ? Lord?
These were later titles that people
    would call him
after they realized who he was . . .
    with new eyes of faith . . .
looking back and remembering . . .

● Mary, the Mother of Jesus

Mary was called by God to be his trusting servant, woman of strength, faithful mother. Mary was one who remembered much . . .

"My heart praises the Lord;
my soul is glad because of
God my Savior,
for he has remembered me,
his lowly servant!
From now on all people will
call me happy,
because of the great things
the mighty God has done
for me."

Luke 1:46—49

Friends and Followers

There were others who
remembered . . .
They had answered his invitation,
"COME, FOLLOW ME"—
the apostles and disciples,
ordinary men and women,
capable of mistake and failure.
They trusted him,
listened to his word,
then turned to share it with others.

There were also other friends and
followers who remained faithful in
spite of opposition.

As the members of the Council listened to
Stephen, they became furious. . . .
Then they all rushed at him at once,
threw him out of the city, and stoned
him. . . . They kept on stoning
Stephen as he called out to the Lord,
"Lord Jesus, receive my spirit! . . .
Lord! Do not remember this sin
against them!" He said this and died.

Acts 7:54, 57—59, 60

● Church—A Community

The faithful Jewish community continued to
grow.

Sometime later, another young man, a fiery
persecutor of the Jews, PAUL,
experienced God's call and became a
preacher of the Good News to Jew and
Gentile alike!

After this, Paul left Athens and went on
to Corinth. There he . . . held
discussions in the synagogue every
Sabbath, trying to convince both Jews
and Greeks.

Acts 18:1—2, 4

The community of believers continued
to expand believing that the new covenant
had begun in Jesus. The young Church had
experienced the Spirit. They tried to live
the law of love Jesus had given them, with
the recognition that compassion for
others was an essential characteristic of
the Kingdom of God. They were now a
community.

This is how we know what love is: Christ
gave his life for us. We too, then, ought to
give our lives for our brothers!

1 John 3:16

Gradually, the understanding grew that
the new People of God would include *all*
who had been changed this way by belief in
Jesus.

■ Read this passage from Paul's letter and write two statements about the main point in your own words. What do you think this helps us to understand about the Christian community?

So we are to use our different gifts in accordance with the grace that God has given us. If our gift is to speak God's message, we should do it according to the faith that we have; if it is to serve, we should serve; if it is to teach, we should teach; if it is to encourage others, we should do so. Whoever shares with others should do it generously; whoever has authority should work hard; whoever shows kindness to others should do it cheerfully.

Romans 12:6—8

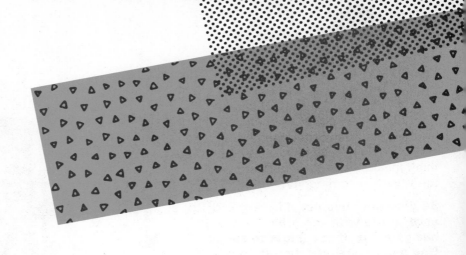

The End Is But the Beginning

So ends the first phase of the story of our roots, of our beginning as the Catholic Christian Community. As a new era began, the rest of the story is but a further unfolding of a familiar pattern. Our relationship with God continues and deepens as all persons without exception are called to share in his life and love. In Jesus a new covenant or relationship began. His followers became the new people of God. Today, we are people of the new covenant in Christ.

Like the early Christians, we, too, are called to create Christian communities. These are environments where people believe, think, value, and live as Jesus would. Most of us as Catholics live in a Christian community called the parish, which we will examine in Chapter 10. One important purpose of the Christian community is to help its members experience Jesus Christ with each other. One way that this is accomplished is by helping people to see that the message of Jesus is alive and applicable today. Many young persons today have caught the spirit of Jesus and are reaching out to serve people in a variety of ways.

In one school which is very sports-oriented, a group of students sponsored a school-wide talent show to raise money for a refugee family. The talent show had a two-fold purpose. It also provided an opportunity for recognition of students' musical talents that otherwise were unknown.

A parish youth group organized a program for prayer, service, and educational enrichment. Some of the terrific things they have done include:
• singing for the elderly in the local nursing home;
• planning and providing the music for liturgies and reconciliation services;
• meeting regularly for Prayer and Share sessions;
• inviting speakers on contemporary topics affecting their religious and moral lives;
• and simply sharing fun together.

These young people and many others like them are living and shaping the story of the Christian community together.

Challenges

The statement, "we are what we are because of our past," can be said about each one of us, as well as about the whole Christian community. How has this chapter helped you to feel more a part of the Christian community story? Can you recall any experiences of people you know who have had to risk believing in someone else and found that their relationships grew stronger as a result?

Choose two or three individuals from your own parish, neighborhood or town, or groups of persons whom you feel are trying to help build a community living the story together. Write a brief description of each one.

What important needs do you see that are not being met in the area where you live? Is it possible that you and your friends might organize a youth group to offer some assistance? Why or why not?

Prayer
Reflection

As we look back and re-read our story, and
as we look forward to shaping and sharing
our part of that story, we are aware that
we are loved tremendously by God.

With grateful hearts we share the prayer that
Paul expressed for his people:

**We must thank God at all times for you
. . . whom the Lord loves. For God chose
you . . . to be saved by the Spirit's
power to make you his holy people and
by your faith in the truth. God called you
to this through the Good News we
preached to you; he called you to possess
your share of the glory of our Lord Jesus
Christ. So then . . . stand firm and hold
on to those truths . . . .**

**May our Lord Jesus Christ himself
and God our Father, who loved us and in
his grace gave us unfailing courage and
a firm hope, encourage you to always
do and say what is good.**
                  2 Thessalonians 2:13—17

6 Sharing Our Story

A New Impression

Jerry had really had his eyes opened this semester. What he had thought would be a real drag had turned out to be almost as incredible as a soap opera. The story of the Church through the ages was unbelievable! This just convinced Jerry that there had to be a God whose Spirit must be working constantly in and through the whole thing. Nothing else could have kept this whole Church going for 2000 years! It's funny, he mused. He had always thought of the Church as popes, priests, scholars, and saints—sort of perfect people. They never made mistakes. They never did anything wrong. They must have had it all together from birth and then spent the rest of their lives sharing their virtues and wisdom with the rest of the world. Jerry had always thought he could never be like those plaster-of Paris saints.

Well, he had certainly created quite a few pedestals, he thought, and placed God's people well out of *his* reach. And yet, one thing that now amazed him was how much like himself each of these holy people were. Jerry had discovered that these people whose lives had influenced so many others were ordinary people, just like himself. They each had to struggle with their human foibles and weaknesses just as he did. What seemed to make the difference was the way in which each of them had let the power of God work in their lives. Jerry noticed that throughout history God had not chosen perfect people, but rather willing ones. Only then did God's power and presence reach out to others through them.

Another big discovery to Jerry was the similarity of events that reoccurred often throughout the story, as well as a reoccurring cycle within those events. It was almost as if a pattern kept repeating in different eras. He remembered seeing such a cycle when they had studied the Old Testament: fidelity and prosperity, followed by infidelity and disaster, then repentance, conversion and peace, and the cycle continued. Jerry had noticed a similar pattern as the Church's story continued into the twentieth century: fidelity and prosperity; materialism, decline and decay; conversion, renewal and reform and spiritual growth; peace and progress.

Jerry began to recall the panorama of persons and events that made up the story of the Church community. In this chapter we will see some of the ones that impressed Jerry most.

■   What do you think may have caused Jerry to think about the Church in such a stereotyped way? How do you think this may have been prevented? Reflect for a few moments about your own images of the Church and its history so that you may be more open to encountering a positive experience with the ways of God's people just as Jerry did.

almost *overdid* in his enthusiasm and zeal. As a young person, Paul arrested and persecuted Jesus' followers. Because of this, when Paul was touched by God and changed his life, he met a great deal of opposition. People found it hard to believe in him and Paul was opposed, ridiculed, and rejected. Yet he never gave up because of his burning love for Christ.

■ As you recall the stories of Paul's conflicts, think for a moment about people you know who are not afraid to say what they believe. Choose one and write a brief description about what you most admire about that person.

Persecution: Love Is Stronger Than Death

The faith of Jesus' followers was tested and proven stronger than death itself. The way of life in Roman society was a marked contrast to the lifestyle of a Christian. The practices and lives of the Christians may have bothered the consciences of the Romans. However, it was primarily the differences about worship that evoked the persecution and death of Christians. The Christians refused to worship and offer sacrifices before the images of the Roman emperors as gods. This refusal was considered a political threat to the empire. Christian believers worshiped God alone in spirit and in fellowship, without any false images.

Peter and Paul: Success and Failure

Let us begin with Sts. Peter and Paul—both of whom did great things, yet also made many mistakes.

Peter, impulsive and headstrong, seemed to have a knack for saying the wrong thing at the wrong time when Jesus was alive. He often missed the point, and spoke too soon. Despite all this, Peter was able to say "I'm sorry," pick up the pieces, and start over again each time he failed. Jesus continually called Peter to new growth and gave him more opportunities for his faith to develop in spite of Peter's human weaknesses. Paul, on the other hand, was an arrogant firebrand. Whatever he did, he

The Christians' faithful practice of meeting in homes for the eucharist was looked upon with suspicion and viewed as superstitious barbarism by the Romans. Ironically, it was the eucharist that was the Christians' source of life and courage and hope through these difficult times. In their communal sharing, they found the strength that was needed.

Courageous faith characterizes the people of this era. They chose to stand up and live what they believed in opposition to the accepted popular attitudes. This is a situation which we have seen repeated in this century many times. Modern-day martyrs, Christians who are living up to and speaking out about their beliefs, are being put to death in many areas of the world today, such as the Congo, the Philippines, and Central America.

■ Research one of these places of modern day persecution of the Church. Find out the causes of the conflicts, and what is being done about them. Discuss your findings in class.

What do you think is the meaning of the statement, ''The blood of the martyrs is the seed of the Church''?

Freedom and Recognition: New Life, New Errors

A movement out of prisons and secret fidelity into open practice of the faith marks the start of the fourth century. Civic buildings were given to the Christians for their worship by the Roman Emperor Constantine. He decreed official recognition of the Church in 313 A.D. in his Edict of Milan and gave Christians the right to worship freely.

Many who had witnessed the courage of the Christians in silent admiration joined their ranks. As the young Church expanded a number of serious errors crept in. These errors, condemned as heresies, were serious threats to the truths within the Church's story. These truths were very precious, especially those which dealt with Jesus and his relationship to God. They had become what are called official doctrines or teachings of the Church.

Chief among the heresies, for example, was that of Arianism. This erroneous teaching insisted that Jesus the Son could not be equal to God the Father, and therefore was not fully God. An earlier heresy known as Gnosticism had paved the way for confusion by suggesting a number of muddled beliefs about Jesus' human nature.

However, out of these seeming misfortunes a greater good emerged. A creedal summary of the Church's beliefs was set down in writing. The Emperor Constantine convened the first general council of the Church at Nicaea in 325 A.D. to resolve these disputed questions. From this assembly of over 300 bishops emerged something which was sorely needed, a clearly formulated written statement of doctrinal belief. This statement was called the Nicene Creed.

Imagine what a job that must have been for those bishops! It reminded Jerry of how hard it was to write essays that described your philosophy of life—in so many words or less. Jerry was able to see why the Creed is included in the Sunday liturgy: so that all Christians may regularly affirm their testimony of faith together.

■   Bring a copy of the Creed to class and take a closer look at this summary of our chief doctrines of faith. Is there any single aspect of the Creed that is especially appealing to you? Why?

Making a Difference

Before proceeding further in our story, we should spotlight two important behind-the-scenes persons. Two devoted mothers prayed very earnestly about each of their sons that the power of God would touch each son's life. Both mothers' prayers were answered. One of these mothers was St. Helena, whose son Constantine we have already read about. The other mother, St. Monica, had a brilliant son named Augustine. His light eventually illumined this period of trial and error in the Church. Perhaps it was partly because he himself had lived in darkness for a good part of his life. Augustine revealed the shameful story of his wasted early years in his classic autobiography, *Confessions of St. Augustine.* In this book, he confesses to having lived a sinful way of life. The important thing is that Augustine learned a great deal from this experience. He grew in his understanding about the intimate relationship between the human person and God.

When Augustine finally turned full face to the God from whom he had been hiding, he realized that not only was this where his life should have been, but where all persons would find their greatest happiness. In his own words he expressed this basic human experience of longing for God in a way that has spoken to persons of every era since then: "Thou hast made us for thyself, O God, and our hearts are restless until they rest in thee."

One of Augustine's other books, the *City of God,* was an important contribution to the thinking of the Church. In it he described so well the struggle that Christians have between the desires of the secular world and their inner desire for the eternal kingdom. He saw that each person has to live with one foot in each world, so to speak. This great work earned for Augustine the title "Doctor of the Church."

■ Imagine that you are doing an interview with Augustine for a magazine. Prepare a set a questions for the interview and then conduct it as you think Augustine would have responded. In writing your article be sure to include for your readers an explanation of Augustine's quote.

Monasticism: A Counter-culture Movement

The next period in the Church's story reveals the steadily decaying society of the Roman Empire, and the smoldering conflict between the Church in the East and the Church in the West. Throughout this era as well as others like it, one observable element is the wave of spiritual renewal

which might be seen as a counter-culture movement. God calls forth individuals to follow him. In order to follow him, these individuals chose a stricter, more spiritual response to the gospel message than might be found in the existing culture. They "go against the grain," so to speak, in living differently from the prevailing culture. To do this often requires some kind of separation from the society in order to become more fully a member of that society—a paradox of dying and living. In the fourth to sixth centuries, some individuals chose to live a solitary life of prayer and communion with God as hermits. They lived very austerely in the desert or in mountain caves.

Others formed communities with kindred persons who also were seeking greater spirituality. These groups usually lived together outside of the towns in places called monasteries. They followed a rigid daily routine of work and prayer. Their purpose and structure were set down in a strict rule which governed their way of life, and they promised to obey the leadership of one person who presided over the group, called the abbot. One of the chief founders of this tradition known as monasticism was St. Benedict, who started the religious group named after him, the Benedictines. The spirit of monasticism caught on.

Civilization had reached an all-time low and all but died out except for the spark of life quietly growing in the hilltop monasteries. A new form of life was emerging. It was to flourish in the Middle Ages. Paradoxically again, the groups who went apart were the ones whose presence ultimately saved the society. The orderly, regulated life of the monks provided stability for a floundering population. The monasteries became centers for spirituality. The monks would counsel people who came to them for spiritual direction, that is, instruction on how to progress in prayer, in one's relationship with God, in overcoming a moral failing or in developing a good habit.

Monasteries also became centers for learning. Peasants came to learn the skills of farming and other trades; the illiterate came to learn how to read and write, and also to expand their knowledge from that of the learned monks. Great literary works might have been lost forever by the hordes of barbarians who pillaged Europe had it not been for the monks' painstaking work of copying manuscripts by hand.

All over the world even today groups of Benedictines live a prayer-centered life according to the Rule of St. Benedict. Weston Priory in Vermont is one such example. Although the works and appearance of the monks are very contemporary, the Benedictine spirit of hospitality and prayer permeates the atmosphere at Weston Priory just as it did the sixth-century monasteries. It has become a place for spiritual refreshment and renewal for many other persons who come to share in liturgy and prayer with the monks.

■ Jerry had been amazed to learn how far people would travel to go to Mass at Weston Priory. What do you think draws people to go to such a monastery for prayer? Why do you think there has been such a renewed interest in prayer and spirituality recently? What do people seem to be looking for?

Saints and Scholars: A New Mood
The twelfth century saw many persons being called by God and inspired by the spirit of St. Benedict to start new religious communities. Since the mood of the times was different so also did the structure of the religious orders change. Instead of the people of the towns and villages going to the monks who lived apart from them, the new religious groups lived and worked among the townspeople. In return for their preaching, teaching, and spiritual services, the religious depended on the generosity of the people for their means of support. Followers of this form of religious life were called "mendicants" or beggars.

Two young persons who responded to God's call to "leave all things" were St. Dominic and St. Francis, both of whom started new mendicant orders. Francis had been a very popular and wealthy nobleman. He was accustomed to a very luxurious and enjoyable lifestyle. He shocked the world when he chose to live in extreme poverty for the sake of Christ. The main work of his followers, the Franciscans, was to live poorly among the townspeople, letting the simplicity of their lifestyle witness to the more important values of the gospel. Francis and his followers believed that the fewer things you possessed, the more free you were to love others.

Dominic's monks, on the other hand, were trained in a highly organized intellectual program and became an order of traveling preachers and teachers throughout the towns of Europe. Learning had become an important part of life in the Middle Ages. The simple instruction within the monasteries had sparked the origin of many cathedral schools and universities. Being a scholar or a thinker was an admirable profession. A person's scholastic reputation was judged by the school of thought one followed, much like people today might be known by their clubs or organizations.

One of the greatest contributions to this age of learning came from an unlikely person, a young Dominican monk named Thomas Aquinas. Thomas would probably have been voted the person "least likely to succeed" by his peers. His appearance and manner earned him the title the "Dumb Ox." Yet Thomas did not give in to peer pressure. This quiet thinker developed and wrote a systematic three-volume work on the whole scope of truth and reality called the *Summa Theologica*.

A *Summa* was a system of thought that combined in one all facets of learning and reality—science, art, ethics, law, philosophy, and theology. Thomas based his massive work on the philosophy of Aristotle but went beyond it to give it a Christian perspective. Sadly, Aquinas' work was not fully appreciated by the Church until centuries later when it was then used as a norm. Thomas is a good example of someone who did not give up!

The Church reached out in many different ways to help educate its people. One way to share its most important values as well as to protect and preserve them was to set them down as laws or precepts. This would guarantee that people of every era would encourage others to learn these laws as well as to practice them. All members of the Church community would know clearly what their essential duties were, and keeping those duties would help them to live according to the values and spirit of Jesus.

Jerry now had a new insight into the meaning of the precepts of the Church. He had never really understood the reason for these laws. He now realized that the important thing was not the laws themselves but the values underlying them. These basic duties expected of Catholic Christians today include the following. (Those traditionally mentioned as precepts of the Church are marked with an asterisk.)

● To keep holy the day of the Lord's Resurrection: to worship God by participating in Mass every Sunday and Holy Day of Obligation: * to avoid those activities that would hinder renewal of soul and body e.g., needless work and business activities, unnecessary shopping, etc.

● To lead a sacramental life: to receive Holy Communion frequently and the sacrament of Reconciliation regularly—minimally, to receive the sacrament of Reconciliation at least once a year (annual confession is obligatory only if serious sin is involved). *— minimally, to receive Holy Communion at least once a year, between the first Sunday of Lent and Trinity Sunday.

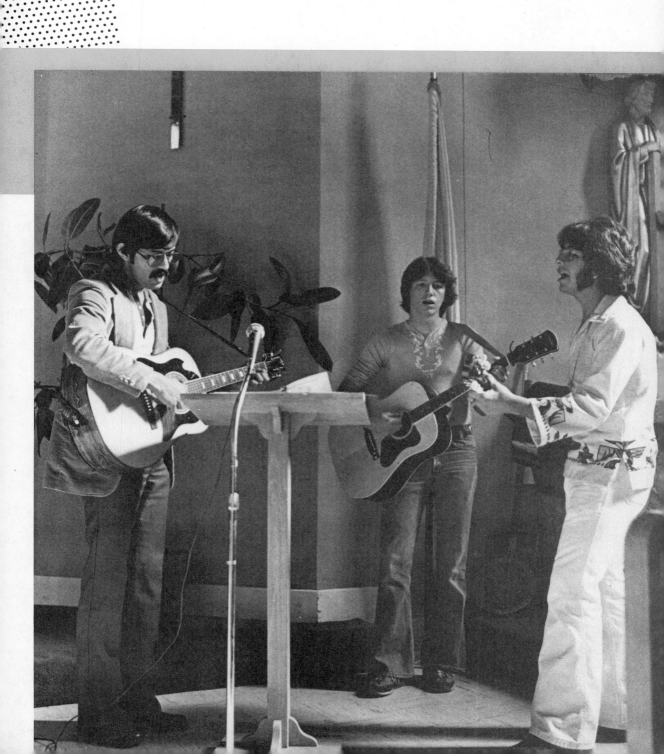

● To study Catholic teaching in preparation for the Sacrament of Confirmation, to be confirmed, and then to continue to study and advance the cause of Christ.

● To observe the marriage laws of the Church: * to give religious training (by example and word) to one's children; to use parish schools and religious education programs.

● To strengthen and support the Church: * one's own parish community and parish priests; the worldwide Church and the Holy Father.

● To do penance, including abstaining from meat and fasting from food on the appointed days. *

● To join in the missionary spirit and apostolate of the Church.

■ As you reread each of the precepts of the Church, think about the underlying value of each one. How would you describe that value to someone who did not understand the Church's laws? Are there any other duties which you think should be added to these seven basic ones? Why?

From Peak Times to Bleak Times

Philosophy and learning had liberated the spirit of the medieval people. The Crusades had drawn their attention to other people and cultures in the East, and sparked their interest in exploring the new world. Christianity, culture, and civilization were flourishing. The soaring spires and graceful structures of their Gothic cathedrals testified to the upward spirit and noble ideals of this age. Yet, a familiar pattern of infidelity and corruption was becoming widespread. Disaster and reform were not too far behind!

Because the Church had been such a stabilizing influence, it had become the ruling power in Europe. Religion and politics did not mix! Some Church leaders ruled and lived like princes. They began to put power and kingly favors ahead of spiritual concerns. Bishops, priests, and even popes were being placed into office by kings, with little or no preparation. Some popes began to sell spiritual benefits to make a profit. The ceremony of the pope's inauguration resembled the coronation of a feudal king, complete with crown and homage.

Inside the lofty cathedrals, the altars too began to look like thrones. The clergy and people became more and more separated by distance and railings. The eucharist began to be worshiped with homage rather than shared in community with others.

To add to this bleak picture, the long-smoldering feud over authority between the Eastern and Western Churches had become a raging inferno, and in 1054 the two churches split. The Greek Orthodox Church wanted no further ties with the Roman Catholic Church in the West. A struggle for power was at the heart of the problem in the East-West dispute. Unresolved rivalry persisted between the heads of each capital, Constantinople and Rome. Clashes over minor differences in language, customs, and traditions fanned the flames, and caused the Church leaders to lose sight of the more important beliefs which they shared in common. Fortunately people in the twentieth century have rediscovered the richness of both traditions, and there have also been efforts towards mutual recognition of each Church. It was an historic moment when Pope Paul VI embraced the eastern Patriarch Athenagoras at Istanbul in the 1960s.

A split also occurred within the western Church itself. Because of nationalistic tensions the popes took up residence at Avignon in France for almost 70 years. After the young Dominican mystic, Catherine of Siena, went boldly to Avignon and persuaded the pope to return to Rome, three men claimed to be pope! Successive popes in turn kept excommunicating one another. People hardly knew which pope was the rightful one. The times were ripe for reform, but people were hardly prepared for the way it would happen.

■ Are you familiar with any efforts of Christian churches today to join together for occasional projects or prayer? Describe those for the class. Suggest other activities that might help to foster Christian unity.

Division: Wounds in Need of Healing

A Dominican preacher named Tetzel was traveling throughout Europe selling indulgences in order to raise money for the rebuilding of St. Peter's Basilica in Rome. A bold young Augustinian priest, Martin Luther, became so disturbed about this that he challenged Tetzel to a public debate. Luther wrote out his list of needed improvements—*95 Theses*—and nailed it to the door of Wittenberg Cathedral. That was the beginning of the Reformation.

Luther refused to take back his condemnations and the pope excommunicated him. Deep anger and an intense personality eventually brought Luther to separate from the Church. He started his own Church, with similar Christian beliefs and practices, and took much of Germany with him. This mood of "protest" and separation spread and hundreds of small protest groups sprang up all over Europe. Hence they became known as *Protestants*. The Calvinists in Switzerland and the Presbyterians in England were two of the major reformed Christian churches. The call for reform was heard. The Council of Trent (1545-1563) strongly condemned the abuses that had been allowed to creep into the Church practices, and more importantly, this council clearly formulated all of the Church's teachings.

Shortly after, God called other reformers. Underlying the abuses that called for reform in this era was a crying need for spirituality once again. A young soldier and nobleman, Ignatius of Loyola, attracted a large group of followers and started a new religious order called the Society of Jesus. Ignatius set down a rigorous program of spiritual exercises by which a person would undergo self-examination and growth in Christian faith and love while in a prayerful setting.

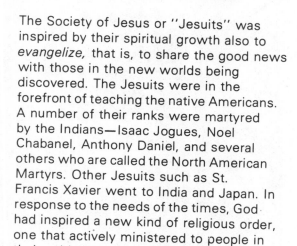

The Society of Jesus or "Jesuits" was inspired by their spiritual growth also to *evangelize,* that is, to share the good news with those in the new worlds being discovered. The Jesuits were in the forefront of teaching the native Americans. A number of their ranks were martyred by the Indians—Isaac Jogues, Noel Chabanel, Anthony Daniel, and several others who are called the North American Martyrs. Other Jesuits such as St. Francis Xavier went to India and Japan. In response to the needs of the times, God had inspired a new kind of religious order, one that actively ministered to people in their spiritual and intellectual needs.

Many other new religious orders began to appear as the great masses of people were in need of help.

While revolution began to be a recurrent event in Europe, the Church in America slowly began to grow. It was a Church made up of immigrant people who came by boat much like the refugees today. People were poor and struggling. Again, God called forth individuals to serve these needs.

The late nineteenth and twentieth centuries saw a number of women starting religious communities—Elizabeth Seton, Rose Hawthorne, Cornelia Connelly, and Mary Dannat Starr, to name but a few. They reached out to the poor with compassion and love. Eventually their ministries evolved into the work of educating the masses of people in formal schools.

As in preceding eras, great spiritual giants emerged in the twentieth century. Their giftedness continues to enrich the lives of others today: Thomas Merton, the young convert who became a Trappist monk—his story and his later writings continue to touch people; Teilhard de Chardin, the Jesuit scientist, poet, philosopher, theologian—his insights and reflections about the evolutionary process of life continue to influence and shape modern thinking; Pope John XXIII, who some said became pope when he was "too old" and "too simple" startled the world by convening the Second Vatican Council, "to open the windows and let fresh air in" to the Church. As some older institutions collapsed or were eliminated from the Church's practices, new structures have been established since Vatican II. These new structures seem to be recapturing the spirit of the early Church community. A good example of the

broad outreach of the Church can be seen in Pope John Paul II who like Peter and Paul is journeying to see his people all over the world.

Our loving God continues to be with us in his community of followers. He continues to give each era people of vision and hope who inspire and give example. They are with us today. We may not recognize them—yet. Remember, as Jerry came to realize, God does not call only perfect people. He often calls the least likely. He needs only willing hearts.

Challenges

Choose three persons mentioned in this chapter. How would you describe them and their work to someone who does not belong to the Roman Catholic Church?

Choose an era or a situation treated in this chapter and prepare a research report about it. What significant people or events shaped this era? Be prepared to share your report with the rest of the class.

Prayer
Reflection

O God our Father, we know that you continue to be with us in your people. You make your presence known to us and you continue to save us through your people. We see that you call individuals to serve in different ways according to their unique gifts. You continue to give us people of hope and vision whose lives inspire and give example to us; you continue to give us people of peace whose zeal for justice challenges the wrongs in society; you continue to give us people of compassion who move to respond to the changing needs of people as they find them. Help us, Father, to remember that you call ordinary people like ourselves and that through your power we may become extraordinary. Open our eyes and hearts, Father, to be able to recognize the giftedness of others, even those whom we may have overlooked. And help us to recognize our own giftedness that we might share it with others. Amen.

7

Proclaiming Our Story

The Great Commission

Advertising and public relations are important fields today. Companies spend large amounts of money publicizing their products or changing their images for a mass audience. Agents may use TV, billboards, news media, popular magazines, etc., to introduce a new star and tell his or her story to millions of people. Think how it might have been in Jesus' time:

The Scene: Early morning in Jerusalem. A young man approaches Jesus and asks for a few minutes of his time.

Young man: Teacher, I hear you have a message you really want to get across. Here is my card. I represent the Mediterranean Division, Rapid Herald Service, and I think we can help you. We have a central office in Rome—and rapid runners and boats who can take your message quickly to all the major cities. From there it will be rushed to the villages by our speedy network of qualified messengers. Our people are quick, intelligent, and dramatic. They can

proclaim any message with conviction! And thousands of hearers know it. I'm sure you'd be satisfied. We can make your name a household word overnight! And our services are reasonable . . . only . . .

Jesus: Thank you, but I really don't need your services. I already have a plan.

Y.M.: Then how *do* you expect to get your message around?

Jesus: I'll have my followers do it.

Y.M.: You must have a lot of them!

Jesus: Well, I'm counting mostly on twelve.

Y.M.: Twelve! They must be very capable!

Jesus: That may seem extraordinary to most people, but I think that they can meet the challenges I've given them.

Y.M.: I'll bet most of them don't even speak Greek. Are you sure you don't want to reconsider?

Jesus: No. These are a group of men who have been with me from the beginning.

Y.M.: I see. Then you feel that they really have a grasp of your message?

Jesus: Not totally, but that will come. I think they'll be able to carry my message to the ends of the world. You see, I'll be with them.

Y.M.: Well, thanks for your time. I'll be anxious to see your followers in action.

Jesus: **"Go, then, to all peoples everywhere and make them my disciples: baptize them. . . . and teach them . . . And I will be with you always, . . ."**

Matthew 28:19–20

This is the great commission Jesus gave his followers. At Pentecost, filled with the Holy Spirit, they began their task. Peter's first sermon (Acts 2:22–36) was the first time the community publicly proclaimed its story. It became a model for later preaching, and ultimately for the gospels.

To do both of these things well, the early Christians had to reflect on their own experience and understanding of Jesus and his message. They had to enrich their personal stories with the stories of others. This sharing enriched the early sermons and eventually the written gospels.

As Christians we, too, are called to personally reflect on the gospels and sometimes to share our reflections with others. How? Perhaps during a retreat, a class, or in a small informal group.

As we read and reflect on the gospels, new things strike us, things which can help us to bring our lives into more Christian patterns. Christian life is a process of such continual conversions, or changes. It is a process of becoming aware, both as an individual and as a community, of those patterns that need changing. It is turning toward Christ and his ways.

Jesus continues to have meaning for his followers in every age, though each age may find different ways of expressing this meaning.

■ Think of your favorite scene from the gospels, or a favorite way of picturing Jesus, or a favorite way of thinking of him. If you were given the task of telling another person who had never heard of Jesus before about your favorite scene, where would you begin? What would you hope that person would learn about Jesus?

■ In this sermon we can discover what the crowd found so exciting about Jesus Christ. What do you think people today find exciting about Jesus? Why?

The Message and the Person
When we speak of the Church in this task of proclaiming the good news to the world, we call it the ministry of the word.
Ministry of the word among Christians, then and today, is a twofold task:
● to proclaim the *message* of Jesus, the things he taught during his years on earth;
● to proclaim the *person* of Jesus, who he is and what he does.

122

Perhaps you would want to lead the student to understand and experience the story of Jesus. The apostles faced the same task. They wanted to lead the people to whom they preached to experience faith in Jesus. Only with faith could people understand Jesus' message and live it. What the Church wants to do in proclaiming its story today is to lead persons to this faith—to experience a personal relationship with God and his Son Jesus. Our need is not only to know *about* Jesus. We need to meet and know him, and then to grasp what his message means. In preaching the story of Jesus, the Church invites people to believe in Jesus—because that is the best way to answer the deepest questions of life—and to participate in God's life. Clues about proclaiming the kingdom and about how to do it come from the ministry of Jesus himself.

Jesus Proclaims the Kingdom

Jesus preached about the coming of the Kingdom of God. He made it very clear that this was not the earthly kingdom, not the territorial kingdom which many persons expected. He told Pilate:

"My kingdom does not belong to this world. . . ."

John 18:36

We might better understand kingdom as the reign or rule of God over the hearts of persons. The early Church believed that this kingdom had come in Jesus' time, and that his task and now theirs was to help establish this reign of God within the hearts of all people through conversion. For a Church which calls itself People of God, whose story begins in the Hebrew Scriptures, this notion is central.

The Bishops of the Second Vatican Council called the Church both a sign and an instrument of the kingdom. Their thinking might be diagrammed like this:

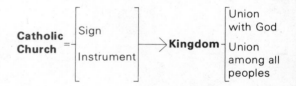

The Church is meant to be both a sign pointing to the kingdom, and a means of reaching the fullness of the kingdom. The kingdom means the reign of God over the hearts of men, women, and children. Though it is present now, it is not present in its fullness. The kingdom looks forward to a time when all people will live in union with God and their fellow human beings forever. To understand this better, we need to hear what Jesus had to say about the kingdom.

Jesus taught about the kingdom largely through the use of parables. A parable is a story or a comparison usually about incidents from everyday life, but the parable usually has a surprise result or an exaggeration that startles its hearers. It challenges them to think about the incident in a different way. Sometimes the parable is followed by an explanation showing how the Christian community understood it.

Sharing the Light of Faith gives us guidelines for proclaiming our story of Jesus and the Church. In speaking of the Church's nature and mission, it says that they:

''. . . are best captured in scriptural parables and images, taken from ordinary life, which not only express truth about its nature but challenge the Church: for example, to become more a People of God. . . .'' (#63)

■ Each of the parables listed below speaks about the Father and the kingdom. But each also tells us something about the nature of the Church and even challenges the Church members. Choose any two of these parables. Read each carefully. Where the same parable is given in several gospels, all references are given. Jot down in a few sentences the meaning of the parable as you understand it, and what it says to you about Church.

● Example: Wheat and Weeds
Matthew 13:24−30 (Mark 4:26−30)
Explanation: Matthew 13:36

The weeds are not pulled up. Both wheat and weeds are able to grow until the harvest. When they are gathered the weeds are burned; the wheat harvested.

The Church is not perfect. It has saints and sinners, good persons and not-so-good all at once. The latter will not be weeded out until the harvest. Thinking about this can help us not to expect the Church and all of its members to be perfect.

● Parable of the Sower
Matthew 13:1−9 (Mark 4:1−9; Luke 8:4−8)
Explanation: Matthew 13:18−23; (Mark 4:13−20; Luke 8:11−15)

● Parable of the Mustard Seed
Matthew 13:31−32 (Mark 4:30−32; Luke 13:18−19)

● Parable of the Yeast/Leaven
Matthew 13:33 (Luke 13:20−21)

● Parable of the Treasure
Matthew 13:44

● Parable of the Pearl
Matthew 13:45

The Church Proclaiming Its Story
While the Church recognized that the kingdom had come in Jesus, the task remained to bring news of this kingdom to the rest of the world.

First, the Church proclaimed its story by word of mouth—oral preaching. This was the way Jesus had taught. Later, the Church proclaimed its story by writings to accompany its preaching and to reinforce it. The message was put into written form to preserve it and to make it more available to people. The gospels were written years after Jesus' death and resurrection. They grew out of the Christian community's reflection on Jesus—what he said and did and its meaning for them.

Gradually Christian beliefs were formulated into doctrines and creeds. The Christians tried to apply their beliefs by the way they lived. Some backed up their beliefs by even dying for what they believed.

Many ways have been used to proclaim the gospel through the ages. These include hymns, songs, poetry, and symbols. Great

cathedrals also have been built, and famous works of art such as mosaics, paintings, and sculpture have been fashioned. Morality plays, novels, dramatic presentations, and even cartoons (for example, *The Gospel According to Peanuts*) have also been used. *Godspell* is a musical play that has attracted much attention to the gospel message.

Each age has used the media at hand to communicate the gospel. Today, with the capabilities of electronic media at our disposal, we have even more possibilities for presenting the gospel message to more people through film, TV, and electronic sound.

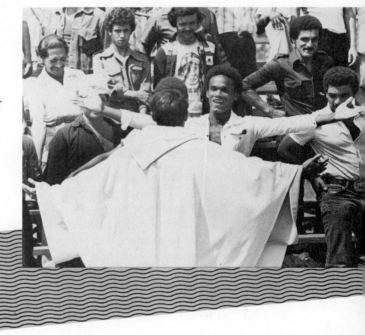

■   How many ways can you tell a story? Can you think of a film that has brought the gospel message home to you this past year? TV programs? Music?

Evangelization—Proclaiming the Message

Today we call the initial preaching of the good news *evangelization*—proclaiming Jesus Christ to those who have not heard of him or experienced him. From earliest times, missionaries traveled much of the world preaching the gospel, winning followers, and establishing small communities of believers in Jesus Christ. St. Paul tells us how necessary such preaching is:

. . . **faith comes from hearing the message, and the message comes through preaching Christ.**

. . . **how can they believe if they have not heard the message? And how can they hear if the message is not proclaimed? And how can the message be proclaimed if the messengers are not sent out? . . .**

Romans 10:17, 14–15

This encounter with the word leads to a change of heart, a conversion, a turning to Christ in faith, a giving of ourselves to Christ. If the person is not baptized, the Church will begin to prepare the person for participation in the community of the Church. The Church does this through a process described as the *Rite of Christian Initiation of Adults.* Through this rite the individual begins to become familiar with the Church itself and is made to feel welcome in the parish community. The components of this process will be explained in Chapter 10.

The Church is aware that many who have been baptized have not *really heard* and *experienced* the message of Christ in such a way as to change their lives. Though most of us have been baptized as infants and grown up in familiarity with Christ's message, we could miss the full impact of Christ for our lives. Reading and listening prayerfully to the gospels can enable us to find Christ in their pages. We can keep our hearts continually open to welcome his message.

Catechesis—Deepening the Message

Catechesis is the time of instruction and deepening of faith as a person learns more about Christ and how to live as a Christian together with others. Catechesis is also a part of the Church's ministry of the word. Along with bishops, priests, and religious, more and more laity share in this ministry . . . people like:

- Joe, a corporation lawyer who teaches a ninth-grade religion class every Sunday evening;
- Jim and Mary, a young couple who have a group of seventh graders in their home weekly for gospel study;
- Colleen, a graduate student in chemical engineering who works with second graders preparing for the sacraments;
- June, who conducts a Bible group for a number of senior citizens.

Any parish has a group of such persons whose faith is important to them, so important that they want to share it with others in a catechetical program. These persons, called *catechists,* have given considerable time to study and training for this ministry.

The primary requirement for anyone who would proclaim the Word is to have heard the Word oneself. What is good news for the catechist is more likely to become good news for the hearers. We cannot give what we do not have.

An individual or community proclaiming the Word must first have listened to it carefully and reflectively. The Church reaffirmed at the Second Vatican Council the central place of the Bible in Catholic life and worship:

• Catholics are urged to read and study and pray with the Bible;

- The change in the readings at Mass to a three-year cycle means that we will hear more of the Bible proclaimed at the liturgy;
- The homily is to be based on the scripture readings to help us understand and apply them to life more effectively;
- Many new, modern translations of the Bible are available to us;
- Courses, books, and articles about scripture are readily available.

□ The Bible is our story. The more we penetrate it and the story of our Church, the more we feel a sense of belonging to it, and the more the story belongs to us. How do you think you can more clearly feel a part of the Christian community? Are there passages from the Bible (or passages from the Scriptures that appear in this book) that help you to feel that you belong? What are they?

129

Shout the Gospel with Our Lives

He was a young French ex-soldier, discharged from the Army for disorderly conduct. When fighting began again, he convinced the Army to let him re-enlist. On assignment in Algeria, he was so impressed by the faith of Moslems and Jews that he began his own search for the God he had abandoned years ago.

That search eventually led him back to God, to his family, to the Catholic Church, to the priesthood, and to the life of a solitary hermit in the desert in Africa. His name was Charles de Foucauld.

One day in prayer he felt he had heard these words from Jesus:
"Your vocation is to
shout the Gospel
from the rooftops
not in words
but with your life."

And he did—living a life of poverty and prayer among the desert tribes. Charles acquired such a great reputation for holiness that he was finally murdered by members of a fanatic religious sect in 1916. Though he had no followers during his lifetime, the Little Brothers and Sisters of Jesus were founded through the inspiration of his writings. While working for a living, they fulfill their vocation by living and working among the poor of the world as persons of prayer. These followers of Jesus truly shout the gospel with their lives.

The bishops at the Second Vatican Council addressed this point when they said:

"The very testimony of their Christian life, and good works done in a supernatural spirit, have the power to draw men to belief and to God; for the Lord says, **'Even so let your light shine before men, in order that they may see your good works and give glory to your Father in heaven'** (Matthew 5:16)."

Every Christian is called to proclaim the gospel this way! In his talk to youth in America, Pope John Paul II stated:

"Dear young people,
By a real Christian life,
by the practice of your religion
you are called to give witness
to your faith.
And because actions
speak louder than words,
you are called to proclaim
by the conduct of your daily lives
that you really do believe
that Jesus Christ is Lord."

A Story to Ponder

Throughout this book we have stressed the importance of our own story within the Christian community. When our stories blend together we can experience the real and true effects of living in community with one another. Sometimes, however, the community's growth is slowed. This can happen when misunderstandings occur and when members of a community experience difficulty in listening to one another. Consider this story of a sixteen-year-old girl who experienced such feelings of regret:

This girl, who did not wish to be identified by name, wrote a letter to a newspaper after reading about religious cults. In her letter, she mentioned that she had been raised in a good Catholic home by wonderful parents. They had been strict, she said, but there had been lots of love in her home. She attended Mass weekly, and her parents never encouraged her to join any other religion. Yet the girl had decided that when she became old enough to leave her parents' home, she would also leave the Catholic Church. (She had not planned on joining a cult.)

She went on to say that, in her opinion, the Catholic Church had failed in trying to deal with children and young adults. She believed that the Catholic religion was a religion for adults. She mentioned that her parish provided no parish-sponsored programs except for a CCD class every other week.

She also said that when she attended Mass on Sundays, she found herself listening to a sermon for adults. She did not recall ever hearing the parish priest talk to the young people in the congregation about the problems they had to deal with—things like peer pressure, drinking, drugs, and "cults." As another example, she wrote that the readers and ushers were always adults. Children rarely participated, unless one happened to be an altar boy.

The girl concluded that there seemed to be no place for the young in the "Catholic adult religion." She added that, as teenagers, they leave the Church they feel has rejected them for too long. However, because they may have learned that religion itself is good, some head for a "cult"—a cult that welcomes them with open arms.

Instead of ending her letter there, the girl provided further comment and some solutions to the problem she had identified.

She called today's young people "the future Catholic Church of tomorrow." She feared, however, that many priests would pass them by, without greeting them or speaking to them. In her opinion, they did not see them as persons.

She suggested that churches invest time and money, not in studying cult groups, but on parish programs such as retreats and socials. She felt that these would be appealing to young people. She also said that if the Church would stop offering only "adult religion," the cults would soon fade away.

Her feeling was that such programs for young people should begin in the middle and junior high grades. Her reasoning was that if young people could become interested in Church activities at an early age they would continue during the remaining high school years. She felt it would be too late to start at the senior year level.

The girl ended her letter by stating her hope that perhaps Church leaders would someday see how desperately all members of the Church—including young people— need their leadership.

In a postscript, she requested that her name not be used—she did not want her parents to know of her plans to leave the Church.

■ In what ways would you agree with the girl? Do you think she wants the same kind of Church you would like to have? In what ways do you disagree with her? Why?

Can you write an answer to this girl which might prove helpful to her? In your answer try to bring in those things from your own experience or from the previous lessons on Church which would speak to her experience.

Challenges

Earlier in this chapter it was stated that the early Christians had to reflect on their own experience and understanding of Jesus and his message. Has your understanding of Jesus helped you to gain a better understanding of what it means to be Christian? Of what it means for you to be a member of a community that calls itself Christian? Explain your answer.

Evangelization and catechesis are both central to the continuous development of our faith. What do you know about people who help others discover the gospel of Jesus? In your opinion, what is it about the message of Jesus that motivates these people to share their own lives the way they do? Do you see this as a responsibility of all Christians? Are there other ways to minister? Explain.

What do you think can be done by adults and young people, together and separately, to strengthen the Christian community? What influence can you and your friends have in your parish? If you feel your influence may be limited, what can be done to change the situation?

Prayer Reflection

Paul's prayer for the Ephesians might be our own as we think over this chapter—the need for conversion to Christ implied in proclaiming the gospel with our words and with our lives:

I ask God from the wealth of his glory to give you power through his Spirit to be strong in your inner selves, and I pray that Christ will make his home in your hearts through faith. I pray that you may have your roots and foundation in love, so that you, together with all God's people, may have the power to understand how broad and long, how high and deep, is Christ's love. Yes, may you come to know his love—although it can never be fully known—and so be completely filled with the very nature of God.

Ephesians 3:16—19

8

Celebrating Our Story

Celebrate!
Skies
and flowers
air
and sun,
light laughing on my face—
I am
crying to be free
with the wind
laughing,
running,
and wanting
oh!
so much
to touch
GOD!

"I am,"
he said,
"everywhere you touch,
in your running
and crying
and singing
and laughing.
I love being your God,
celebrating myself.
Come!
Celebrate with me. . . ."

Learning How to Celebrate
Think of how you feel on the first warm
sunny day of spring . . . or when you bite
into a juicy apple . . . or when you feel
the majesty of a clear night sky . . . or
experience the might of an ocean.

Think of an experience that made you feel
good inside, or one that filled you with
awe, or provided a pleasant surprise.

Think of how you wanted to respond.
Perhaps it was with a laugh,
    a shout of joy,
    a shiver of excitement.
Perhaps you wanted to paint the scene,
    or write a poem,
    or sing.
Maybe you just wanted to stay there in quiet
appreciation.

Often we think of celebration in a more formal way and forget that all through life there are things to celebrate. There are small occasions when something touches us with wonder, gives us an insight into life, and makes us want to say "Yes" to it. The poem at the beginning of the chapter is an example of such a moment.

■ Can you think of any time when something like this has happened to you? Can you think of ways that a person might celebrate . . .
a rose?
a spring day?
a good night's sleep?
a new baby in the family?

getting an "A" on a math test?
the peace that comes when you are forgiven?
recognizing that a painful experience really helped you grow?

Many of our works of art, our poetry and literature, our music and songs have been inspired by a desire to celebrate some aspect of life, beauty, or truth and lead others to share the feeling. Have you any favorites that do this for you?

For the religious person, celebrating events or moments leads naturally to celebration and praise of God. Many of the Psalms, the prayer poems of Israel

Persons who have learned to be open to celebrate life are more ready to celebrate the liturgy. They have an attitude of celebration. Their readiness to see and celebrate God's love in the world around them helps them to celebrate God's love in the "good news."

We can learn to open our eyes and ears and hearts to the beauty of nature, or persons, and of life. We can become familiar with ways others have celebrated life in the fine arts: painting, sculpture, music, drama, dance, architecture. Sensitivity to the life and beauty around us enables us to be better "celebrators"—an attitude that will carry over into our planning and celebration of liturgy.

Celebrating with Others
People who have an experience together which means much to them often feel the need to celebrate it together:
- countries and states celebrate independence or statehood;
- husbands and wives celebrate anniversaries;
- families celebrate birthdays.

Have you ever thought of celebrating something ordinary, like rain? Or something unusual, like a mistake?

Every year one family celebrates a disaster—the day a pipe broke and flooded part of their house. They had to eat outside, and had so much fun doing it, they celebrate the date every year with a picnic.

which the Church uses in its liturgy, express such a celebrative attitude toward life. One of the most beautiful of these is Psalm 8:

O LORD, our Lord,
your greatness is seen in all
the world! . . .

When I look at the sky, which you
have made,
at the moon and the stars,
which you set in their
places—
what is man, that you think of
him;
mere man, that you care for
him?

Psalm 8:1, 3—4

Celebrations like these are a means of reliving a past event that was full of meaning for us. Almost always the celebration has eating and drinking connected with it, and often the foods are special. Sometimes there are traditional acts or "rituals" which add to the meaning, and without which the event would seem incomplete.

In celebrations like this there is often:
● a looking back to a past event;
● a looking forward to a time in the future;
● a celebration in the present with a particular group of people done in a particular manner.

Often our celebrations help us to look back or ahead. For example, when we celebrate New Year's we tend to look back at the past year, and ahead to the coming one with expectation for what it will bring. We celebrate it in the present, perhaps with fun and noisemakers, food and drink, and song. In many of our celebrations there are elements which remain essentially the same from year to year so that we come to expect and feel comfortable with them. But also, because celebrations are with people in historical time, there are elements in the celebrations which change from year to year.

■ Try to think of some event you may have recently celebrated. What made the celebration so special? What was it about the celebration that made it different from others you have shared in?

Celebrating Our Story

Israel as a people views the Exodus/Passover event as essential to her meaning and identity. Faithful to the Lord's command, she celebrates this event every year even to the present time. Through the Passover meal and the ritual which surrounds it, the Jews recall and renew themselves as God's covenant community. But the celebration does not just recall the past event; it makes the past event present in the lives of the people who celebrate.

At the Last Supper, Jesus' final meal was within a Passover context. Together with his apostles, he celebrated the Passover ritual, but he added something new:

While they were eating, Jesus took a piece of bread, gave a prayer of thanks, broke it, and gave it to his disciples. "Take it," he said, "this is my body."

Then he took a cup, gave thanks to God, and handed it to them; and they all drank from it. Jesus said, "This is my blood which is poured out for many, my blood which seals God's covenant."
Mark 14:22–24

Through these ritual actions Jesus made himself present to his followers under the form of bread and wine.

After Jesus' death and resurrection, the early Christian community recognized the importance of what Jesus had done at the Last Supper. He had said, **"Do this in memory of me" (Luke 22:19).**

So from the earliest days, the followers of Jesus who were still regularly attending synagogue services met later in a home to celebrate the breaking of the bread as Jesus had done. Thus they recalled and made present Jesus' death and resurrection. They viewed this simple ritual as a celebration of who they were as followers of Jesus.

The Mass as we know it today evolved from this simple breaking of the bread ceremony of the early Christian community. Through this celebration we recall the Paschal Mystery of Jesus' passion, death, and resurrection and make it work among us here and now. The Mass is a celebration of who we are as followers of Jesus. The Mass is the primary way in which the Christian community celebrates its story. Liturgical celebrations such as the other sacraments, praying the Liturgy of the Hours, and observing the liturgical seasons are also ways of celebrating the story and are related to the Eucharist.

■ Name a liturgical celebration that has had great meaning for your life. Are there "special people" who come to mind when you think of that celebration? How have they contributed to your life story?

What Is This Celebration About?
Perhaps you are saying: "Wait a minute! Yes, I know the Mass is supposed to be a celebration. But is it really? Do most people come to celebrate? And do most Masses seem to be celebrations?"

What do you really think about the Mass? How would you answer? Divide a piece of paper into three columns. At the top of the column on the left write the word "Always." Put the word "Seldom" on top of the middle column, and "Never" on the far right. Then read each of the numbered statements that appear below, and indicate your attitude about the Mass by checking the appropriate column on your paper.

1. Mass is a celebration for me.

2. Mass is boring for me.

3. Mass is an obligation for me. I go because I have to.

4. Mass is worship for me. I find the time goes quickly.

5. Mass is a waste of time. I do not get anything out of it.

6. Mass is a real need for me. It helps me to live and act like a Christian.

7. I get something out of the Mass.

In any group there are probably varying opinions about the Mass. Some people may not feel happy about their answers, but that is the way it is right now for them. Discuss your answers with others in your group. Do you all think alike—or are there different opinions about the liturgy in your group?

Suppose we are part of the liturgy planning committee for a parish. What might we do to help change things for the better? We might begin by asking ourselves: What are some of the elements of a good celebration? How do we achieve them? Every good celebration, like every good liturgy, must be carefully planned. The Constitution on the Sacred Liturgy from Vatican II tells us that all people should be helped "to that full, conscious, and active participation in liturgical celebrations which is demanded by the very nature of liturgy."

Baptism has made us a part of the people with a story to celebrate, but it does not insure us full, conscious, and active participation. That is something we all have to learn. One way is to become more aware of the world around us, its beauty and its hidden goodness. A way of becoming more aware is to take an awareness walk. Go for a ten or fifteen minute walk alone. Try to be very aware of how you feel as you begin. As you walk, open your senses to all the impressions which come, being as aware of them as you can. Smell the smells, notice the things you would not normally see, listen to the sounds around you. When something catches your interest stop and pay attention. You are not

walking to get any place, only to become more aware. At the end of the walk, think for a few moments of the good things you have perceived . . . traces of God in his world. Spend a little time thanking and praising him.

The Meaning of the Eucharist
Eucharist comes from a Greek word. The Hebrew verb which it translates means both praise and thanks. Mass is meant to be a thankful praise celebration of the good things God has done for us. A celebrating attitude leads to thanksgiving. We need to bring a celebrating attitude to Eucharist. The more we feel thankful and praise-full about life, the more will we be able to join in celebration. The exercise above helps us become more aware of God in the world around us, and of his goodness to us. The Scripture readings and the Eucharistic Prayer remind us of the good things God has done for us that are part of our story. Both can lead us to celebration, especially as we grow in awareness. There is much in our story to celebrate. There is much to make us say in union with our fellow Christians: "Happy are we who are called to share in the banquet of the Lord."

Celebrating the Story
The Liturgical Year: Our Great Cycle

Imagine a world where every day was sunny and warm. Imagine that this continued for month after month, year after year. We would soon find sunny, warm days monotonous. We are used to a rhythm in nature, a change of seasons, expected, yet different each year. Where the seasons are clearly defined and different, we live through the expectation of winter, to rebirth of life in the spring, to full growth in summer, and harvest in the fall. The rhythm and repetition add variety and challenge to life.

Each year the Church helps us to relive our story through a similar rhythm. In Advent we recall the centuries of expectation and preparation for the Messiah; at Christmas we celebrate his coming; and during the next weeks we walk with him in his life through to his passion, death, and resurrection at Easter. We see him send his Spirit at Pentecost to remain with his Church and lead it to holiness. We celebrate the fullness of Christ's kingship on the last Sunday of Ordinary Time in November. Each year we are led through

our story again, not just to remember the past, but to enter into the story more fully.

Seasons of the Church Year

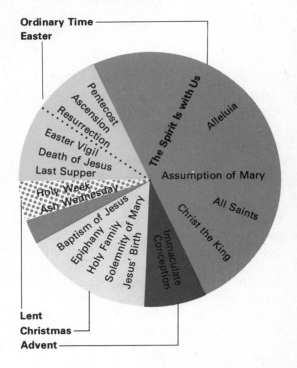

Each of the liturgical seasons has a
special spirit, special scriptural readings,
special feasts, and special symbols. All of
these can help us enter more deeply into
the mystery of Christ. In addition, different
ethnic groups may have special customs
or devotions attached to certain feasts.

⌐ Ask yourself which season of the
Church year listed below has most meaning
for your faith:
Ordinary Time
Advent
Lent
Easter
Christmas

Reflect why and how it has meaning for
you. What special customs in your parish,
family, or ethnic group add to its
meaning for you?

The Sacraments

The Church celebrates our story as it touches individual members at key times in our lives. We believe that Christ acts through these sacred signs, the sacraments. Through Christ, what the sacred sign symbolizes actually happens. Because the individual is a member of the community, celebrating the sacraments is something which the community participates in also.

- *Baptism*
(New life—fellowship with God—membership in the community)
How might we ritualize this new life that centers on our fellowship with God and membership in the Christian community?

For adults, the *Rite of Christian Initiation of Adults* provides for a number of times when the parish community celebrates with persons (catechumens) on their journey toward full membership in the Church. A series of stages in the preparation are marked by these celebrations. The rite culminates in the catechumens' celebration of Baptism, Confirmation, and Eucharist at the Easter Vigil.

For infants, parishes often celebrate the baptism at a parish liturgy, or have a group ceremony once a month for all the infants to be baptized and for their families.

- *Reconciliation*
(Sinfulness — forgiveness — mercy — penance)
How might we celebrate together God's forgiveness of our sinfulness? The father of the prodigal son had a great celebration when his son returned home.

Many parishes often schedule group or communal celebrations of the sacrament of Reconciliation, emphasizing the fact that sin affects the whole community, as well as the sinner's reconciliation with God. Readings and songs are chosen to highlight the theme of God's mercy and love.

- *Anointing of the Sick*
(Illness—weakness—support of the community—healing)
Though this sacrament is often conferred privately when a person is ill or in danger of death, there is encouragement to have group ceremonies of anointing for older persons, or for those who are ill, in parishes, nursing homes, and hospitals. Often these take place within a eucharistic liturgy.

The Christian community has always been more involved in the celebrations of the other sacraments: Confirmation, Eucharist, Holy Orders, and Matrimony. Even here, however, the community aspect has been heightened. Prayers of the community are asked for those who are preparing, and community approval through applause is often sought during the ceremony itself. In this way we, as the Christian community, become more conscious that sacramental celebrations are celebrations of our story.

Eucharistic Liturgy: The Mass
The Eucharist is the center of Christian life both for the whole Church and for the parish, since it brings us closest to Christ. Earlier we spoke of celebrating the Mass as an entering into our story because we celebrate the passion, death, and resurrection of Jesus. The scriptural readings and prayers are chosen to reflect the spirit of the liturgical year.

The Mass has two principal parts: the Liturgy of the Word and the Liturgy of the Eucharist. Both parts together form a whole. Within each, there is an interaction between God and his people; within each, there is a rhythm of proclamation of the word or story, and response. People who plan liturgies need to be aware of the movement, the rhythm, and the high points, so that the participation and music will enhance the celebration of the story.

In every Eucharist the individual Christian joins with the community in offering Christ's sacrifice to the Father, and receiving Christ in communion. The dismissal indicates that this is not an end but a beginning: "Go in peace to love and serve the Lord."

The love and service take place within the context of our everyday lives. The bishops at Vatican II said:

"The liturgy is . . . the outstanding means by which the faithful can express in their lives, and manifest to others, the mystery of Christ and the real nature of the true Church."

Diagram of the Mass

Introductory Rites
Entrance
Penitential Rite
Gloria
Prayer

Liturgy of the Word
First Reading
Responsorial Psalm
Second Reading
Gospel Acclamation (Alleluia)
Gospel
Profession of Faith
Petitions of Faithful

Eucharistic Prayer
Preparation of Gifts
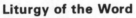
    Holy Holy Holy
    Narration of Institution
    Acclamation
    Doxology
    Great Amen

Communion Rite
    Lord's Prayer
    Sign of Peace
    Breaking of Bread
    Reception of Communion
    Prayer after Communion

Concluding Rite
Blessing
Dismissal

■   With the preceding list of various elements of the Mass you might get the impression that so many separate actions have merely been joined together. This, however, is not the case. What do you see as the central aspect(s) of the Mass? What part of the Mass celebration has special significance for you?

A Note on Celebrations
Good liturgy does not just happen. The key lies in planning carefully and well. Understanding the liturgy itself, the people who will be celebrating together, and knowing the place where the celebration will be held are all essentials to good planning. The Christian community can celebrate its story in many ways. When we are responsible for helping to plan a celebration, we should be prepared to make careful use of the many options that we have, so that the celebration will reflect the lives of those who are participating. It will express their understanding of the Christian story, and at the same time, will deepen their understanding, and enable them to live the story more effectively in the service of others.

Challenges

The theme of celebration has been central to this chapter. What do you think it means to be a good "celebrator"? You might become a good celebrator by choosing one of the following and reporting on it to your class:

● Attend a communal celebration of a sacrament in your parish.

● Participate in a group Morning or Evening Prayer—or pray one of these privately for a week.

● Look over the Rite of Christian Initiation of Adults and attend one of the meetings of the catechumenate in your parish, or a celebration connected with it.

● Plan a eucharistic liturgy for your class or school; your own wedding liturgy; your own funeral liturgy.

You are called to develop an "attitude" of celebration. What do you think this means? How can the way you view the meaning of celebration affect the way you worship? What is your attitude toward participating in a worshiping community?

When you celebrate with others at Mass you are celebrating your own story of faith and the story of the Christian community. What part do the Eucharist and the other sacraments now play in your own story?

Prayer
Reflection

The following brief prayer of St. Augustine
can help us to be people of celebration. It
is followed by a prayer that calls us to
celebrate who we are.

"All you who are reborn in Christ, hear
        me.
Sing to the Lord a new song! . . .
Sing with your voice
    but also with your heart and deeds.
Do you want to sing God's praises?
Then, be what you sing;
    Be the praise of God
        by living in God."

Celebrate yourself!
You are the miracle.
You, who can breathe good air,
    drink cold water,
        smell clean smells and
        feel the coolness
        of rain against your face.
You are unique in all the world!
    God has called you forth
        with your gifts to give,
        your talents to use,
        your potential to love,
        to give and receive.
Celebrate yourself!

9 Acting on Our Story

Discovering Through Experience

Cathy was a freshman in high school, a quiet but involved young person. She lived in a suburban town, and participated regularly in her parish youth program. One evening, Cathy's parish scheduled a special presentation on social justice and service given by a group of young adults who worked for her diocese.

When she walked into the parish hall that evening, she was given a special colored name tag. She noticed that the name tags were in three different colors; hers was green. For the first part of the evening, Cathy listened quietly to the presentation and watched a filmstrip on the social problems being faced by people in the United States as well as around the world.

At the break, an announcement was made that special refreshments were available in the next room for all the participants. As they walked into the room, Cathy noticed that the food tables had different colored tablecloths, each of which matched the

colored name tags of the participants. The participants were directed to go to their respective refreshment table according to the color that corresponded with each of their name tags. As she moved among her friends, she noticed first the red table. It was filled with homemade cookies, fresh donuts, soda, and all kinds of appealing snacks. Cathy's mouth began to water.

The red table had only four chairs around it. Cathy walked past the red table toward the blue one, which had eight chairs. The blue table contained one plate of cookies, one bowl of potato chips, and eight cans of soda. Cathy walked past the blue table and came to her table, the green one. Many people seemed to be going to her table. She noticed that only four people went to the red table and only eight people went to the blue one; everyone else was at hers. The forty people at her table had only a pitcher of water with three or four paper cups, and one paper plate filled with saltine crackers. There were no chairs at this table. Cathy's shoulders sagged.

After a period of time, the participants were called back to the meeting room. The young adult leaders then asked the group to describe how they felt and what they had experienced during the break. Slowly, the participants shared their feelings, especially those at the tables which had too many people and very few refreshments. Some said they were surprised; others disappointed, confused, wondering. Slowly, a realization began to grow among the group. They were asked if they thought this had any purpose. Cathy raised her hand and said very quietly, "Hardly anyone in our town ever goes hungry. Just as each of us received a color that we did not choose when we entered the room tonight, people are born into our world without being able to choose whether they will live in a wealthy family or in a poor one." The leader commented that Cathy had accurately described the purpose of the activity. Cathy then asked if there might be something that the people in her town could do about the problem of hunger. Others in the group expressed a similar interest. That night Cathy stood at the door saying good-bye to people, and collected names and phone numbers of those who

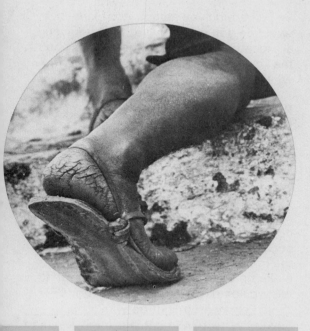

"I, your Lord and Teacher, have just washed your feet. You, then, should wash one another's feet. I have set an example for you, so that you will do just what I have done for you."

John 13:14–15

Throughout the entire history of the Church, and very dramatically in this century, the Church community has been a voice of concern. It has been an agent of Jesus Christ in trying to meet the needs of the poor, the hungry, the oppressed, and those who are alone in the world. As men and women of every era have been touched by the Spirit of Jesus, their response to the gospel message has led them to reach out in a variety of ways to persons in need.

■ Have you ever participated in a "hunger banquet" similar to the refreshment table that Cathy was assigned to? Imagine yourself trying to explain this idea to your pastor, your principal, or to the parents' organization in order to get permission to provide a similar experience. Choose one of these persons and write up an appropriate explanation that will arouse their interest and their support.

Put yourself in Cathy's shoes at the refreshment table. What do you think your own reactions would have been? Do you think that the people at the red and blue tables shared their food with those at the table with only some water and crackers? Explain your response. What do you think the group leaders wanted Cathy and her friends to learn from this experience?

wanted to do something. For the next six months, Cathy and her parish youth group worked with other youth groups in town to organize a hunger walk. From this walk, they were able to raise several thousand dollars for the hungry.

Without consciously realizing it, in this project Cathy and her friends were doing the work of Jesus Christ and the Christian community in their own town. Jesus spoke often about his concern for the poor, and said that this same concern should characterize those who follow him. As Jesus said:

Where Do You Stand?

The world we live in today is faced with many awesome problems. It is a world in which countless people:

- do not have enough food to eat;
- do not have adequate health care and medical facilities;
- do not have good housing;
- do not receive a good education so that they may qualify for a good job;
- do not have a homeland, and are forced to wander the earth as refugees.

We live in a world which is sometimes at war or close to war. In some countries, people must live with the threat of cruel political oppression. At least two thirds of the world's people suffer because they do not have a way to meet the most basic of human needs. Often, many of us may take for granted the basics of living, such as food, water, medical care, housing, education, and occupation.

At the same time in this troubled world there are signs of hope. We are members of a Christian community which has taken a stand on these problems, in both its teachings, and its actions. As *Sharing the Light of Faith* states:

"Action on behalf of justice is a significant criterion of the Church's fidelity to its missions. It is not optional, nor is it the work of only a few in the Church. It is something to which all Christians are called according to their vocations, talents, and situations in life." (#160)

■ Where do you stand? What kind of world do you want to live in? When you are faced with making tough choices about the kind of world you want to grow up in, what will you choose?

Social Values Auction

A few years ago there was a hit song that encouraged people to envision an ideal world where all persons would live as one. Perhaps the reason for its popularity lies in the fact that we all seek a better world, and we all desire to live in peace and harmony with one another. There is such a dream in each one of us. How to reach such a goal is the challenge for us. What are the important parts that are needed to make up the whole picture of the world we would imagine as a "better world"? Which elements might be within our power to shape? What things might seem to be more important or more desirable than others? What would benefit the greater number of people?

Let us begin this dream right now. Imagine that you are at a Social Values Auction. Before the auction takes place there is some preliminary work to do.

Step 1—Read through the following list of values that might characterize your ideal world. Choose the five that you feel are most important. On a piece of paper list your top five in order of importance to you. You may find it difficult to choose among the values that are listed. Take your time and think about it.

- A job for every family that would be adequate to provide its basic needs of food, clothing, and shelter.

- Freedom from violent and criminal actions such as theft, mugging, murder, rape.

- The elimination of racial and sexual discrimination in employment, housing, and educational opportunities.

- Appropriate respect, care, and services for handicapped and retarded persons.

- Elimination of civil and international wars.

- Freedom from worry, plus good physical and emotional health.

- Equal opportunity for a meaningful education for all people.

- A guaranteed job and a yearly income of $50,000 for life.

- The elimination of all pollution from the air and the water.

Step 2—Join with three or four other students to share your list of the top five priorities, that is, the values which you consider to be most important.

Step 3—After each person has shared his/her ranking, develop a list of the five values the entire group agrees on. Now you are ready for the auction.

Step 4—Your group has received $200 for bidding on your five values. Select someone in your group who will serve as your bidder. Then assign to each of your five values the highest amount of money you are willing to bid on it in the auction. During the auction, try to win your values for as little money as possible. For example, if you win a value for $30 even though you were willing to spend $40, you have $10 left over to assign to another value that you also want to win.

Step 5—After the auction is over, it is time to reflect on what happened.
● Why did you choose the five values you did? What made these five so important?
● Why did your group choose the five values they did? What made these five so important?
● Do your five values reflect priorities in your own life? How can you make them real?

■ Take one of your most important values (e.g., eliminating pollution) and develop a research project on it. Find out as much as you can about it. Gather concrete facts and data on the problem. Read at least three magazine articles about it. Conduct interviews with people who are knowledgeable on the subject. Investigate what is currently being done about the problem. Be sure to find out what the Church in your area is doing about this problem. Suggest ways that you and your friends could work on solving the problem. Develop and submit a full, written report on your findings. You might want to work with two or three other students on your research project.

Jesus the Servant

Jesus did not offer us a detailed blueprint for solving the complex problems of the twentieth century, but in his words we can clearly see his priorities of service. From the beginning of his public ministry, Jesus identified his mission as especially bringing the good news to the poor, proclaiming liberty to captives, healing the blind and sick, and setting free those who were oppressed. Jesus offered himself to all persons:

"Come to me, all of you who are tired from carrying heavy loads, and I will give you rest. Take my yoke, and put it on you, and learn from me, because I am gentle and humble in spirit; and you will find rest. For the yoke I will give you is easy, and the load I will put on you is light."

Matthew 11:28–30

The Beatitudes—A Story of Hope

Jesus challenged people to think about the conditions of their life situation in what are called the Beatitudes. In the Sermon on the Mount, he spoke of God's great love, and his own hope and concern for all persons:

Jesus saw the crowds and went up a hill, where he sat down. His disciples gathered around him, and he began to teach them:

**"Happy are those who know
     they are spiritually poor;
the Kingdom of heaven
   belongs to them!**

**"Happy are those who mourn;
  God will comfort them:
"Happy are those who are
    humble;
   they will receive what God
   has promised!
"Happy are those whose
    greatest desire is to do
   what God requires;
  God will satisfy them fully!
"Happy are those who are
   merciful to others;
  God will be merciful to them!
"Happy are the pure in heart;
  they will see God!
"Happy are those who work for
    peace;**

**God will call them his
    children!
"Happy are those who are
    persecuted because they do
   what God requires;
  the Kingdom of heaven
   belongs to them!**

"Happy are you when people insult you and persecute you and tell all kinds of evil lies against you because you are my followers. Be happy and glad, for a great reward is kept for you in heaven. . . ."

Matthew: 5:1—12

It is difficult to imagine how powerful the words of Jesus are. As his words touch peoples' hearts and persons move towards a closer living of these Beatitudes, hope is being born anew continually in the lives of other persons, especially the poor, the hungry, the rejected, and the oppressed. The dynamic of God's love inspiring faith and hope in others can be as startling as a news bulletin that could literally change the focus of their lives.

■ Choose three of the Beatitudes of Jesus and identify three specific problems facing society today which might relate to each of these Beatitudes. For each of the specific problems you have identified, suggest some concrete ways to solve or at least improve each problem area. Try to be very specific and explain who would have to be involved in solving this problem, as well as what their tasks would be. During your planning, remember that you and others who are helping you are members of the Christian community.

The Good Samaritan—A Story of Love

It is not enough for us to know of God's love and concern for those in need; we are called in our lives to live out that love and concern. What are the demands of love? This is the question that a teacher of the Law asked Jesus. The teacher knew by heart what the scriptures taught:

" 'Love the Lord your God with all your heart, with all your soul, with all your strength, and with all your mind'; and 'Love your neighbor as you love yourself.' "

Luke 10:27

In fact, he had often taught people this very commandment himself. Yet he pressed on, hoping to justify his own lax behavior, and asked Jesus, "Who is my neighbor?" In reply, Jesus told the teacher of the Law a parable.

The story is familiar to most of us: how a Samaritan stopped to bandage the wounds of a man who was attacked and beaten, after a priest and Levite had passed by. For centuries, the Samaritans were despised by the Jews because of certain infidelities in the past. Most Jews avoided

any contact with the Samaritans. In this story Jesus told, a Samaritan went out of his way to care for the man in need, even to the extreme of paying for his room and board while the man recovered.

164 As the story ended, Jesus asked the teacher of the Law, "Which one of these three acted like a neighbor toward the man attacked by the robbers?" The answer was obvious. Jesus instructed the teacher to go out and do the same. The Samaritan knew what it meant to love one's neighbor and he acted on it. This is a story of love in action. Jesus tells us that to practice love of one's neighbor means to help the needy whatever their social condition, race, or religion.

■ Think of some individuals that you might call "Good Samaritans" in your school or neighborhood. Why are each of them thought of this way? Describe each one's activities. What effect does each one seem to have on other people?

The Final Judgment—A Story of Challenge

Before his passion and death, Jesus described the qualities of those who will live forever with him in the Kingdom of God. He said that when we feed the hungry, give a drink to the thirsty, receive the stranger in our home, clothe the naked, care for the sick, and visit those in prison, we are living a life of service to others. Jesus was less concerned with a precise list of things to do than he was with active concern and love for those in need. It is up to us in the Church community to find out the specifics of where and how people are in need, and then to serve them in the manner Jesus described.

■ Take time now to select scripture stories which illustrate Jesus' ministry of service. Find examples where Jesus fed the hungry, healed the sick and troubled, loved the outcast, forgave the sinner, and cared for persons in need. Write a brief description of each incident. Be sure to mention the specific qualities in Jesus that you observed in each of these stories.

The Ministry of Service Today

To continue Jesus' ministry of service today, the Christian community has proclaimed the message of justice and love and shown its active concern for those in need through positive statements and actions. To follow Jesus faithfully, the Church must live a life of service to the world. A concern for justice must clearly be seen in the Church's actions. The story of the Church must be a story of speaking out for justice in the world. The necessity to do this was dramatically confirmed by the American bishops in *Sharing the Light of Faith*. The bishops cited this statement from the document *Justice in the World:*

"Action on behalf of justice and participation in the transformation of the world fully appear to us as a constitutive dimension of the preaching of the Gospel, or, in other words, of the Church's mission for the redemption of the human race and its liberation from every oppressive situation."

Thus, anytime that the Church members speak out about injustice, they are fulfilling one of the essential dimensions of participation in the Church.

Helping the Poor

The Church community has sought many different ways to meet the needs of poor persons in this nation. At times, the Church takes up special collections in every parish throughout the United States as one way of responding to poverty in different areas of the country. Other responses take the form of specific programs whose purpose is to improve the quality of human life in our nation.

Through the activities of the Church in promoting justice, new jobs have been found for people and the rights of workers have been enhanced; rural farmers have been given assistance to buy their own farms; cooperatives have been formed in places such as Appalachia so that people could buy coal cheaply for heating their homes. There have been countless stories of justice, of people who were given the freedom to determine their own future. These stories are an example of the Church community carrying out the special mission of Jesus to proclaim good news to the poor, liberty to captives, and freedom to the oppressed.

Helping Migrant Workers

Low wages, poor housing, poor education for children, and little security describe the life of migrant workers and their families in the United States. When the families in Cabrillo Village, Saticoy, California received eviction notices from the lemon company which owned their homes, as well as unemployment notices for the men who worked in the fields, they decided to take action. The average yearly income of families in Cabrillo village was $6000. Yet they decided to take a stand. With help from Church programs, and federal and state funds, they bought the company's village and made it their own. For the first time, these families were taking control of their lives.

Traditionally, farmworkers have not had the power to make decisions which affect their lives. Now, Cabrillo members sit on local and state boards ranging from the housing board to a nutrition council. Cabrillo villagers were given the chance to determine their own lives; the results were very impressive. This is another example of the Church community supporting the cause of social justice.

Aiding Health Care

From the beginning, the people of Epes, Alabama had several social strikes facing them. They were from one of the poorest regions in the rural south. They had no friends in high places. They had no money, only a dream and fierce determination.

The people of Epes were always bypassed when funding grants were distributed. So for nearly two years, they raised money and built a health center. With a grant from the Catholic Church and other groups, the center opened and now serves the health needs of this rural area. This health center is seeking to overcome major health problems in an area in which one fourth of the people cannot read, and half live in poor housing. Prenatal health classes, taught by a full-time nutritionist, help to reduce the infant mortality rate which is 2.5 times the national average.

Helping Communities

Darlene Morse went out to her first movie in 25 years. Myrtle Fox is no longer afraid to go home at night. There are 47 new street lights in her neighborhood. Daniel Saenz watched his car insurance rates drop from $480 to $360 a year. What do they all have in common? They are all members of community organizations that the Church has funded to help people make a better life for themselves and their community.

Working for Justice:
Your Story in the Church

High school students like yourself have often been leaders in developing service projects to respond to community and even global problems. The story of Cathy which began this chapter was one example of a young person who heard the call to serve. *Sharing the Light of Faith* stresses the importance of service projects in high schools by noting that:

"one measure of a school's success is its ability to foster a sense of vocation, of eagerness to live out the basic baptismal commitment to service, . . ." (#232)

In high schools and parish youth programs across the country, young people are involved in service projects with the elderly of their community, in raising money to donate to the hungry of the world, in organizing recreational and educational programs, in developing special programs for the handicapped, and in assisting in various parish projects. Through works of service, young people like yourself are showing what it means to love one's neighbor and serve those in need.

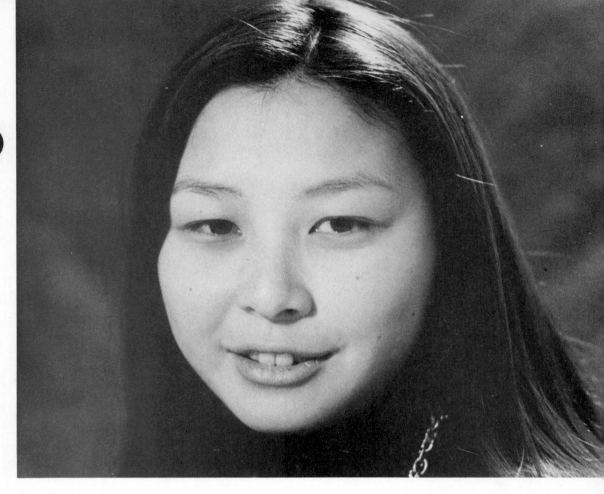

Challenges

What are some ways in which your school participates in service projects? How would you determine what needs of the community are being met by these service projects? What might be some additional ways in which your school could meet some of the crying needs for greater justice and love in the world?

After having studied this entire chapter, look back at the values that you ranked in the Social Values Auction. Are there any changes that you would now make in the ranking? Why? Explain what may have brought you to this.

In your opinion, in what way can people today live more in the spirit of the Beatitudes? Do you think the Beatitudes are as challenging today—or more challenging—as they were in Jesus' time? Explain your response.

Prayer
Reflection

Jesus said:
"When you give a lunch or a dinner, do
not invite your friends or your
brothers or your relatives or your rich
neighbors—for they will invite you
back, and in this way you will be paid for
what you did. When you give a feast,
invite the poor, the crippled, the lame,
and the blind; and you will be blessed,
because they are not able to pay you
back. God will repay you on the day the
good people rise from death."
Luke 14:12—14

May we be unafraid to face the challenge of
Jesus and the Church to seek social
justice throughout our world. May we be
given the courage to speak out and to act
positively to promote justice. May we
never be the cause of injustice to others—or
hardship, especially to those who have
been most neglected by society. May
each one of us be the promoter of justice for
all persons in the world. May we never
miss an opportunity to serve faithfully the
poor and the needy of the world. With the
presence of the Spirit and the story of
the Son, help us, Father, to do your will in
the Church and in the world. Amen.

Our Story Takes Shape

What's a Parish All About?

Chris Stowe looked at the Church as a genuine mystery, not in the sense of awe, but a mystery in the sense of why anyone would want to go to Church. He remembered that, as a child, he went to Church with his parents, but now that he was in high school, it just did not seem as important or useful to go to Church. The homilies during the Sunday liturgy did not speak to his life. It seemed that his parish was only interested in the adults.

Beth Morton belonged to a different parish from Chris. Her parish seemed to be one of the great things in her life. Every Sunday evening, she had the opportunity to worship at a special Mass that was just for youth. In Beth's parish, the youth were considered so important that a committee of high school students helped to prepare the Sunday liturgy. They also spent considerable time working on special service projects to meet some of the community needs.

Chris and Beth's experiences in their parishes seemed very different from Brian's understanding of his parish. Brian's parish was composed of several predominant ethnic groups, and families usually went to Church together. Although there was no separate youth Mass, the liturgies were developed in such a way that they seemed to draw the people closer to each other and to God. Brian was somewhat uncertain about all the aspects of the Church, but his family tried to always worship together and it seemed like a good thing to him.

■ Take turns interviewing each other about your parish. Report these interviews in a format such as you might find in a newspaper or interview magazine. Learn from each other. What is most important about your parish? What should be changed to make the parish better? Why do you feel a part of the life of your parish or separated from your parish?

Parish Is a Mosaic

In this final chapter we will look at the Church as we experience it in our parish community. It may be said that the parish is a mosaic of many different elements which make up what it is. In this mosaic, you can find so many different expressions of what the Church is, and even what the Church can be. In this mosaic, you can easily identify some of the more striking aspects of parish life. There are also several empty spaces in the mosaic. The reason for this is that the parish is not yet complete. It, too, is in the process of journeying and has a story still to be told. That story is the part that you and your generation will play.

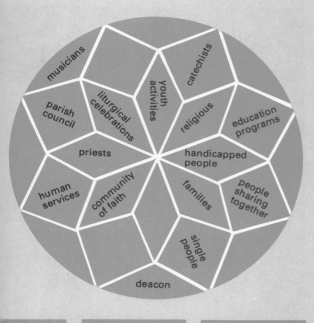

The mosaic labels read: musicians, catechists, youth activities, liturgical celebrations, parish council, religious, education programs, priests, handicapped people, human services, community of faith, families, people sharing together, single people, deacon

Story of the Parish/Story of the Church

The story of the parish actually becomes the story of the Church. Just as Jesus reminds us that he is present whenever two or three are gathered together in his name, the parish community becomes the Church for us whenever it gathers to tell and to live the story of Jesus. The parish, called the local church, is linked by its common beliefs, traditions, and stories to the Church that encompasses the entire world. We often refer to it as the universal Church. The parish is not merely a subdivision of the universal Church. The parish is actually the Church in microcosm, because it is where persons who believe in Jesus celebrate his story and the ways in which his story has been understood and lived for nearly 2000 years.

Each parish is part of a diocese, which is a grouping of different parishes in the same area of a particular state. Sometimes an entire state might be only one diocese. Just as most parishes are under the leadership of a priest, called the pastor, the diocese is under the leadership of a bishop, often called the "ordinary" of the diocese. The universal Church receives special leadership from the successor to Saint Peter, the pope. The pope, the Holy Father, is also the Bishop of Rome. The pope in consultation with the other bishops of the world governs the universal Church. This principle of bishops all working in conjunction with one another for the good of the whole Church is known as collegiality.

You should be able to find most of the elements in your own parish in this mosaic. Each parish will probably have a different kind of mosaic that describes it—just as each of you has a different story that describes who you are. The beautiful thing about the parish mosaic is that it is a story that continues to grow and change in order to meet the needs of the parish members.

■ On a piece of paper, sketch your own mosaic of your parish, in any shape you wish. Do a little creative daydreaming and suggest some fill-ins for the empty spaces that will become your part of the mosaic's story.

Through these special positions of leadership within the Church, the continuing will of God and the work of the Spirit are given special prominence. The story of the Church is continually clarified through the teachings of these leaders in the Church.

Sharing the Light of Faith expresses this special teaching role this way:

''The pope and the bishops in communion with him have been anointed by the Holy Spirit to be the official and authentic teachers of Christian life. . . . It is their office and duty to express Christ's teaching on moral questions and matters of belief. This special teaching office within the Catholic Church is a gift of the Lord Jesus for the benefit of all His followers in their efforts to know what He teaches, value as He values, and live as free, responsible, loving, and holy persons.'' (#104)

In the life of the Church, the pope and the bishops have been given the role of:

''. . . teaching, sanctifying, and governing the Church, and enjoy the gift of infallibility in guiding the Church when they exercise supreme teaching authority.'' (#93)

This special teaching quality of infallibility means that the Church will proclaim clear and undisputed truth to the world when speaking on matters of faith and morals. This truth is going to be proclaimed to the members of the local Church by ordained priests and deacons. The seeking and speaking of truth is not a task only for the pope, bishops, priests, and deacons but also for all the people of God.

Why is the Church so confident about the truth that it presents to the world? Quite simply, it is because God's story has become part of our story through the action and life of the Holy Spirit in the activities of the Church. This means that the Church can change some of the ways that it views itself in the world because the Spirit continues to help the Church members meet the new and different demands of each particular age and society.

■ How does the Church teach the world? Use the library to research and discover ways in which the Church has sought to be a teaching force for good in the world. Note carefully which persons are speaking out in the name of the Church. What level are they speaking on: parish, diocesan, national, or universal?

Parish: Persons, Programs, and Priorities

In your parish, as in every parish, there is a range of talents and giftedness among the persons who make up the membership. Some of these persons are professionally prepared with years of specialized training. Others are parish members who have volunteered their services, time, energies, and insights to the life of the parish. In fact, one sign of a successful and alive parish is the extent to which as many persons as possible participate in the life of the parish.

Persons

Let us look at the roles of some persons in the parish in order to understand what the programs and the priorities of the parish will be.

There are several persons in various leadership roles in many parishes. We will discuss some of these persons. There may be other roles in your parish which you can add to this listing:

● *Pastor:* a priest with the overall spiritual leadership of the parish. In some parishes, rather than having a pastor, a team ministry is established where the various parish leaders share in the overall leadership of the parish. Whether the overall leadership comes from a pastor or a team ministry, the first priority for the leaders is clear: to preach and live the story of Jesus Christ and the Church community.

● *Associate Pastor:* a priest who ministers with the pastor in the leadership and activities of the parish.

- *Sisters:* vowed religious women who have committed themselves to public and lifelong service to the Church. They minister in a variety of ways. They frequently teach in or administer schools and hospitals, and exercise a variety of spiritual and social ministries for all persons in the community.

- *Director of Religious Education:* a relatively new position in the life of the Church; a person who has been trained to give direction and resource help to all of the catechetical programs of the parish. This person, often referred to as the *DRE,* or parish coordinator, is expected to develop the many dimensions of total parish catechesis.

- *Catholic School Principal:* the instructional leader of the parish elementary or high school. By special training, this person seeks to bring the best of education and the story of the Church to the students, parents, and staff of the parish school.

- *Deacon:* a person called to serve others through a ministry of the word, of liturgy, and of charity. The deacon may be either a permanent deacon (intending to remain in the order of deacon for life), or a temporary deacon (intending to remain in the order of deacon until being ordained to the priesthood).

- *Minister of Music:* a person who has the responsibility to prepare and to lead the music in such a way that it will not only be appropriate for the particular group at worship, but it will also motivate persons to praise God through their music and singing.

- *Parish Council President:* a person elected to lead the parish council, a group of elected and appointed individuals who act in an advisory capacity for the life of the parish. The parish council provides necessary expertise to the parish leaders so that it will not only be a means of establishing effective programs and worthwhile priorities, but will also be a way for all parish members, including youth, to have a voice in the life of the parish.

All of the positions in the parish that we have studied fit into the mosaic that makes up our parish. With so many different kinds of positions, it can even get a little hectic and disorganized. As long as persons remember that they are all to share in telling the story of Jesus and the Church community as part of their own story, then the parish will be united. To the extent that such unity and life is seen in the story of the parish, then that parish is truly participating effectively in the story of Jesus.

■ There are probably some positions in your own parish that were not included in the previous list. Write down these positions and give a brief description of their functions. There may also be roles in the life of the parish that you believe should exist in each parish. Also write down these roles and explain precisely what these new roles could do or achieve in the life of the parish.

Programs

Any organization, including the parish, often has to develop its approach through different kinds of programs. Mary and Stan Chambers had always been the kinds of persons who liked to get involved. They had recently moved into a new community and became members of Corpus Christi parish. Their parish had an extensive religious education program, a Catholic school, social programs to meet the needs of the elderly in the community, and also groups of parish members who sponsored food and clothing drives. Mary and Stan were eager to help, and were happy to learn that the parish council always was trying to get more people involved in the parish activities. The parish council was working in five main areas of parish life: religious education, ecumenism, worship, social justice, finances, and buildings and grounds. Let us look at some of these key areas of parish life.

Committees of the Parish Council:

● *Religious Education:* The persons working in this area suggest policies and develop programs in all areas of relgious education. They are responsible not only for a variety of strong programs of religious education, but also have the responsibility to motivate parish members to be involved in this important aspect of parish ministry. This committee works closely with the pastor and director of religious education in a total approach to religious education—in other words, a lifelong approach to learning about and being part of the story of Jesus and his Church. The persons who teach in a religious education program are called catechists because they helped to catechize or instruct parish members in the story of Jesus and his Church.

● *Ecumenism:* This committee in the parish gives attention to ecumenical activities and programs. The members of this committee meet with leaders from other churches within the community, frequently to develop common approaches to community needs. Often, the Ecumenism committee will develop special prayer services to enable members of different churches to gather together for prayers seeking Christian unity, or an end to violence or war in our society.

● *Worship:* This parish council committee has the overall direction of the public prayer life as its foremost concern. The members of this committee work together with the minister of music to develop liturgies and prayer services that will foster the spiritual growth of the parish members. This committee is one of the groups that must take special care to meet the needs of young people so that it can do an effective job of reaching all persons within the parish. The committee members need to meet and work with the priests and

deacons of the parish in selecting appropriate themes and approaches to the liturgy.

● *Social Justice:* In some ways, the members of this committee might be said to prod the consciences of all the parish members to address social justice concerns. The function of this committee is to provide ways of raising the consciousness level of parishioners about social justice concerns and to provide opportunities for them to *do* something about these problems. These concerns may be local ones, such as inadequate housing or health care for persons within the community, or they may be world-wide problems such as hunger relief, disarmament, or government spending. Some may involve specific moral issues such as abortion, racial discrimination, or poverty.

● *Finances:* The members of this committee have the responsibility to prepare the annual parish budget and to determine if the collections of the parish are sufficient to meet the program requirements of the parish. Often, the members of this committee have financial expertise from their business experiences that will permit them to bring special skills in this necessary area of parish life. A parish may desire tremendous programs, but without sufficient funds, that parish's story will not be realized.

● *Buildings and Grounds:* While we know that the Church is more than just buildings, it is important for the members of this committee to see that the parish buildings and grounds are properly maintained and repaired when necessary. Practical matters such as adequate lighting, sound systems, and heating are important because they provide a setting that is conducive to sound liturgical celebrations. Members of this committee also may be active in planning building renovations or suggesting ideas for the future space needs of the parish.

The above descriptions of the different committees on the parish council give some practical understandings of some of the different dimensions of parish life. The mosaic of the parish is composed of persons and programs in order to let the story of the parish, the story of Jesus and his Church, be told consistently and fully.

■ Divide into small groups with no more than three persons in a group. Try to imagine what you would like your ideal parish to be like. Think about this in terms of the persons involved and the description of their roles, and what programs should be essential components of parish life. When you have finished with this exercise, share your main ideas with the rest of the class. Take time to find some common themes that may have surfaced in the different groups in the class. Then try to discover any similarities you have with the parishes in which you are members, and what are the differences between your ideal parish and the parish you are in. For each of the differences, try to decide whether your parish could be better if it was developed according to the ideas of you and your class. Keep in mind that the purpose of the parish is to bring people together to live and to understand the story of Jesus and his Church.

A New, Yet Old, Part of the Story

One of the most exciting things to happen to parish life has been the developing understanding of a special document called the *Rite of Christian Initiation of Adults,* issued by the universal Church to help not only those who wish to become members of the Catholic Church, but also to deepen the faith of those who are parish members. It might seem strange to hear that a document is going to be an exciting source of change and growth in the Church, but this is precisely what is happening. The following is an explanation of the overall structure of this special approach to sharing in the story of the Church.

Structure of the *Rite of Christian Initiation of Adults* (RCIA)

The RCIA discusses four periods of spiritual growth during the individual's journey in faith. These periods are joined together by a series of three stages, which are steps that celebrate liturgically the movement of the individual's growth in the Christian life. The stages not only celebrate the growth in faith of the believer, but also serve as "gateways" to the next period of Christian formation.

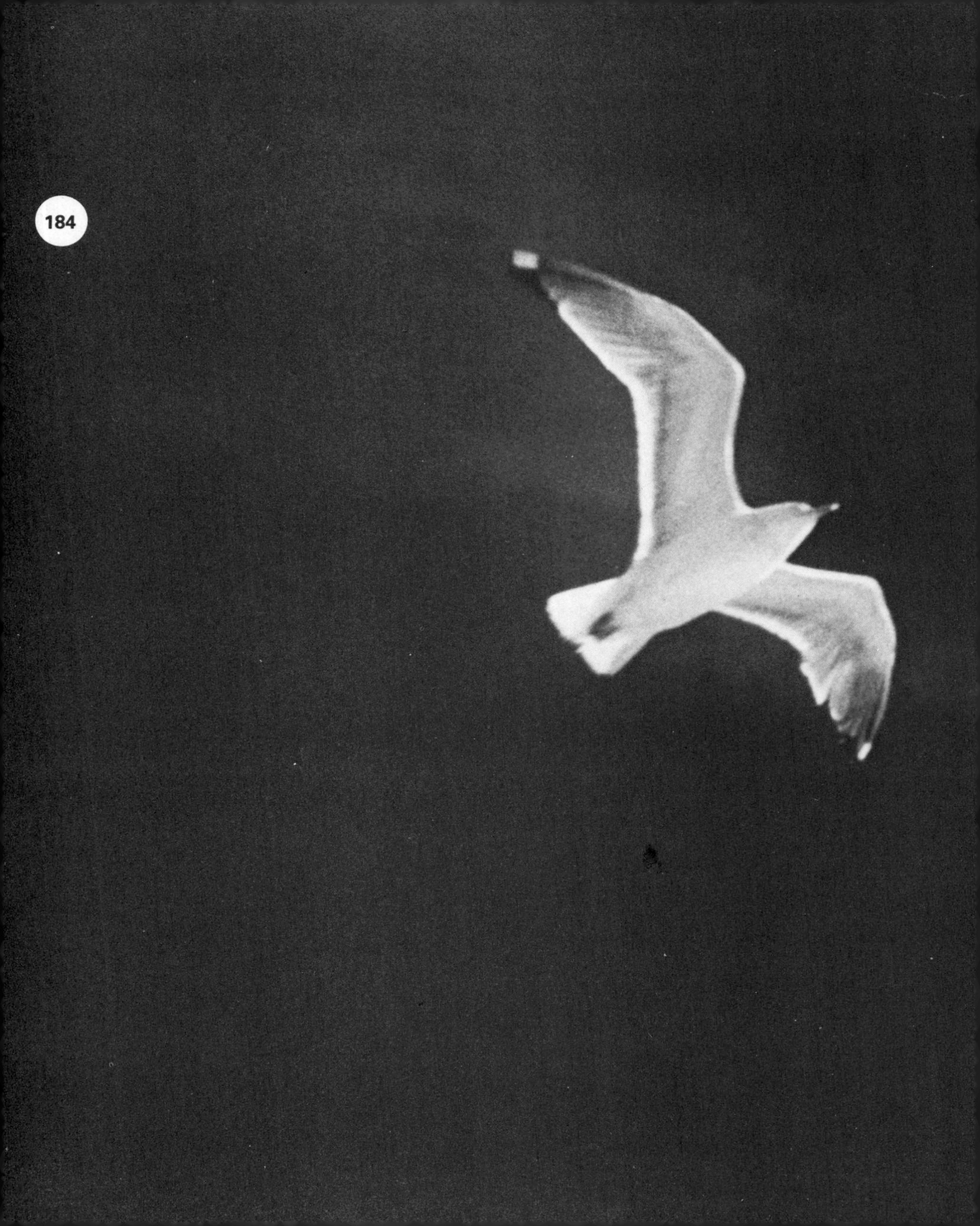
184

The first period is the time during which the individual inquires about the faith and begins to hear the good news of Jesus Christ. This period is concluded by what is called the first stage, which celebrates the individual's entrance into the catechumenate.

First Stage: Rite of Becoming Catechumens

In this first stage, the catechumens indicate that they have accepted the proclamation of God and have a basic faith in Jesus Christ as our savior. The members of the parish are expected to share their own faith and religious knowledge with the catechumens in order that the story of their faith might be told and received by others with eagerness and joy.

The second period of the journey in faith commences with this entry into the catechumenate. Note that the word catechumen refers to the person seeking to become a full participant in the life of the Church, and catechumenate refers to the process of education in the story of the Church for the catechumen and growth in the Christian life. This period leads to the celebration of the Rite of Election.

185

Second Stage: Rite of Election or Enrollment of Names

This rite usually takes place at the beginning of Lent. The community hears the witness of godparents and catechists as to the faith of the catechumens. The community is expected to pass a judgement as to whether or not the catechumen can proceed to receive the sacraments and to full participation in the life of the community. The catechumens give their names in response to the call of God. The Church community not only recognizes but also encourages these "elect" to progress eagerly toward the celebration of the sacraments of initiation.

With the celebration of the Rite of Election at the beginning of the Lenten Season, the remaining weeks of Lent become a period of purification and enlightenment, or "illumination." The purpose of this period is to acquaint the catechumens with the mystery of sin and the need to put one's life in the trust of God.

The catechumens are expected to proceed to a greater knowledge of themselves and a spirit of penance that will remind them of the true values for those journeying towards the Kingdom of God. In this period, the catechumens assess their own progress and are spiritually strengthened as followers of Christ. They are also formally presented with the Creed and the Lord's Prayer, expressions of basic and essential elements of Catholic belief and practice.

Upon the completion of spiritual preparation during this period of illumination, the catechumens moves to the next stage of the process of initiation.

■ Catechumens are reminded of "true values" as they progress in their journey in faith. What values do you think are important for living a Christian life?

Third Stage: Celebration of the Sacraments of Initiation

In this stage, the catechumens celebrate and receive the sacraments of initiation, which are Baptism, Confirmation, and Eucharist. The ideal time for this to take place is during the Easter Vigil on Holy Saturday, which recalls most vividly the death and the resurrection of Jesus. This Vigil is most significant for the catechumens who are about to experience a regeneration of life in Christ, the confirming of this life in the Spirit, and a first full sharing of it in the Eucharist. The person has now become fully initiated into the Christian community.

Once the catechumens have participated in these sacraments of initiation, there is a time for postbaptismal instruction called the *mystagogia*. This is a period to continue to learn more profoundly the story of Jesus and the Church. This is also an important time for the Church community to express and foster a deeper concern for the newly-baptized Christian and to offer guidance for the individual to grow in faith and knowledge.

What makes this rite so exciting for the parish today? What could make this rite so exciting for you? Quite simply, it is a challenge not only for those who are catechumens, but also for every person who considers himself or herself to be a Catholic Christian. We are all challenged to take seriously the story of Jesus and the Church. This *Rite of Christian Initiation of Adults* is not celebrated in a quiet ceremony with only a few relatives and close friends in attendance. The entire parish community is encouraged to participate in this rite and when they participate they are consciously being asked to share and to deepen their involvement in the story of Jesus and the Church. It is a time, paradoxically, of serious joy. It is serious because a commitment to Jesus and the Church is a serious and responsible decision to make. It is joyful because it celebrates the story of the good news of God's love for all people.

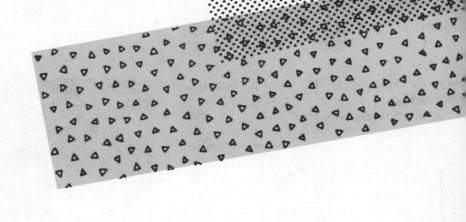

You will probably be part of liturgies where this rite is celebrated in your parish. Think about what it means—not only for the catechumens, but also for you—because you are saying, through your participation in the rite, that as a Catholic Christian you want to continue to grow in the knowledge and experience of Jesus Christ in this world. Why is this worth sharing in?

Priorities: Where Is the Parish's Story Going?
The future of the parish in the Church community will have many aspects that are the same as they are today, and it will probably have many aspects that will grow and change. Some that obviously must remain as important priorities are worship, a sense of Christian community, a structure in parish life, an awareness of the local Church as well as the universal Church, and a sense of social justice. However, it seems that there are new priorities that will continue to develop in the life of the Church as Catholic Christians discover new and fuller means to their story in the Church. Some areas of new

Church life that are just beginning to be experienced by many parishes include:

● greater attention to the special ministry required of adult persons who are single;

● more emphasis on ministry to the divorced and separated;

● more social and pastoral programs for senior citizens;

● greater priorities for youth ministry;

● more emphasis on adult and family education without losing sight of the need to educate persons at all levels of Church participation;

● more attention to the Church's role with those who are handicapped.

Parishes will continue to explore ways to make their liturgies more meaningful to their people. Many parishes will start to evaluate the quality of parish life, and offer more opportunities for spiritual enrichment. All of these priorities and more will be part of the continuing story of the Church and of *your* life in the Church. For the story of the Church in the future is the story of your future, too.

Challenges

Based on what you have learned from reading this chapter, what do you think might be some of the future concerns of the Church community? Are there areas that concern you that you have not found in this chapter?

Part of this chapter dealt with the Rite of Christian Initiation of Adults, *a process of initiating new members into the Christian community. What do you see as the high point of your own journey in faith so far? What role has the Christian community (family, friends, parish staff members, and so on) played in helping you to grow in the Christian life? Do you see all of life as a journey in faith? Why or why not?*

Prayer
Reflection

We have spent time reflecting on practical
and lifelong concerns in the story of the
Church as we read this story in our
parishes. Time spent in thinking can turn into
ways to pray—about parishes, about
people, about programs, about priorities in
the life of the story we call the Church.

And so we pray:

Give us patience, Lord,
for those who do not understand—
and let us give thanks for those
who do understand.
Give us the words to tell the story,
the hearts to feel the story,
and the vitality to live the story.
We ask all of this in the name
of Jesus Christ,
our Lord and Brother. Amen.

192

Acknowledgments

Excerpts from the *Good News Bible.* Copyright © American Bible Society, 1966, 1971, 1976.

Excerpts from *Sharing the Light of Faith:* National Catechetical Directory for Catholics of the United States, copyright © 1979, by the United States Catholic Conference, Department of Education, Washington, D.C., are used by permission of copyright owner. All rights reserved.

Michael Warren, "Touching the Stories of Young People." *New Catholic World,* April-May, 1979. NY: Paulist Press.

J. Schaupp and D. Griggs, *8 Simulated Activities* (New Testament). Livermore, CA: Griggs Educational Service.

D. Griggs, *20 New Ways of Teaching the Bible.* Livermore, CA: Griggs Educational Service.

Excerpt from "The Church in Our Day": Pastoral Letter of American Bishops, 1968. Reprinted with permission of the United States Catholic Conference, Washington, D.C.

Walter Abbott. *The Documents of Vatican II.* Wilton, CT: Association Press, Follett Publishing Company.

Anne Powell, r.c. "Alive." Reprinted with permission of *Encounter,* a Cenacle publication, Brighton, MA.

Adapted with permission from Charles R. McCollough, *Morality of Power: A Notebook on Christian Education for Social Change.* Copyright © 1977 by the United Church Press.

Photo Credits

The photographs reproduced on the pages listed are from the following sources:
Waring Abbott: 106.
Peter Arnold, Inc.: Ginger Chih 37, 89; Richard Choy 4; Gerhard E. Gscheidle 44; James H. Karales 123, 181; Yoram Lehmann 156; George Roos 57; W.u.C. Schiemann 146–147; Sybil Shelton 78, 121, 179, 180; Erika Stone 25, 35, 40, 105.
Joyce Crider: cover.
Design Conceptions: Jock Pottle 137.
DPI: Robert Crawford 13; Darst-Ireland 76; EMA 24, 47; Harold Fay 184–185; Jerry Frank 157; Joel Gordon 173; Syd Greenberg 86; William Koplitz 110–111; Grete Mannheim 55; Abraham Menashe 169; Janet Nelson 62; Chris Reeberg 107; Leeanne Schmidt 67; Jean-Claude Seine 31; Simark 170; SUVA 52–53; Darwin Van Campen 82.
Editorial Photocolor Archives: Daniel S. Brody 164–165; Ann Chwatsky 163; Laima Druskis 183; HJM Photos 20; Jan Lukas 65; Doug Magee 102; Susan McKinney 27, 190; Linda Rogers 14–15; Michos Tzovaras 152.
John Lei: 69.
Mark Mittelman: 187.
Monkmeyer: Irene Bayer 11; Tom Carew 28; David C. Conklin 75; Paul S. Conklin 19, 38, 63, 131, 159; Jim Cron 115; Edward L. DuPuy 32–33; Sam Falk 58; Marion Faller 93; Will Faller 143; Mimi Forsyth 6, 9, 42, 43, 48, 61, 73, 79, 90–91, 96, 101, 109, 118, 120, 128–129, 141, 149, 151, 155, 174, 176; Nancy Hays 10; Michal Heron 160, 167; Hugh Rogers 17, 41, 100; David S. Strickler 51, 154.

Omni-Photo Communications, Inc.: Ann Hagen Griffiths 23; Lea 81.
Nancy Palmer Photo Agency Inc.: Michael Lloyd Carlebach 119; Jim Jowers 139; Kenneth Murray 127.
Religious News Service: 29, 113, 142, 189.
Rick Smolan: 5, 80, 87, 99, 116, 138.
SYGMA: William Karel 85; J.P. Laffont 70–71.
Taurus Photos: Clifton Studio 66; Eric Kroll 161; Mike Wannemacher 145; Shirley Zeiberg 7, 49.
United Press International: 125.
Woodfin Camp: Timothy Eagan 134; Gianfranco Gorgoni/Contact 133; Michal Heron 95; Sylvia Johnson 124.